Plays from The Bridge

Plays from The Bridge

Drama and comedies
dealing with American history
written to be performed
on the Bridge Theater in
Whitehall, New York

2000-2009

Cover design by The Troy Book Makers
Cover graphic artwork by Nils Lommerin

Royalty quotes and acting copies are available for productions both
in professional and community theaters.
Call 518/461-5411

This book is published for:
Riverview Entertainment Productions, Inc.
E-Mail: markell2@localnet.com

ISBN: 978-1935534-92-1

Special thanks to:

The Bridge Theater
Whitehall NY
David Mohn, Managing Director

Steamer No. 10 Theater
Albany NY
Ric Chesser, Producing Artistic Director

Discover Quincy—Adams National Park
Quincy MA
Jennifer Logue, Executive Director

Albany Civic Theater
Albany NY
Carol King, Artistic Director

Some of the plays in this book
were given premieres at the above theaters
for which the playwrights are indeed grateful.

Contents

-THE BRIDGE THEATER-

For nine years the Bridge Theater was 'America's Most Unique Theater' but while the producers prepared to open its 10th year in 2009 of bringing the arts and entertainment to the Adirondack north country, a structural flaw was found on the Champlain Canal bridge located over Lock 12 of the canal. New York State was forced to close the bridge and end activities in the theater.

Imagine! A theater on a bridge! How did this unusual theater in Whitehall, New York, get its start? How did this come about?

In the fall of 1998 a group of local business men and women got together in a 'brain storming session' in order to come up with a plan to rejuvenate the beautiful historic, but economically depressed, downtown area of Whitehall. A performing arts center was one of ideas discussed by the group, but where would this theater be located?

Following up on an unusual idea, and with the splendid cooperation of the New York State Department of Transportation, the unused vehicle bridge over Lock 12 on the Champlain Canal in Whitehall was obtained on a year-to-year lease basis. Later in the fall of 1998, the non-profit Arts & Recreation Commission of Whitehall, New York, Inc. (ARCW) organization was established.

With a major grass roots effort and many long volunteer hours, the theater designed by local engineer David Mohn, was built on the vehicular structure and opened in July, 2000.

The Bridge Theater had been born!

Part of the motivation for the building of this theater was the production of a new play about Benedict Arnold at a local restaurant by the Riverview Entertainment Productions theater troupe. The Albany, New York based company first appeared at the Whitehall venue in 1999.

During the ensuing years, this professional company has been the resident theater troupe and has presented a number of historical plays (including five contained in this book) especially written for Whitehall's Bridge Theater.

"A Marriage of True Minds"

Rita Russell and William Hickman *(above)* portray Abigail and John Adams in the first performance of "A Marriage of True Minds" at the Bridge Theater in Whitehall NY.

"Hostess To History"

Carol King *(right)* appears as Dolly Madison in the first production of "Hostess To History" at The Bridge Theater.

"Champlain Onward"
Act One "Discovery of Lake"
Carol Jones and Richard Harte *(above)* appear as French
settlers in the first act of "Champlain Onward."

"Champlain Onward"
Danielle Ingerson and Ted
DeBonis (right) perform
as Samuel de Champlain
and his wife, Helene.

"Champlain Onward" Act Two "The Land of Skene"
Richard Harte and Janet Stasio *(above)* appear as
Colonel Skene and his sister, Elizabeth.

"Champlain Onward" Act Two "The Land of Skene"
Janet Stasio, left, as Elizabeth Skene greets her niece,
Kathi Skene played by Danielle Ingerson.

"Champlain Onward" Act Three "Victory in Defeat"
Ted DeBonis, left, performs as Benedict Arnold with
Susan Ingerson as Molly Sampson and Richard Harte as
Silas Perkins.

"Champlain Onward" Act Three "Victory in Defeat"
In a previous version of the Benedict Arnold saga the
company consisted of (from left) William Hickman, Carol
Jones, Michael Ryan, Donna Hatch and
Barry Corlew.

"Champlain Onward" Act Four "Whither Whitehall"
The Cast
(front, from left) Rie Lee, Susan Ingerson, Danielle Ingerson, Carol Jones, Ted DeBonis, Brittany Hurlburt, Janet Stasio *(rear)* Richard Harte, Gary Hurlburt

"Cases On The Canal"
(From left) Susan Ingerson, Douglas Bates, Danielle Ingerson, William Hickman and Janet Stasio perform in a scene in the play about Prohibition in Whitehall.

"Cases On The Canal"
The cast appears backstage on the bridge with Lake Champlain in the background. *(From left rear)* William Hickman, Danielle Ingerson, and Douglas Bates. *(Front)* Janet Stasio and Susan Ingerson.

"Cases on the Canal"
Danielle Ingerson *(left)* enjoys William Hickman's story about selling bootleg gin in a scene between niece and her wayward uncle.

"Cases on the Canal"
Danielle Ingerson *(right)* is aghast at story being told her by the showgirl friend of her uncle, performed by Janet Stasio.

"Cases on the Canal"
Susan Ingerson threatens to hit her bootlegging brother, played by William Hickman.

Cast members perform in a previous musical play, "Whither Whitehall" that was adapted without music and used as an act in "Champlain Onward." The actors, *(from left)* are: Barry Corlew. Bonnie Williams and Carol Jones.

Rita Russell and William Hickman, as John and Abigail Adams, perform in "A Marriage of True Minds" at a Quincy, Massachusetts theatre.

"A Marriage of True Minds"

A play based on the letters of John and Abigail Adams

By Martin P. Kelly

Performers in first production of the play in Whitehall, NY

John Adams...............*William Hickman*

Abigail Adams............*Rita Russell*

Note from the Author

In 2003, I suffered a fall that resulted in a severely broken leg that after several surgeries required almost seven months of recuperation.

While resting at home, I busied myself by working on the computer where one day I ran across the letters of John and Abigail Adams.

There were about 1,100 of them on the web site of the Massachusetts Historical Society and as I read them, I found myself drawn deeply into their lives and was particularly impressed with Abigail's writings.

What I more fully realized was that during a period from 1774 to 1784, these two people were separated for almost seven of those ten years.

John Adams was either in Philadelphia with the Continental Congress or later, serving as emissary in France, Holland and then England. Abigail Adams was at home in Quincy, Massachusetts caring for the couple's four children and other members of their families during severe weather and often deadly illnesses in the community.

Through all of this, Abigail Adams was still able to maintain the family farm and property as well as supervise the schooling of the children. She was a woman you could admire deeply across the span of several centuries.

The letters brought out the love each had for the other and the love of country expressed most ardently in their letters.

In essence, "A Marriage of True Minds" is, with their words, a play built around their lives during this important historical era with a continuity that exposed their tragic moments, their periods of happiness but, most of all, their love of country and each other.

The borrowing of Shakespeare's words for the play's title seemed most appropriate for what I felt about them and their relationship.

But most of all, we stand indebted to them and their compatriots of the late 18th century.

MARTIN P. KELLY

About John and Abigail Adams

John and Abigail Adams exchanged more than 1,100 letters prior to and during their marriage, beginning with their first meeting. The letters that form the first act cover a period beginning in 1774 and carrying through mid-1777. The second act is indebted to their correspondence from 1777-1784.

John Adams, born in 1735, graduated from Harvard with a law degree and advanced from circuit lawyer, covering New Hampshire and Massachusetts, his native colony, to become its representative in Congress. As such he led in the writing the Articles of Confederation and the Declaration of Independence in Philadelphia. From that time, he and Abigail, parents of four children, were apart for almost seven years during his service to his country, both in America and abroad.

Abigail Adams, born in 1744, was the daughter of the Rev. William Smith and Elizabeth Quincy Smith. She was educated with the help of her grandmother, Elizabeth Norton Smith, and the many books in her father's extensive library.

In her husband's absence, Abigail kept their home intact and tended their farm despite British occupation of the Massachusetts colony, shortages of food and commodities and the ravages of diseases during the American Revolution.

She also had the distinction of being the wife of the second president of the United States - John Adams—and the mother of the sixth president, her son—John Quincy Adams. The only other woman to share this distinction of having a husband and a son serve as presidents of this country is Barbara Bush.

Abigail Adams died of typhoid fever in 1818 at age 74, eight years before her husband. He died in 1826 on the same day that Thomas Jefferson also passed away. Ironically, it was July 4. Both were writers of the Declaration of Independence and both served as presidents of the United States.

John Adams died while his son, John Quincy, was serving as president.

The italized word(s) following the character's name and prior to the individual speech indicates for the actor the tone and impact of the particular speech.

The actors pretend to write their individual speeches when, in reality, they are reading them. So, as one pretends to write, the other actor is listening as if pretending to read it.

Then, the second actor repeats the routine when he or she writes a letter.

ACT ONE

(At curtain, Abigail and John are sitting at desks on opposite sides of the stage. She is looking at a miniature of her husband. She puts it on the desk and then begins writing)

ABIGAIL: *(Anxious)* The great distance between us makes the time appear very long to me. It seems already a month since you left me. The great anxiety I feel for my country, for you and for our family renders the day tedious, and the night unpleasant.

JOHN: *(Pleased but apologetic)* I received your letter at New York and it is not easy for you to imagine the pleasure it has given me. I have not found an opportunity to write since I left Boston. I don't choose to write by post for fear of foul play. But, as we are now within 42 miles of Philadelphia, I hope there to find some private hand by which I can convey this.

ABIGAIL: *(Stoic)* I have taken a very great fondness for reading ancient history since you left me. I am determined to go through it if possible in these my days of solitude. We have had a charming rain which lasted 12 hours and has greatly revived the dying fruits of the earth.

JOHN: *(Sense of pride)* Your account of the rain refreshed me. The summer heat here in Philadelphia can be unbearable. Still, the spirit of the people wherever we have been seems to be very favorable. They universally consider our cause as their own, and resolve to abide the determination of the Congress.

ABIGAIL: *(Concerned, comforting)* I wish you every private blessing and wisdom to guide you in these difficult days. The little flock remembers Poppa, and kindly wishes to see him. So does your most affectionate...Abigail Adams.

JOHN: *(Fatherly)* Remember my tender love to my little Nabby. Tell her she must write me a letter. I am charmed with our little Johnny.

I am glad to hear he is so good a boy as to read to his Momma for her entertainment and to keep himself out of the company of rude children. Kiss my little Charley and Tommy for me. Tell them I will be home by November, how much sooner I know not.

ABIGAIL: *(Chiding)* Five weeks have passed and not one line have I received. I had rather give a dollar for a letter by the post though the consequences should be that I eat but one meal a day for those three weeks to come.

JOHN: *(Restrained apology)* It is a great affliction to me that I cannot write to you oftener than I do. There are so many hindrances. It would fill volumes to give you an idea of the scenes I behold and the characters I converse with.

ABIGAIL: *(Somewhat peevish)* Everyone I see is inquiring about you and when did I hear. All my intelligence is collected from the newspaper and I can only reply that I saw by that, that you arrived on such a day. I know your fondness for writing and your inclination to let me hear from you by the first safe conveyance. This makes me suspect that some letter or other has miscarried. I hope now that you have arrived at Philadelphia you will find means to convey me some intelligence.

JOHN: *(Begins to orate)* I am very well: write me as often as you can. I know not how we can live without the British government. But, the experiment must be tried. Let us eat potatoes and drink water. Let us wear canvass and undressed sheepskins, rather than submit to the ignominious domination that is prepared for us.

ABIGAIL: *(Wryly)* The British Governor is making all kinds of warlike preparations such as mounting cannon upon Beacon Hill, digging entrenchments above Boston, and camping a regiment there. The people are alarmed.

This past Sunday about 200 of our men, preceded by a horse cart, marched down to the powder house in Charlestown and took the powder and placed it in a secret place. They do not want the Tories to get it.

There is not a Tory but hides his head. The church parson thought they were coming after him and hid in his garret while another jumped out his window and hid in the corn and still a third crept under his bed and prayed his beads.

JOHN: *(Explanatory)* Sitting down to write to you is a scene almost too tender for my state of nerves. It calls up to my view the anxious, distressed state you must be in, amidst the confusion and dangers which surround you. I long to return and administer all the consolation in my power but when I shall have accomplished all the business I have to do here I know not. If it should be necessary to stay here till Christmas, or longer, in order to effect our purposes, I am determined patiently to wait.

ABIGAIL: *(Longing)* I dare not express to you at 300 miles distance how ardently I long for your return. I have some very miserly wishes; and cannot consent to your spending one hour in town till at least I have had you twelve.

JOHN: *(Frustrated)* The business of the Congress is tedious, beyond expression. This assembly is like no other that ever existed. Every man is an orator, a critic, a statesman, and therefore every man upon every question must show his oratory, his criticism and his political abilities. The consequence of this is that business is drawn and spun out to an immeasurable length. I believe that we even moved and seconded a resolution that three and two make five.

ABIGAIL: *(Time wears heavy)* Ten weeks absence knows not how to brook restraint any longer but will break forth and flow through my pen. May like sensations enter thy breast and mingle themselves with those I wish to communicate. In giving them utterance, I have felt more sincere pleasure than I have known since the 10th of August.

JOHN: *(Concerned)* At a time when my friends and country are in such keen distress, I am scarcely ever interrupted by apprehensions for my personal safety. I am often concerned for you and our dear babes, surrounded as you are by people who are too timorous and too much susceptible of alarms. I hope you will not be impressed by them.

ABIGAIL: *(Didactic with humor)* I greatly fear that the arm of treachery and violence is lifted over us as a scourge and heavy punishment from heaven for our numerous offences, and for the misuse of our advantages.

If we expect to inherit the blessings of our Fathers, we should return more to their primitive simplicity of manners, and not sink into inglorious ease.

I rejoice at the favorable account you give me of your health; may it be continued. My health is much better than it was last fall. Some folks say I grow very fat. Let me know when you think of returning to your most affectionate… Abigail Adams.

JOHN: *(Anxious instruction)* The trials of our unhappy and devoted people are likely to be severe indeed. God grant that the furnace of affliction may refine them. God grant that they may be relieved from their present distress. In case of real danger, fly to the woods with our children. Give my most tender love to them, and to all.

ABIGAIL: *(Alarmed)* Last Sunday morning when I awoke at 6 o'clock, I was told that the drum had been some time beating and alarm guns were fired. The Weymouth bell was ringing. The whole town was in confusion. Three sloops and a cutter dropped anchor and 300 British troops prepared to march into town. Our house was a scene of confusion with soldiers coming in for lodging, for breakfast, for supper, for drink. Sometimes refugees from Boston, tired and frightened, seek asylum for the night or a week. You can hardly imagine how we live.

JOHN: *(Concern)* We had yesterday a report of a battle at Bunker Hill and Dorchester Point with three colonels wounded, one mortally. God Almighty's Providence preserve, sustain and comfort you.

ABIGAIL: *(Saddened)* My father has been more affected with the destruction of Charlestown, than with anything that has taken place. The city of his fathers' sepulchers lies in waste and the gates thereof are consumed by fire.

(Upset) We live in constant expectation of hostilities. The British delight in molesting us on the Sabbath. Two Sabbaths we have been in such alarms that we have had no meeting.

JOHN: *(Sympathizes)* It is not at all surprising to me that the wanton, cruel and infamous conflagration of Charlestown, the place of your father's nativity, should afflict him. It is a disreputable method of conducting war but every year brings us fresh evidence that we have nothing to hope for from our loving mother country but cruelties more abominable than those practiced by savages. The distresses of the worthy inhabitants of Boston and the other seaport towns are enough to melt a heart of stone.

Our consolation must be that cities may be rebuilt, and a people reduced to poverty may acquire fresh property. But a constitution of government once changed from freedom, can never be restored. Liberty once lost, is lost forever. When the people once surrender their share in the legislature, and their right of defending the limitation upon the government, and of resisting every encroachment upon them, they can never regain it.

ABIGAIL: *(Caring)* You would laugh to see our children all run upon the sight of a letter—like chickens for a crumb when the hen clucks.

'Tis exceeding dry weather! Even as the meadow has been mowed, the crop will not be as last year's. Pray let me hear from you by every opportunity till I have the joy of once more meeting you.

JOHN: *(Tenderly)* My dear Nabby, Johnny, Charley and Tommy: I long to see you, and to share with your Momma the pleasures of your conversation.

(Comforting) Tell them the clergy here, of every denomination, not excepting the Episcopalian, thunder and lighten every Sabbath. They pray for Boston and Massachusetts—they thank God most explicitly and fervently for our remarkable successes—they pray for the American army.

ABIGAIL: *(Uplifting)* I have this afternoon had the pleasure of receiving your letter by your friend Mr. Collins. It was next to seeing you, my dearest friend. Mr. Collins could tell me more particularly about you and your health than I have been able to hear since you left me. I rejoice in his account of your better health, and your spirits, though he says I must not expect to see you till next spring. I hope he does not speak the truth.

JOHN: *(Weary)* It is now almost three months since I last left you, in every part of which my anxiety about you and the children, as well as our country, has been extreme. The business I have had upon my mind has been as great and important as can be entrusted to one man.

We have 50 or 60 men to form a great empire, at the same time a country of 1,500 miles extent to fortify, men to arm and train, a naval power to begin, an extensive commerce to regulate, numerous tribes of Indians to negotiate with, and a standing army of 27,000 men to raise, pay, and feed. Pity these 50 or 60 men.

ABIGAIL: *(Saddened)* 'Tis with a sad heart I take my pen to write to you because I must be the bearer of what will greatly afflict and distress you. Your brother Elihu lies very dangerously ill with the dysentery. His life is despaired of. He is calmly resigned to the will of heaven. Woe follows woe.

My dear mother's kindness brought her to see me and our little Tommy when I was ill. She has taken the disorder and lies so bad that we have little hopes of her recovery. She is possess'd with the idea that she shall not recover, and I fear it will prove but too true.

JOHN: *(Surprised)* This morning I received your two letters and the intelligence they contain came upon me by surprise, as I never had the least intimation before, that any of our family was ill. You can easily conceive the state of mind in which I am at present.

I thought of setting off immediately for Braintree. Yet, the state of public affairs is so critical that I am half afraid to leave my station. I rejoice that Nabby and her brothers have hitherto escaped and pray God that His goodness may be still continued to them.

ABIGAIL: *(Weary)* 'Tis a fortnight tonight since I wrote you a line during which, I have been confined with the jaundice, rheumatism and a most violent cold. The great and incessant rains we have had this fall may have occasioned some of the present disorders. The jaundice is very prevalent.

Colonel Warren dampened my spirits greatly by telling me that the colony had prolonged your stay in Philadelphia another month. I was pleasing myself with the thoughts that you would soon be upon your return. I hope the public will reap what I sacrifice.

JOHN: *(Concerned)* The nation is embraced most vigorously by a social infirmity that I must attribute to a local attachment, as is my overweening prejudice in favor of New England. The people here are purer English blood, less mixed with Scotch, Irish, Dutch, French, Danish, and Swedish than any other; and descended from Englishmen who left Europe, in purer times than the present and less tainted with corruption, than those they left behind them.

ABIGAIL: *(Informative)* There have been movements amongst the British troops as if they mean to evacuate the town of Boston. Between 70 and 80 vessels of various sizes lay in a row all of which appear to be loaded in fair sight of this place.

By what can be collected from our own observations and from deserters, they have been plundering the town. That they will leave appears to be the prevailing opinion of most people. Orders are given to our army to hold themselves in readiness to march at a moment's warning.

JOHN: *(Orates)* I sent you from New York a pamphlet entitled "Common Sense" written in vindication of a common faith to repel encroachments of tyranny and depredations of oppression. This common faith will prevail unless the cunning British ministry, by proposing negotiations and terms of reconciliation, should divert the present current from its channel.

Reconciliation, if practicable, and peace, if attainable, you very well know would be agreeable to my interest as to any man's. But I see no prospect, no probability, no possibility. I detest the hypocritical heart which pretends to expect it when in truth it does not.

ABIGAIL: *(Spirited)* Firing was occasioned by our soldiers taking possession of Nook Hill which they kept in spite of the British cannon barrage. This has really obliged our enemy to decamp this morning aboard the transports. To what a contemptible situation are the troops of Britain reduced. They have carried off everything they could possibly take, and what they could not they have burnt, broke or hove into the water. Here from Penns Hill we have a view of the largest fleet ever seen in America. You can count upwards of 170 sail. They look like a forest.

JOHN: *(Apologetic)* The enclosed papers will inform you where the British fleet is. You ask what sort of defense Virginia can make. I believe they will make an able defense. Their militia and Minute Men have been some time employed in training themselves. North Carolina which is a warlike colony, has several battalions ready at Continental expense and a pretty good militia.

ABIGAIL: *(Controlled)* I feel very differently at the approach of spring to what I did a month ago. I think the sun looks brighter, the birds sing more melodiously, and nature puts on a more cheerful countenance. I long to hear that you have declared an independency.

In the new code of laws which I suppose it will be necessary for you to make, I desire you would remember the ladies, and be more generous and favorable to them than your ancestors. Do not put such unlimited power into the hands of the husbands. Remember all men would be tyrants if they could. If particular care and attention is not paid to the ladies, we are determined to foment a rebellion.

JOHN: *(Whimsical, yet didactic)* As to the Declaration of Independence, be patient. As for your extraordinary code of laws, I cannot but laugh. We have been told our struggle has loosened the bonds of government everywhere: That children and apprentices were disobedient, that schools and colleges were grown turbulent, that Indians slighted their guardians. But your letter was the first intimation that another tribe more numerous and powerful than all the rest has grown discontented. This is rather too coarse a compliment but you are so saucy. I won't blot it out. Depend on it. We know better than to repeal our masculine systems. Although they are in full force, you know they are little more than theory. We dare not exert our power in its full latitude. We are obliged to go fair, and softly. In practice you know we are the subjects. We have only the name of masters, and rather than give up this, which would completely subject us to the despotism of the petticoat, I hope General Washington and our brave heroes would fight and, every good politician would plot as long as he would against this despotism.

ABIGAIL: *(Determined)* That your sex is naturally tyrannical is a truth so thoroughly established as to admit no dispute. But as you wish to be happy, then willingly give up the harsh title of Master for the more tender and endearing one of Friend. Why then not put it out of the power of the vicious and the lawless to use us with cruelty and indignity with impunity.

Men of sense in all ages abhor those customs which treat us only as the vassals of your sex. Regard us then as beings placed by Providence under your protection and in imitation of the Supreme Being make use of that power only for our happiness.

JOHN: *(Comforting)* It gives me concern to think of the many cares you must have upon your mind. Your reputation as a farmer, or anything else you undertake, I dare say, exceeds your partner's character as a statesman.

As to my return, I have not a thought of it. Journeys of such a length are tedious and expensive both of time and money neither of which are my own. I hope to spend the next Christmas where I did the last, and after that I hope to be relieved of these duties.

But, if my countrymen insist upon my serving them another year, they must let me bring my whole family with me. Indeed I could keep house here with my dear partner, four children and two servants as cheap as I maintain myself here with two horses and a servant at lodgings.

ABIGAIL: *(Lonely)* How many are the solitary hours I spend, ruminating upon the past, and anticipating the future, whilst you, overwhelmed with the cares of state, have but few moments you can devote to any individual. All domestic pleasures and enjoyments are absorbed in the great important duty you owe your country.

Thus, I do suppress every wish, and silence every murmur, acquiescing in a painful separation from the companion of my youth, and the friend of my heart.

JOHN: *(Enthused)* The late Act of Parliament has made so deep an onerous impression upon people's minds throughout the colonies, it is looked upon as the last stretch of oppression. We are hastening rapidly to great events. Governments will be up everywhere in the colonies before midsummer and an end to royal style.

ABIGAIL: *(Resolved)* A government of more stability is much wanted in this colony, and they are ready to receive it from the hands of the Congress. Since I have begun with maxims of state I will add another: that a people may let a king fall, yet still remain a people, but if a king lets his people slip from him, he is no longer a king. And as this is most certainly our case, why not proclaim to the world in decisive terms your own importance!

JOHN: *(Explanatory)* In one or two of your letters you remind me to think of you as I ought. Be assured there is not an hour in the day, in which I do not think of you as I ought, that is with every sentiment of tenderness, esteem and admiration.

When I consider the great events which are passed, and those greater which are rapidly advancing, and that I may have been instrumental of touching some springs, and turning some small wheels, which have had and will have such effects, I feel an awe upon my mind which is not easily described.

Great Britain has at last driven America to the last step, a complete separation from her, total absolute independence, not only of her parliament but of her crown.

ABIGAIL: *(Softly pleading)* Your letters alleviate a tedious absence. I long earnestly for a Saturday evening and to experience a similar pleasure to that which I used to find in the return of my friend after a week's absence. The idea of a year's absence dissolves me.

JOHN: *(Stirring)* The Second Day of July 1776 will be the most memorable epoch in the history of America! I am apt to believe that it will be celebrated by succeeding generations, as the great anniversary festival. It ought to be commemorated, as the Day of Deliverance by solemn acts of devotion to God Almighty.

It ought to be solemnized with pomp and parade, with shows, games, sports, guns, bells, bonfires and illuminations from one end of the continent to the other from this time forward forever more. Yesterday, the greatest question was decided, which ever was debated in America, and a greater perhaps, never was or will be decided among men.

A resolution was passed without one dissenting colony *(orates)* "that these united colonies, are, and of right ought to be free and independent states, and as such, they have, and of right ought to have full power to make war, conclude peace, establish commerce, and to do all the other acts and things, which other states may rightfully do."

You will see in a few days a Declaration setting forth the causes which have impell'd us to this mighty revolution, and the reasons which will justify it, in the sight of God and man.

ABIGAIL: *(Proud)* By yesterday's post I received two letters dated 3rd and 4th of July and though your letters never fail to give me pleasure yet it was greatly heightened by the prospect of the future happiness and glory of our country; nor am I a little gratified when I reflect that a person so nearly connected with me has had the honor of being a principal actor in laying a foundation for its future greatness. May the foundation of our new constitution, be justice, truth and righteousness. Like the wise man's house may it be founded upon those rocks and then neither storms nor tempests will overthrow it.

JOHN: *(Forlorn)* This has been a dull day for me. I waited the arrival of the post with much solicitude and impatience, but his arrival made me more solicitous still. If you were too busy to write, I hoped that some kind hand would have been found to let me know something about you.

Do my friends think that I have been a politician so long as to have lost all feeling? What have I done, or omitted to do, that I should be thus forgotten and neglected in the most tender and affecting scene of my life. Don't mistake me! I don't blame you! Your time and thoughts must have been wholly taken up with your own and your family's situation and necessities.

ABIGAIL: *(Disarming)* I have no doubt that my dearest friend is anxious to know how his Portia does, and his little flock of children under the operation of a disease once formidable. I have the pleasure to tell him that they are all comfortable. Nabby has been very ill, but the eruption begins to make its appearance upon her, and upon Johnny. Tommy is so well that the doctor inoculated him again today fearing it has not taken. Charley has no complaints yet, though his arm has been very sore.

JOHN: *(Thankful)* I suspect that you intended to have run slyly through the small pox with the family, without letting me know it, and then have sent me an account that you were all well.

This might be a kind intention which has made me very joyous.

ABIGAIL: *(Cheerful pride)* Last Thursday after hearing a very good sermon I went with the multitude into Kings Street to hear the proclamation for independence read and proclaimed. Field pieces were brought there, troops appeared under arms and the inhabitants assembled there. Great attention was given to every word. When the reading was ended, a cry of "God Save Our American State" was heard along with cheers which filled the air. Bells rang, cannons were fired and platoons marched. Every face appeared joyful.

JOHN: *(Wryly)* Went this morning to the Baptist meeting, and the minister disappointed. His action was violent to a degree bordering on fury; his gestures unnatural and distorted. Not the least idea of grace in his motions, or elegance in his style. His voice was vociferous and boisterous, and his composition almost wholly destitute of ingenuity. I wonder extremely at the fondness of our people for southern preachers. There is no one thing in which we excel them more, than in our university, our scholars and our preachers.

If ever I get through this scene of politics and war, I will spend the remainder of my days, in endeavoring to instruct my countrymen in the art of making the most of their abilities and virtues, an art which they have too much neglected.

Oh! Too many of my countrymen lack art and address. These imperfections must be remedied. New England must produce the heroes, the statesmen, the philosophers, or America will make no great figure for some time.

ABIGAIL: *(Advocacy)* I most sincerely wish that some more liberal plan might be laid and executed for the benefit of the rising generation and that our constitution may be distinguished for learning and virtue.

If we mean to have heroes, statesmen and philosophers, we should have learned women.

The world perhaps would laugh at me, and accuse me of vanity. But you, I know, have a mind too enlarged and liberal to disregard the sentiment. If much depends, as is allowed, upon the early education of youth, great benefit must arise from literary accomplishments in women. If you complain of neglect in education in sons, what shall I say with regard to daughters who every day experience the want of it.

JOHN: *(Anxious)* If you will come to Philadelphia in September, I will stay, as long as you please. I should be as proud and happy as a bridegroom.

ABIGAIL: *(Emphatic)* I have no thoughts of coming to Philadelphia, even if you had not thoughts of returning till December. I live in daily expectation of seeing you here. Your health I think requires your immediate return. Nabby is poorly this morning. The pox is near the turn, 6 or 7 hundred boils are no agreeable feeling. You and I know not what a feeling it is. The town, instead of being clear of this distemper, is now in the height of it, hundreds having it in the natural way through the deceitfulness of inoculation. Adieu, ever yours.

JOHN: *(Solemn)* Yesterday morning I took a walk to Mr. Charles Wilson Peele's painting room to see his large picture containing a group of figures which upon inquiry, I found were his family. One moving picture by this patriot was of his wife, all bathed in tears, with a child almost about six months old, laid out upon her lap.

ABIGAIL: *(Anxiety)*. I hear what I have feared for some time. I was certain that your nerves must be so sorely tried, and your constitution now depleted, to continue well throughout a load of business. Such intense application, in such a climate through the burning heat of summer, 'tis too much even for a constitution of steel and ought not to be required. I entreat you to return and that speedily. Is there any assistance you can think of that I can procure for you? Pray, let me know. Our colony court does not set 'til the 28th of this month of August so no delegates can be chosen to relieve you till then. But, if you are low in health do not wait for that.

JOHN: *(Informative)* This day is most remarkable as a result of a message from Lord Howe desiring to have an hour's conversation on Staten Island with some of the members of Congress. We have spent three or four days debating here in Philadelphia whether we should appoint any members to confer privately with his Lordship.

It was decided to appoint a committee of their body to wait on him, to know whether he had power to treat with Congress upon terms of peace and to hear any propositions that his Lordship may think proper to make. When the Committee came to be balloted for, Dr. Franklin and your humble servant were unanimously chosen. Mr. Edward Rutledge of South Carolina was voted as the third member of the committee.

ABIGAIL: *(Worried)* I sit down this evening to write you, but I hardly know what to think about your going to New York. Your letter dampened my spirits. When I had no expectation of your return till December, I endeavored to bring my mind to acquiesce in the too painful situation. I have every letter expected to find the day set for your return.

JOHN: *(Informative)* We met Lord Howe and had about three hours' conversation with him. As a result of the interview it is now plain that his Lordship has no power, but what is given him in the Act of Parliament. His commission authorizes him to grant pardons upon submission, and to converse, confer, consult and advise upon American grievances with such persons as he may think proper.

ABIGAIL: *(Anxious)* I cannot consent to your tarrying much longer. I know your health must greatly suffer from so constant application to business and so little exercise.

Whilst you are engaged in the Congress, your own domestic affairs require your presence at home, and that your wife and children are in danger of wanting bread.

Unless you return, what little property you possess will be lost. The house in Boston is going to ruin. It is so exceeding damp being shut up, that the floors are mildewed, the ceiling falling down, and the paper moldy and falling from the walls. I know the weight of public cares lie so heavily upon you that I have been loath to mention your own private ones.

JOHN: *(Somewhat teasing)* I suppose your ladyship has been in the twitters for some time past because you have not received a letter by every post. But I am coming to make my apology in person. I yesterday asked and obtained a leave of absence. It will take me till next Monday to get ready, to finish off a few remnants of public business, and to put my private affairs in proper order. On the 14th day of October I shall get away. But I don't expect to reach home in less than a fortnight, perhaps not in three weeks, but before Thanksgiving, as I shall be obliged to make stops by the way.

ABIGAIL: *(Weary)* We have had very severe weather almost ever since you left us again after the holidays. About the middle of February came a snow of a foot and a half deep and with the wind made the banks five and six feet high. There is such a cry for bread in the town of Boston. The bakers deal out but a loaf a day to the largest families. The meat carried to market is miserably poor, and so little of it that many people say they were as well supplied during the siege.

JOHN: *(Melancholic)* When I reflect upon the prospect before me of so long an absence from all that I hold dear in this world, those who contribute to my private personal happiness, it makes me melancholy. When I think of your circumstances I am more so, and yet I rejoice in these reflections in spite of all this melancholy. God Almighty's Providence protect and bless you and yours and mine.

The Presbyterian Meeting House where we now meet in Baltimore stands upon a hill just at the back of the town, from whence we in Congress have a very fair prospect of the town, and the water upon which it stands. I shall take opportunities to describe this town and state more particularly to you hereafter

ABIGAIL: *(Miffed)* I received a letter dated February 10th and not being franked, it cost me a dollar. If it had contain'd half as much as I wanted to know I would not have grumbled, but you do not tell me how you do, nor what accommodations you have, which is of more consequence to me than all the descriptions of cities, states and kingdoms of the world.

JOHN: *(Apologetic)* I am now situated in a pleasant part of town, in Walnut Street in the south side of Philadelphia. The landlady buried four husbands, one a tailor, two shoemakers and one Gilbert Tennent, and still is ready for a fifth, and well deserves him too.

Still, I long for rural and domestic scenes, for the warbling of birds and the prattle of my children.

ABIGAIL: *(Anxiety)* As the summer advances I have many anxieties. I must summon all the strength I am mistress of since what cannot be help'd must be endured. Mrs. Howard, a lady for whom I know you had a great respect, died yesterday. She was delivered of a son yesterday week but a mortification of her bowels occasioned her death.

Everything of this kind naturally shocks a person in similar circumstances. How great the mind that can overcome the fear of death!

How anxious is the heart of a parent who looks upon a family of young and helpless children and thinks of leaving them to a world full of snares and temptations. I have enjoyed as much health since the small pox as I have known in any year.

For about three weeks past I have got the better of color and a clumsy figure which make their appearance so much as Master John says: "Maar, I never saw anybody grow so fat as you do."

Remember the loving sentiments from her who knows no earthly happiness equal to that of being tenderly beloved by her dearest friend.

JOHN: *(Anxious)* My mind is again anxious, and my heart in pain for my dearest friend. Three times have I felt the most distressing sympathy with my partner, without being able to afford her any kind of solace, or assistance; when the family was sick of the dysentery, and so many of our friends died of it; when you all had the smallpox. And now I think I feel as anxious as ever.

ABIGAIL: *(Weary calm)* I should greatly rejoice to see you. I know of no earthly blessing which would make me happier. No separation has been more painful to me than the last. May the joy of meeting again be equal to the pain of separation.

I regret that I am in a situation to wish away one of the most precious blessings of life. Yet, as the months pass, I count them up with pleasure and reckon upon tomorrow as the fifth which has passed since your absence.

Good night! 'Tis so dark that I cannot see to add more than that I am with the utmost tenderness: yours, ever yours.

JOHN: *(Compassionate)* Oh, that I could be near, to say a few kind words, or show a few kind looks, or do a few kind actions. Oh, that I could take from my dearest, a share of her distress, or relieve her of the whole.

ABIGAIL: *(Anxiety)* I sit down to write you this post, and from my present feelings, it's the last I shall be able to write for some time, if I should do well. I have been very unwell for this week past, with some complaints that have been new to me, though I hope not dangerous.

I was last night taken with a shaking fit, and am very apprehensive. As I have no reason today to think otherwise, what may be the consequences to me, Heaven only knows. I know not of any injury to myself, nor anything which could occasion what I fear.

This day, ten years ago, Master John came into this world. May I have reason again to recollect it with similar gratitude. Adieu!

JOHN: *(John opens an envelope and reads aloud with his back three-quarters to the audience)*

July 13, 1777

Sir:

The day before yesterday, Mrs. Adams was delivered of a daughter; but it grieves me to add, sir, that it was stillborn. It was an exceedingly fine looking child.

Everything I can do that respects her comfort, or that respects the children, shall be attended to by your most obedient servant,

J. Thaxter.

ABIGAIL: *(Calmly)* Join with me, my dearest friend, in gratitude to heaven that a life I know you value has been spared and carried through distress and danger although the dear infant is numbered now with its ancestors. My heart was much set upon a daughter. I had had a strong persuasion that my desire would be granted me. I feel myself weakened by this exertion, yet I could not refrain from the temptation of writing with my hand to you.

Adieu, dearest of friends, adieu. Yours most affectionately....

JOHN: *(Angry with himself, John turns slowly to the audience)* It is intolerable that the time I should enjoy with my wife and children upon my little farm, should pass away and laugh at me, for laboring day after day and month after month in a conclave where neither taste, nor fancy, nor reason, nor passion, nor appetite can be gratified.

(John steps toward audience) Posterity! You will never know how much it cost the present generation to preserve your freedom! I hope you will make a good use of it. If you do not, I shall repent in heaven, that I ever took half the pains to preserve it

(John looks to where Abigail remains seated with head bowed as lights dim to....)

End of Act One

ACT TWO

(John and Abigail return to the desks they occupied during Act 1)

ABIGAIL: *(Upbeat)* There has been much noise in the town for weeks. You must know that there is a great scarcity of sugar and coffee, articles which the female part of the state are very loath to give up, especially whilst they consider the scarcity occasioned by the merchants having hidden a large quantity. A number of females, some say a hundred, assembled with a cart and wagons, marched down to the warehouse and demanded the keys which the eminent, wealthy, and stingy merchant refused to deliver, upon which one of the women seized him by the neck and tossed him into the cart.

Upon his finding no quarter, he delivered the keys, whereupon they opened the warehouse, hoisted out the coffee themselves, put it into the wagons, and drove off. A large gathering of men stood amazed, silent spectators of the whole transaction.

JOHN: *(Amused)* You have made me merry with the coffee frolic but I hope the females will leave off their attachment to coffee. I assure you, the best families in Philadelphia have left off in a great measure the use of West India goods. We must bring ourselves to live upon the produce of our own country. Milk has become the breakfast of many of the wealthiest and most genteel families here. Oh! What would I give for some of your cider?

ABIGAIL: *(Worried)* The late evacuation by our troops at Ticonderoga has appeared so alarming to me and given me as much uneasiness as did the commencement of the war. Had the enemy fought and conquered the fort, I could have borne it, but our soldiers to leave it with all the stores before it was even attacked, has excited a thousand suspicions, and gives room for more wrath than suspicions. We look every day for an attack upon us this way. The reports of this week are that a number of transports with English troops have arrived at Newport.

JOHN: *(Informative)* The transports of which you speak, a fleet of 100 sail, was seen off the Capes of Delaware and Chesapeake last Thursday. Lord Howe makes no decision yet. How many of his men and horses will be crippled by this strange coasting voyage of five weeks, one would wonder?

We have given New England men a complete triumph in sending General Gates to Saratoga. Never was a more glorious opportunity than Burgoyne has given us of destroying him, by marching down so far towards Albany. Let New England turn out and cut off his retreat.

ABIGAIL: *(Jubilant)* The joyful news of the surrender of General Burgoyne and all his army to our victorious troops at Saratoga prompted me to take a ride to town to join tomorrow with my friends in thanksgiving and praise to the Supreme Being who hath so remarkably delivered our enemies into our hands. Burgoyne is being marched here in the middle of the week. I have read many articles of capitulation but none which ever contained so generous terms before. Many people find fault with them but perhaps do not consider sufficiently the circumstances of General Gates who, by delaying and exacting more, might have lost all. This must be said of him that he has followed the golden rule.

JOHN: *(Upbeat)* Since a courier goes off to Boston tomorrow, I have seized a moment to congratulate you on the great glorious success of our arms in the north, which will give our country a reputation in Europe.

ABIGAIL: *(Sentimental)* This day, October 25, 1777, dearest of friends, completes 13 years since we were solemnly united in wedlock; three years of this time we have been cruelly separated. I have patiently as I could endure it with the relief that you were serving your country, and rendering your fellow creatures essential benefits. May future generations rise up and call you blessed, and the present generation behave worthy of the blessings you are laboring to secure for them. Then, I shall have less reason to regret the deprivation of my own particular felicity.

JOHN: *(Pleased)* I am in New Hampshire in good health. My case in Portsmouth comes before my old friend Dr. Joshua Brackett as judge of admiralty. How it will go, I know not. The defendants are said to be very tenacious and have many connections. So that we have prejudice, and influence to fear: Justice, policy and law are, I am very sure, on our side. I have had many opportunities, in the course of this journey, to observe, how deeply rooted our righteous cause for independence is in the minds of the people.

One morning, I asked my landlady what I had to pay? "Nothing!" she said. I was welcome and she hoped I would always make her house my house and she should be happy to entertain all those gentlemen who have been raised up by Providence to be the Saviors of their Country.

ABIGAIL: *(Restrained anger)*

Dear Mr. James Lovell:

Your letters arrived in the absence of Mr. Adams who is gone as far as Portsmouth, little thinking of your plot against him. Oh, Sir! You who are possessed of sensibility, and a tender heart, how could you contrive to rob me of my happiness? I can hardly be reconciled to you, you who so lately experienced, as has my husband, what it was to be restored to your family after painful absence from it. Then in a few weeks you were torn from it by a call from your country. You obeyed the summons to return to Philadelphia but how could you so soon forget your sufferings and place your friend, my husband, in a more painful situation considering the risk and hazard of a foreign voyage.

I know, sir, by this appointment of my husband to the embassy in France you mean the public good, or you would not thus call upon me to sacrifice my tranquility and happiness. I would not wish him to be less deserving of the esteem of his country though I am sometimes almost selfish enough to wish his abilities confined to private life.

(Deliberate calm) I beg you excuse me, sir, for writing thus freely; it has been a relief to my mind to drop some of my sorrows through my

pen, which, had my husband been present, would have been poured into his bosom.

JOHN: *(Upbeat)* We shall soon be on board the Boston, a 24-gun frigate, and may God prosper our voyage, in every stage of it, as much as the beginning. Johnny sends his duty to his Mamma and his love to his sister and brothers. He behaves like a man. Tomorrow morning we sail and within the month arrive in Bordeaux.

ABIGAIL: *(Worried)* I have waited with great patience, restraining as much as possible every anxious idea for three months. But now every vessel which arrives sets my expectation upon the wing, and I pray for the happy tidings of your safety and welfare. My imagination sits you down upon the French shore, a land to which Americans are now bound to transfer their affections. I anticipate the pleasure you must feel and, though so many leagues distant, share in the joy of finding the great interest of our country so generously espoused and nobly aided by so powerful a monarch.

JOHN: *(Concern)* On the 13th of February, I left you. It is now the third of June, and have not received a line, nor heard a word, directly nor indirectly, concerning you since my departure. This is a situation of mind, to which I never was before, and I assure you I feel a great deal of anxiety at it; yet I do not wonder at it, because I suppose few vessels have sailed from Boston since ours.

ABIGAIL: *(Affectionate)* Difficult as the day is, cruel as this war has been, separated as I am on account of it from the dearest connection in life, I would not exchange my country for the wealth of the Indies. Nor would I be any other than an American though I might be Queen or Empress of any nation upon the globe. My soul does not seek pomp or power. Beneath my humble roof, bless'd with the society and tenderest affection of my dear partner, I have enjoyed as much felicity, and as exquisite pleasure from my intimate connection with one who is esteemed worthy of the important trust devolved upon him.

JOHN: *(Exhilirated)* It would be endless to attempt a description of this country. There is so much danger that my letter may fall into malicious hands, that I should not choose to be too free in my observations upon the customs and manners of this people. But this much I may say with truth and without offence. Nature and art have conspired to render every thing here delightful, religion and government excepted. But these are no afflictions to me because I have well fixed it in my mind, as a principle, that every nation has a right to that religion and government which it chooses, and as long as people please themselves in these great points, I am determined they shall not displease me.

ABIGAIL: *(Overjoyed)* Shall I tell my dearest that tears of joy fill'd my eyes this morning at the sight of his well known hand, the first time it has bless'd my sight since his four months' absence. About ten days ago, an English paper given me contained an account under Paris news of your arrival at the abode of Dr. Franklin. And last week, the captain of the Boston informed me he left you well the 11th of March and that he had letters for me but destroyed them when his ship was taken by the British navy.

I have lived a life of fear and anxiety ever since you left me. Not more than a week after your departure, the horrid story of Doctor Franklin's assassination was received from France and sent to Congress. It was nearly two months before that news was contradicted.

JOHN: *(Reportorial)* This country is one great garden. There are no people in the world who take so much pain to please. Their arts, manners, taste and language are more respected in Europe than those of any other nation. Yet, luxury, dissipation and effeminacy are pretty nearly at the same degree of excess here, as in every other part of Europe. Luxury has many bewitching charms. Yet, wherever it goes, it takes from human nature the image of the Divinity. If I had power I would forever banish and exclude from America, all gold, silver, precious stones, alabaster, marble, silk, velvet and lace.

"Oh, the Tyrant!" the American ladies would say! Ay, my dear girls, tyrants, different from me, have banished not gold indeed but other things of greater value...wisdom, virtue and liberty

ABIGAIL: *(With conviction)* I can hear of the brilliant accomplishments of any of my sex with pleasure and rejoice in the accomplishments of the French ladies. In this country, you need not be told how much female education is neglected, nor how fashionable it has been to ridicule female learning. I acknowledge, though, it is my happiness to be connected with a person of a more generous mind and liberal sentiments. A few generous sentiments which I lately read upon this subject by Mr. Thomas Paine who said:. "If women are to be esteemed our enemies, methinks it is an ignoble cowardice thus to disarm them and not allow them the same weapons we use ourselves. But, if they deserve the title of our friends, 'tis inhumane tyranny to debar them from privileges of ingenious education which would also render their friendship so much more delightful to themselves and us!"

JOHN: *(Apologetic)* This is a delicious country. Everything that can soothe, charm and bewitch is here. But these are no enchantments for me. My time is employed in the public business, in studying French like a schoolboy, and in fervent wishes, that the happy time may arrive soon when I may exchange the elegances and magnificence of Europe for the simplicity of our Penns Hill, and trade the glory of war, for the obscurity of private contemplation.

ABIGAIL: *(Wryly)* The morning after I received your very short letter, I determined to have devoted the day in writing to you but I had only just breakfasted when I had a visit from Monsieur Rivers, an officer on board his French warship. He speaks English well and spent the day so I had no opportunity of writing. The gentlemen French officers have paid me several visits and I have dined twice on board in Boston's harbor at very elegant entertainments. Count d'Estaing who commands the French fleet, has been exceeding polite to me. He requested that the family would accompany me on board his ship and dine with him with any friends we chose to bring. We went according to the invitation and were sumptuously entertained with every delicacy that this country produces and the addition of every foreign article that could render our feast splendid.

JOHN: *(Explanatory)* Count D'Estaing is allowed by all Europe to be a great and worthy officer, and by all that know him, to be a zealous friend of America. With regard to my connections with the public business here, which you will be naturally inquisitive to know something of, I can only say that we have many disagreeable circumstances here, many difficulties to accomplish the wishes of our constituents. But from this court, this city, and nation I have experienced nothing but uninterrupted politeness.

ABIGAIL: *(Reportorial)* Count D'Estaing told me that a British fleet of some 15 sail lay upon the watch for him, but a very terrible storm shattered the English fleet. The Somerset was lost upon the Nantucket shoals. Two other British ships are missing, one with 50 guns, and are believed to have sunk. I fed many of the prisoners upon their being marched to Boston. About 40 of their mates drowned..

JOHN: *(Agitated)* There is information that so many of our letters have been thrown overboard to escape capture by our enemies, and I fear you will not have heard so often from me, as both of us wish. I have written often. But my letters have not been worth so much as other things which I have sent you. I sent you a small present by Captain Niles. But, he was captured by a British privateer.

ABIGAIL: *(Unabashed tenderness)* The affection I feel for my friend is of the tenderest kind, matured by years, sanctified by choice and approved by heaven. What care I then for the ridicule of Britain should this testimony of it fall into their hands. Nor can I endure that so much caution and circumspection on your part should deprive me of the only consolation of your absence, a consolation that our enemies enjoy to a much higher degree than I do. Many of them receive three or four letters from their friends in England to one that I have received from France. My mind, as you will easily see, is far from tranquil, and my heart so wounded by the idea of inattention that the very name of my dearest friend would draw tears from me. Forgive me for harboring an idea so unjust to your affection. Were you not dearer to me than all this universe, I could not have suffered as I have done.

JOHN: *(Reasurring)* My anxiety for you is not diminished by time or distance. The great number of disappointments in the course of the last summer is afflicting. But we hope for better luck another year. It seems to be the intention of heaven that we should be taught the full value of our liberty by the dearness of its purchase, and the importance of public virtue by the necessity of it. There seems to be also a further design, that by eradicating forever from the heart of every American, every tender sentiment towards Great Britain, we may sometime or other know how to make the full advantage of our independence by more extensive connections with other countries.

ABIGAIL: *(Saddened)* How lonely are my days. How solitary are my nights? Secluded from all society by the mountains of snow which surround me, I could almost fancy myself in Greenland. We have had four of the coldest days I ever knew, and they were followed by the severest snowstorm I ever remember. The wind blowing like a hurricane for 15 or 20 hours rendered it impossible for man or beast to move outside, and has blocked up the roads so that they are impassible. Can the best of friends recollect that for 14 years past, I have not spent a whole winter alone. Some part of the dismal season has heretofore been mitigated and softened by the social converse and participation of the friend of my youth.

JOHN: *(Severe)* A letter from my dearest friend gave me a pleasure that is in vain to describe but the complaint in it gave me more pain than I can express. This is the third letter I have read in this complaining style, the former two I have not answered. I have written several answers but upon review, they appeared to be such I could not send. One was angry, another was full of grief, and the third was filled with melancholy. So I burnt them all! If you write me in this style, I shall leave off writing entirely. Am I not wretched enough, in this banishment, without these letters? What course shall I take to convince you that my heart is warm? Is it possible you should doubt? I beg you would never more write to me in such a strain for it really makes me unhappy.

ABIGAIL: *(Pointedly)* You chide me for my complaints, when in reality, I had so little occasion for them. I must entreat you to attribute it to the real cause—an over anxious solicitude to hear of your welfare, and an ill-grounded fear least multiplicity of public cares, and avocations might render you less attentive to your pen than I would wish.

This is the year anniversary of a very melancholy day to me. It rose upon me this morning with the recollection of scenes too tender to name. Your own sensibility will supply your memory and dictate your pen a kind remembrance of those dear connections to whom you waved an adieu, whilst the full heart and weeping eye followed your foot steps to the ship until intervening objects obstructed the sight.

JOHN: *(Upbeat)* The Marquis de Lafayette arrived from Boston in January with instructions for Franklin from Congress. I have received intelligence much agreeable, that of being reduced to a private citizen, which gives me more pleasure than you can imagine. I shall therefore soon be present before you, your own good man. Happy—happy indeed shall I be once more to see our fireside. Yet the situation here is painful. I never was in such a situation before. If I should return, and in my absence, orders should arrive here for me to execute, nobody would be here to execute them. They might possibly fail of success for want of somebody with power to perform them. However, upon the whole, as Congress has said nothing to me good or bad, I have no right to presume that they mean to say any thing. Therefore, it is my duty to return to you by the first good opportunity, -- unless I should receive counter orders before that occurs.

ABIGAIL: *(Thrilled)* My own dear friend, I rejoice in the news of your impending return.

JOHN: *(Frustrated)* When I left Paris March 8, 1 expected to have been at home before this May day. I have done my utmost to get to sea, but the disappointments I have met with have been many, very many. But, by the gracious invitation of the king, I am now to take passage in his frigate, the Sensible, with his new Ambassador to America, the Chevalier De La Luzerne. I hope to see you in six or seven weeks. Never has there been any man in such a state of uncertainty and suspense as I have been from last October, entirely uninformed of the intentions of Congress concerning me..

ABIGAIL: *(Exuberant)* I count the days, dear friend, 'til your return!

JOHN: *(Enthused)* My baggage is on board a frigate of the king this day, June 14 and I am to take passage in her. We expect to go to Boston though we may go to Philadelphia. England is torn with distraction, and Spain is expected to declare for us and Holland and the Northern Powers have made declarations which sufficiently indicate their determination favorable to us. Britannia, in short, must soon hearken to reason.

My dear fellow traveler, our little Johnny, is very well and is the comfort of my life. Remember me to his sister and brothers. No words, no actions can express the ardor of affection with which I am theirs and yours.

ABIGAIL: *(Excited)* I thrill at the thought of seeing you again arriving in Boston Harbor holding the hand of our dear Johnny.

JOHN: *(Reserved)* Three months since I returned to our home, my election by Congress as minister to negotiate peace and commerce with Great Britain brings me once again aboard La Sensible in Boston Harbor, preparing for our trip to Paris. I have Johnny and our young Charles with me and they join me in entreating you to keep up your spirits and throw off cares as much as possible. My love to Nabby and Tommy. Yours, ever, ever yours.

ABIGAIL: *(Disconsolate)* My habitation, how disconsolate it looks! My table; I set down to it but cannot swallow my food. Oh, why was I born with so much sensibility and so often been call'd to struggle with it? What a cordial ease to my dejected spirits were the few lines last night received. My dear sons I can not think of them without a tear, little do they know the feelings of a mother's heart. May they be good and useful to their father; then will they in some measure reward the anxiety of a mother.

May God Almighty bless and protect my dearest friend and in his own time restore him to the affectionate bosom of his dear Portia.

JOHN: *(Upbeat)* We escaped the British fleet and are arrived safely in Spain. Ferrol is a magnificent port and harbor, fortified by nature by rows of lofty rocky mountains on each side of the narrow entrance of it. I have never been more pleased with a reception at any place. But, as the frigate will probably not get from this port for two months, I must go by land to Paris over mountains riding mules. Horses are not to be had. I must get some kind of carriage for the children, if possible. Charles sustained the voyage and behaves as well as ever his brother did. They are learning the Spanish language as fast as possible.

ABIGAIL: *(Anxious)* It is now a little more than two months since you left me. You left this coast in the best time that could have been chosen. Winter set in with all its horrors in a week after you sailed, and has continued with all its rigors ever since. Such mountains of snow have not been known for 60 years. Enclosed to you are the journals and newspapers from Mr. Lovell. A ship will sail for Spain in a day or two and Mr. Austin goes with dispatches for you. You will learn from Mr. Austin the state of our currency and taxes and the rate of exchange which renders it needless for me to say anything about the subject.

JOHN: *(Explanatory)* You inquire how you shall pay taxes! I will tell you. Ask the favor of your Uncle Smith or some other friend to let you have silver, and draw your bills upon me. The money shall be paid, in the instant of the sight of your bill, drawn in your own handwriting. Any body who wants to remit cash to France, Spain, Holland or England, will let you have the money, the cash shall be paid here. I suppose, however, that one hundred pounds a year sterling will be as much as you will have occasion for. With silver, you may get your father, or your uncle or brother, to pay your taxes.

ABIGAIL: *(Pleased)* The remittance will render me very comfortable for this 12 months, even though I purchased the land I have written you about which belonged to Nathaniel Belcher. Our currency too is a subject which you must learn from others; if I can procure sufficient to pay my taxes I shall be content. The last year's tax upon only two and one-half acres of meadow in Milton was 60 dollars and parish tax for the land you own in the next parish 50 dollars. This year, it is impossible to say to what amount they will rise. The tenants declare they will quit farming as 'tis impossible for them to pay half the taxes. This letter wholly upon business must conclude with an assurance of the most affectionate regard of your ...Portia.

JOHN: *(Reportorial)* Since my arrival this time I have driven about Paris, more than I did before. There is everything here that can inform the understanding, or refine the taste, and indeed one would think that could purify the heart. Yet, it must be remembered there is everything here too, which can seduce, betray, deceive, deprave, corrupt and debauch it. Hercules marches here in full view of the steps of virtue on one hand, and the flowery paths of pleasure on the other. There are few who make the choice of Hercules. That my children may follow his example is my earnest prayer. But I sometimes tremble, when I hear the siren songs of sloth, lest they should be captivated with her bewitching charms and her soft, insinuating music.

ABIGAIL: *(Pleased)* Last week the Marquis de LaFayette arrived in Boston to the universal joy of all who know the merit and worth of that nobleman. He was received with the ringing of bells, firing of cannon and bon fires. He was kind to forward your letters but his haste to set off for Philadelphia deprived me of the honor of a visit from him at Braintree. All your letters have come safe to me that you have written since you left again, except what may be on board The Alliance, not yet arrived. I will repeat that I requested you to send me 12 yards of black and white striped linen, and 12 yards of lead colored satin for mourning. The first I want for Nabby, the other for myself, as I greatly fear I shall soon have a call for it. Your brother will soon be a widower we all apprehend. His wife is in the last stages of consumption, confined to her room for more than two months, and in circumstances alarming..

JOHN: *(Chiding)* I would not have you draw any more bills. I have no remittance nor anything to depend upon with no line of credit from Congress since I left you. Every farthing is expended and more.

You can have no idea of my unavoidable expenses. I know not what to do.

London, with the first appearance of mobs mixing with the universal discontent of the nation, has broken out into violence. They have burned the Kings Bench Prison, and all the other prisons, letting loose all the debtors and criminals. Many have been killed with martial law proclaimed and many have been hanged. The mobs all cry: Peace with America, and war with France. Poor wretches, as if this were possible!

ABIGAIL: *(Informative)* This state has raised, and is procuring men with vigor to act in concert with the fleet and army of France, our generous ally, which we are impatiently looking for. The importance of immediately recruiting our army in this year 1780 is known to be such, that the demands of pay are exorbitant, yet we fill up at any rate. We pay any price. Government now sees to its sorrow its deplorable mistake in not enlisting an army for the duration of the war. Thousands of lives might have been saved and millions of treasure. We now only patch and patch, find a temporary relief, and at an immense expense give our enemies advantages they could never have obtained if we had possessed a regular army.

JOHN: *(Contemplative)* May heaven permit you and me to enjoy the cool evening of life, in tranquility, undisturbed by the cares of politics or war. And, above all agree with the sweetest of all reflections, that neither ambition nor vanity, nor avarice, nor malice, nor envy, nor revenge, nor fear, nor any base motive, or sordid passion through the whole course of this mighty revolution will stay our dream. The rapid impetuous course of great and terrible events that have attended it, have drawn us aside from the line of our duty and the dictates of our consciences. Let us have ambition enough to keep our simplicity, our frugality and our integrity, and transmit these virtues as the fairest of inheritances to our children.

ABIGAIL: *(Explanatory)* Enclosed is a resolution of Congress with regard to your salary and a copy of their resolve with regard to your accounts. Mr. Lovell wrote me that the treasurer would draw a bill for the balance which I shall enclose as soon as I receive it. Nothing would have been more fortunate for me than the arrival of the few articles you ordered, which bring large sums of money. If you should feel proper to make further remittances, be so kind as to send the following list, in lieu of Barcelona handkerchiefs with which the market is at present glutted. Order 15 yards of thin black calico, ditto white, ditto red, ditto blue, some black satin proper for cloaks and low-priced black lace, and Irish linen which is not higher priced than Dutch, but sells much better.

JOHN: *(Jubilant)* The French and Spaniards have made a haul of 40 to 50 ships from the English. But, this does not make peace. This will never be while the English have one soldier in the United States. I have been here in Holland three or four weeks and I am very pleased. It is a very singular country, like no other with all the effect of industry and the work of art. The new orders I have received from your side of the water, have determined me to stay here in Amsterdam until further orders. Our two boys are at an excellent Latin school, and learning the language of the country. The scholars here all speak French even though France despises the Dutch because they are a smaller nation. The English are totally abandoned and lost. There is no hope for them but in a civil war and maybe not in that either.

ABIGAIL: *(Yearning)* I do not know how to enter into a detail of public affairs. They are not what I wish them to be. The successes of the enemy in the south at Charleston are mortifying. General Gates' misfortune will be announced to you before this reaches you, and the enclosed gazette will give you all the information of the treachery of Benedict Arnold.

Peace, peace, my beloved object, is farther and farther from my embraces I fear. If you bring the olive branch, even at the expense of another year of service, my present sacrifices should be my future triumph.

The fond endearments of social and domestic life, is the happiness I sigh for. Of that I am in a great measure deprived by a separation from my dear partner and children, at the only season in life when it is probable we might have enjoyed them all together. In a year or two, our sons will arrive at an age when a mother's care becomes less necessary and the father's more important. I long to embrace them! The tears my dear Charles shed at parting, have melted my heart a thousand times. Why does the mind love to turn to those painful scenes and to recollect them with pleasure?

JOHN: *(Proud)* I have this morning sent Mr. Thaxter, with our two sons to Leyden, there to take up their residence for some time and there to pursue their studies of Latin and Greek under the excellent masters, and there to attend lectures of the celebrated professors in that university. It is perhaps as learned a university as any in Europe.

The Dutch say that without a habit of thinking of every coin before you spend it, no man can be a merchant or conduct trade with success. It is the sure and certain way for an industrious man to be rich. But, this is an object that I hope none of my children will ever aim at. I would have my children attend to coin and farthings as devoutly as the merest Dutchman on earth, but only if such attention was necessary to support their independence. In our country, any man with common industry and prudence may be independent.

ABIGAIL: *(Consumed with anxiety)* This day, May 25, 1781, my dear friend, completes eight months since the date of your last letter, and five since it was received. You may judge of my anxiety. I think you must still be in Holland from whence no vessels have arrived since that country's declaration of war with England. There are some late arrivals from France, but no private letters. We are anxiously waiting for intelligence from abroad. We shall have in the field a more respectable army than has appeared there since the commencement of the war in the colonies, and all raised for three years service. We wish also for a naval force superior to what we have yet had, to act in concert with our army.

JOHN: *(Depressed)* I am called to Paris in the course of my duty but don't conceive from it any hopes of peace. This desirable object is yet unhappily at a distance, a long distance I fear.

Our dear Charles will go home with Major Jackson. Put him to school and keep him steady. He is a delightful child but is too sensitive to the rigors of our life in Europe. However, our Johnny is gone on a long journey to St. Petersburg in Russia where he will serve as a diplomatic interpreter. He will be satiated with travel in his childhood and care nothing about it, I hope, in his riper years. I am distracted with more cares than ever, yet I grow fat. Anxiety is good for my health, I believe. Oh! But that I had wings, that I might fly and bury all my cares at the foot of Penns Hill.

ABIGAIL: *(In reverie)* Oh! That I could realize the agreeable reverie of the last night when my dear friend presented himself and two sons safely returned in the arms of the affectionate wife and mother. Cruel is it that I should awake only to experience a renewal of my daily solitude. While no very important military events have taken place since I wrote you last, newly appointed General Nathaniel Greene is driving Cornwallis in the south and acting with much spirit and vigor.

JOHN: *(Vigilant)* I can't conceive what the English will do. They are in a strange position at present. They cannot do much against America but I hope, America will take their remaining armies as prisoners in New York and Charlestown. We must not relax, but pursue our advantages.

Your humble servant has lately grown much into fashion in this country. There appears nobody scarcely of so much importance as Mein Heer Adams. Every city and province rings with DeHeer Adams and if I were to judge of things here as we do in other countries, I should think I was going to be received at the Hague in great pomp in a few weeks. There is a national attachment to America in the body of this nation.

ABIGAIL: *(Happy)* How great was my joy to see the well known signature of my friend after a melancholy solitude of many months in which my hopes and fears alternately occupied my mind and spirit. It was January when Charles, our dear son, arrived home. By him, I expected a letter but found not a line; instead of which the heavy tidings of your illness reached me. I then found my friends had been no strangers of what they carefully concealed from me. Your letter to Charles dated November, 1781 was the only consolation I had; by that I found you considered yourself recovering though feeble.

The restoration of my dearest friend from so dangerous a sickness demands all my gratitude whilst I supplicate Heaven for the continuance of a life upon which my temporal happiness rests.

In regard to politics, it is rather a dull season for them; we are still recruiting for the army even as the enemy makes sad havoc with our navigation. It is difficult to get gentlemen of ability and integrity to serve in Congress; few, very few, are willing to sacrifice their interest as others before them. *(Downbeat)* I can also say that I was disappointed when I found that your return to your native land was a still distant idea.

JOHN: *(Quandary)* When shall I go home? If a peace should be made, you would soon see me. I have had strong conflicts about resigning all my employments, as soon as I can send home a treaty. But I know not what is duty. It is not that my pride or my vanity is piqued by the revocation of my envied commission. The American cause has had a signal triumph in this country. If this had been the only action in my life, it would have been a life well spent.

ABIGAIL: *(Proud)* We learn that the Dutch are acquiring a firmness of conduct, that they have acknowledged the independence of America, and are determined to turn a deaf ear to Britain. If this is true, and I sincerely hope it is, I congratulate you upon the success of your negotiations. If I know you are happy, it will tend to alleviate the pains of absence.

What think you of your daughter's coming to keep house for you? She proposes it. She would make a graceful appearance at the head of your table and she frequently mourns the long absence of her father.

JOHN: *(Self-effacing)* You would be surprised to see your friend; he is much altered. He is half a century older and feebler than ever you knew him. The horse that he mounts every day is of service to his health and the air of The Hague is much better than that of Amsterdam. Besides he begins to be a courtier, and sups and visits at court among princesses and princes, lords and ladies of various nations. I assure you it is much more wholesome to be a complaisant, good humored, contented courtier, than a grumbling patriot, always whining and snarling. However, I believe my courtierism will never go any great lengths. I must be an independent man, and how to reconcile this to the character of courtier is the question.

ABIGAIL: *(Firmly)* I repeat my request that I may come to you with our daughter in the spring provided you are likely to continue abroad. I am more desirous to come now that I learn your aide, Mr. Thaxter, is coming home. I am sure you must feel a still greater want of my attention to you.

Remember, that to render your situation more agreeable, I fear neither the enemy nor old Neptune. But then, you must give me full assurance of your entire approbation of my request. I cannot accept a halfway invitation. To say that I am happy here, I cannot, but it is not an idle curiosity that makes me wish to hazard the watery element. I much more sincerely wish your return. Could I hope for that during another year, I would endeavor to wait patiently for that event.

JOHN: *(Excited)* The king of Great Britain, by a commission under the great seal of his kingdom, has constituted his commissioner to meet with the ministers plenipotentiary of the United State of America, and has given him full powers. Thus, Great Britain has shifted suddenly about. From persecuting us, it now unconditionally and unequivocally acknowledges us a sovereign state and independent nation. As to your coming to Europe with Miss Nabby, I know not what to say. I am obliged to differ in opinion so often from Dr. Franklin and French Foreign Minister Count de Vergennes in points that essentially affect the honor, dignity and most precious interest of my country. These personages are little disposed to bear contradiction, and Congress has gone so near enjoining upon me passive obedience to them, that I do not expect to hold any place in Europe longer than next spring.

Write Mr. Jackson in Congress and desire him candidly to tell you whether he thinks Congress will continue me in Europe another year upon terms which I can submit to with honor. If he tells you that I must stay another year, come to me in the spring with our daughter. Leave the boys in good hands and a good school. A trip to Europe for one year may do no harm to you or our daughter.

ABIGAIL: *(Delicately)* Your daughter most sincerely regrets your absence. She has had a strong desire to encounter the dangers of the sea to visit you. I, however, am not without a suspicion that she may lose her relish for a voyage by spring. We have in our circle a gentleman who has opened an office in town. His father you knew, name of Tyler. This young gentleman studied law upon, a warm imagination, he lost his father young and had a very pretty inheritance left him. But, he was rather negligent in pursing his business in the way of his profession; and dissipated two or three years of his life and much of his fortune. At age 23, he took the resolution of coming to Boston and to pursue his studies and his business. His mamma is in possession of a large estate and he is a very favorite child. He has succeeded beyond expectation. He has popular talents, and as his behavior has been exceptional since his residence in town, I early saw that he was possessed of powerful attractions. I thought it prudent to keep as great a reserve as possible. In this I was seconded by the discreet conduct of our daughter.

Yet, I see a growing attachment in him stimulated by that very reserve. His days are devoted to his office, his evenings of late to my fireside. His attachment is too obvious to escape notice. I don't think our little lady is wholly indifferent, yet her reserve and apparent coldness is such that I know he is in miserable doubt.

I told him that I might quit this country in the spring and that I never would go abroad without my daughter. If I did go, I wished to carry her with a mind unattached.

JOHN: *(Lectures)* Your letter concerning Mr. Tyler is never out of my mind. He is of a very numerous family and connections in Boston who have long had great influence in that town. Therefore, if his education has been regular to the bar, as it must have been if he followed his studies regularly, if he has been admitted and sworn with the consent and recommendation of the bar, and if he has health, talents, and application and is a speaker, his relations will easily introduce him to full business.

But, I don't like the trait to his character, his gaiety. He is but a prodigal son, and though a penitent, has no right to our daughter who deserves a character without a spot. A frivolity of mind, which breaks out into such errors in youth, never gets out of the man but shows itself in some mean shape, or other through life. You seem to me to have favored this affair much too far, and I wish it off!

ABIGAIL: *(Apologetic)* The other day, the gentleman I have been speaking of, had a difficult writ to draw. He requested the favor of looking into your book of forms which I readily granted. In the evening when he returned me the key he put into my hands a paper which exclaimed "O! Madam, Madam, I have hopes that I shall one day become worthy of your regard." I daily see that he will win the affections of our fine majestic girl who has as much dignity as a princess.

JOHN: *(Cautious)* Our daughter is a model, as you represent her and as I know her, and is not to be the prize of any even reformed rake. A lawyer would be my choice but it must be a lawyer who spends his midnights as well as evenings over his books and not at any lady's fireside. This youth had a brother in Europe and a detestable specimen he exhibited. Their father had not all those nice sentiments which I wish, although an honorable man. I think he and you have both advanced too fast, and I should advise both to retreat!

ABIGAIL: *(Anticipatory)* Two days only are wanting to complete six years since my dearest friend first crossed the Atlantic. But three months of the six years have been spent in America. Why is that I hear so seldom from my dear John Quincy? Only one letter have I ever received from him since he arrived in St. Petersburg!

JOHN: *(Weary pride)* I have no news from our son since the 8th of December when he was in Stockholm, but hope every hour to hear of his arrival at The Hague. The preliminaries of peace and an armistice were signed at Versailles on January 21 in this year 1783. Thus drops the curtain upon this mighty tragedy. It has unraveled itself happily for us and may heaven be praised.

I would give the world to be with you tomorrow but I have not yet leave from my masters. I don't love to go home in a miff, pet or passion nor with an ill grace, but I hope soon to have leave. If I were to stay in Europe another year, I would insist upon your coming with our daughter.

ABIGAIL: *(Hesitant)* You invite me to you, to follow you, the most ardent wish of my soul is to be with you, but I can scarcely force an idea of the conflict of my mind. It appears to me such an enterprise, the ocean so formidable, the quitting my habitation and my country, leaving my children, my friends, with the idea that perhaps I may never see them again, without my husband to console and comfort me. I feel unequal to the trial. But, on the other hand, I console myself with the idea of being joyfully and tenderly received by the best of husbands and friends, and of meeting a dear and long absent son.

Away ye idle specters! The desires and request of my friend are a law to me. I have already arranged all my family affairs in such away that I hope nothing will suffer by my absence.

JOHN: *(Pleased)* This morning was delivered to me the resolution of Congress that commissions and instructions should be sent to me, Dr. Franklin and John Jay to make a treaty of commerce with Great Britain. The resolution of Congress deserves my gratitude. It is highly honorable to me, and restores to me my feelings which a former proceeding had taken away.

I am now perfectly content to stay in Europe until this business is finished provided you come and live with me. We may spend our time together in Paris, London or The Hague with contented minds.

ABIGAIL: *(Overjoyed)* At length, Heaven be praised! I am with our daughter safely landed upon the British shore after a passage of 30 days from Boston. We had 11 passengers and traveled from the port of Deal to London July 23, 1784 all in one company. What we suffered in sickness and fatigue, I will think no more of it. It is all done away in the joyful hope of soon holding to my bosom the dearest best of friends.

JOHN: *(Contained joy)* Your letter of the 23rd reached me here at The Hague in just three days and has made me the happiest man upon earth. I am 20 years younger than I was yesterday. It is cruel mortification to me that I cannot go to meet you in London, but there are a variety of reasons decisive against it which I will communicate to you here. Meantime, I send you a son who is the greatest traveler of his age and without partiality, I think John Quincy as promising and manly a youth as in the world.

After spending a week or two here, you will have to set out with me to France, but there are no seas between, a good road, a fine reason and we will make moderate journeys and see the curiosities of several cities in our way, including Antwerp and Brussels.

It is the first time in Europe that I looked forward to a journey with pleasure!

Yours with more ardor than ever!

(John and Abigail rise and meet at center stage and embrace while lights dim to out. Lights come up and the two take a paired bow, then individually, then together.)

THE END

"Diplomat Above All"

An appreciation of a president
who is best known
for his service to his country as
a diplomat and congressman

By Martin P. Kelly

Note from the Author

While writing "A Marriage of True Minds," I became more fully aware of John and Abigail Adams' oldest son, John Quincy, who at age 16 traveled to Europe to be with his father and to attend several universities.

It soon became evident in reading and compiling the letters of John and Abigail that their son was an unusual young man, brilliant in his schoolwork and able in his late teens to travel to Russia as a translator for the American ambassador in Moscow.

He became fluent in Russian, French and Flemish and so was able to be an important aide for his famous father who was busy securing European loans for the American Revolution and working with Benjamin Franklin to keep the French nation on the American colonies' side.

When I completed and produced "A Marriage of True Minds," I turned to research on this remarkable young man and his later life. His many services for his country, as president of the United States, and then as one of the finest members of Congress the country has produced, all served to support the fact that he was probably the finest diplomat the country ever produced.

Hence the title: "Diplomat Above All." It was an apt description for there have been few men and women since his time that approached his ability to represent the United States in its dealings with the countries of the European continent, including England where he became a highly respected member of the diplomatic corps.

It was in England that he met the young woman who was to become his wife, Louisa Johnson. The daughter of the American ambassador, Joshua Johnson, and Catherine Noth Johnson, an Englishwoman, Louisa was schooled in France and possessed social graces and artistic talents beyond her peers.

It is also apparent that she was a courageous woman and marvelous mother, particularly evident in one particular incident in her life as the play relates.

In research for this play, I found also that John Quincy and Louisa Adams had as their Washington neighbor Dolly Madison. Both women were fast friends even as they competed to bring Washington society to their salons.

When I read my daughter's (Margaret M. Kelly) play, "Hostess to History," about the widowhood of Dolly Madison, I found that she also incorporated s reference to the friendship Dolly had with John Quincy and Louisa Adams.

In all, I found that John Quincy Adams was a formidable successor to his illustrious parents, carrying the spirit of the American Revolution into the mid-19th century.

MARTIN P. KELLY
June, 2009

ACT ONE

(At curtain rise, three people are on stage. John Quincy Adams sits in a study, stage right, and Louisa Adams is at stage left sitting on a drawing room settee. Abigail Adams sits upstage on a level above the stage floor. The time is 1847, following the observance of the 50th wedding anniversary of John Quincy and Louisa Adams in Quincy, MA. It is late that night following the celebration by family and friends of the couple. John Quincy is now 80 years old, and Louisa is 72. John Quincy is discussing his life with men who have gathered with him for a late night drink. Louisa is enjoying tea with the wives of these men. Abigail has been dead since 1818 so she sits upstage in the netherworld of a blue-lighted area prepared to comment on the couple's conversation. Members of the audience represent the men and women sitting with either John or Louisa)

LOUISA: *(To Women in Audience)* Oh! I am weary from tonight's celebration but so happy that you joined us at this wonderful party. *(Sips tea)* Thank you ladies for sitting with me while I collect my thoughts. Fifty years do seem to pass in a wink. It helped to be reminded of the happiness John Quincy and I have both enjoyed along even with the trials suffered since we married in 1797. It seems now as ages ago.

Gathering with us tonight as you did was so comforting, especially our dear son, Charles, and his family. As you know, Charles is the lone survivor of our four children, but he remains a sturdy oak for us to lean on these past years.

Equally joyous in today's celebration is the realization that my husband has finally been truly recognized with the esteem due him for his long life of service to this dear country.

JOHN: *(To Men in Audience)* Gentlemen, this wine is doubly enjoyable tonight. The tributes at the party outweighed all that I have received in the past, even the kind words of President Harrison who called me "brother." Still, there is sadness tonight, knowing that the dear president is no longer with us nor are my two brothers and loving sister, all passed on too early in life as did my two sons.

(Sips wine) Ah! Despite my 80 years, the flattery of friends is no less pleasing. With due humility, I still could not dispute the claim that I reached the pinnacle of my career as an attorney with the defense of the Africans in the Amistad case. Unworthy as I believed myself to be, I was much pleased by my friends' insistence that I take the case. As you remember, the justices' decision on the Supreme Court supported my plea by an 8-1 vote. It was vindication of my friends' trust and also the preparation I did for the friendless Africans. I dared not think I would gain such support from the sitting justices. *(Sips some wine)*

LOUISA: It was good today, too, for our son Charles to join with our friends in praising his father's triumph in the defense of those slaves who took over the vessel while being transported to Cuba for continued slavery. Oh, my husband's defense of these poor souls evoked pride in my heart. Even as the Africans commanded the two remaining Spanish sailors to take them back to freedom in Africa, they sailed instead to the American shore. How I do recall they were taken by American naval officers and jailed for two years even as lower court judges refused to declare them guilty. My dear husband decried President Van Buren's agreement that they were property as he willingly prepared to return these people to their original Spanish captors

JOHN: We should well know the absurdity of considering living beings as merchandise to be returned to their slave status and then on the other hand be named as persons to be punished for killing the crew. It was made evident by my arguments. My father before me and his peers fought a revolution to overcome the tyranny of denying freedom to individuals. What these Africans did to gain their freedom was no more than our engaging in mortal combat with British soldiers for our freedom from a tyrannical king almost 75 years ago.

That these Africans were freed from jail and permitted to sail back to their native homes is a tribute to the ideals we honor in the Declaration of Independence written by my father and his dear comrade, Thomas Jefferson.

ABIGAIL: *(To Audience)* John Quincy has been his father's son even as I despaired early in his life that he was reluctant to use his full capacity to retain the family's devotion to service to his country.

When my best friend and loving husband brought our young son to Paris with him in 1777, my heart was near broken at the absence of husband and eldest son together. Yet, John Quincy was able to gain a great knowledge of the classics at the schools he attended while with his father. His love of Latin and Greek and his knowledge acquired of languages made him a valuable and loving companion for his father.

Yet, when I learned he accompanied the American Consul to the Russian Court at St. Petersburg, at his tender age, I feared for his safety even as he did charm these foreigners with his knowledge.

It was with joy and some apprehension when his father encouraged me to bring our daughter, Nabby, to Europe after seven years of separation. The perilous ocean trip was soon forgotten the moment I saw a grown-up John Quincy coming to greet us. He had come to England to meet us and bring us to his father in France.

JOHN: Now, little did I know or even believe that as a youth, my time as my father's companion in Paris would lead to what I have experienced through life with great satisfaction. Much of what I learned also is a tribute to my schooling at Harvard where my father attended. Even as I attempted to earn a living as an attorney, I was drawn to writing and artistic endeavors.

Still, I could not refuse President Washington's request that I return to Europe in 1794 to represent the United States as minister to the Netherlands

ABIGAIL: Once again, my John Quincy crossed the ocean. Worried as a mother, I could not as wife of the vice-president deter John Quincy from accepting that post, far from parents and friends. His father was proud of the appointment since it brought further honor to the family and was a position for which John Quincy was well prepared.

JOHN: Almost as soon as I arrived in The Netherlands, the French Army arrived to take over the country. As a result, I was frequently called to England, there to help the American consul, Joshua Johnson, the father of three charming daughters. The Johnsons' extravagant lifestyle seemed dictated by the tastes of his English wife. American males often suffer by marrying extravagant European woman. Still, I could not be but charmed by the Johnson's daughters, particularly Louisa, who had a spirit I admired.

ABIGAIL: When I learned of John Quincy's infatuation with the Johnsons' daughter, I reminded him Louisa Johnson, while born of an American father, had been brought up by her mother in a style dictated by passion and beauty, strictly alien to natives of Massachusetts. I reminded him that sensuality and beauty soon fade. Therefore, a good marriage need be founded on friendship.

JOHN: Gentlemen, how I remember as a boy in Europe, my mother's letters urging attention to my need for purity of person and desire for success. I could but be surprised when she graphically described the pitfalls presented even to the best-prepared male. Lust, a word I heard most often, I believed I could manage, if only women would cooperate through calm and reticent behavior.

LOUISA: My mother-in-law took great pains, I am told, to stress to her sons that she came to her marriage as a virgin. I can attest it was also true of me although she never spoke to me of this admonition. I would have told her European women also possessed good moral stature.

JOHN: I became fully aware of the objections my mother had about my marrying in Europe. But I also remembered her success several years earlier in having me give up my deep and loving relationship with Mary Frazier, a young woman I met when I first practiced law north of Boston. With this memory, my dear mother's determination to deter marriage to Louisa only made me more anxious to marry. If

I waited to find a wife based on my mother's requisites, I would be doomed to permanent celibacy. *(Laughs, sips wine)*

As to Mary, all my hopes of future happiness in this life did center in the possession of that girl. When I could not avoid my mother's admonitions, Mary bid farewell to me because, she said, I was still dependant too much upon my parents. When I told my mother of Mary's action I could not avoid assuring her that she would have understood my weakness if she had but met the young lady.

LOUISA: While I was well aware of John Quincy's interest in me when he dined with my family in London, he also knew I was captivated by his intellect and his love of things artistic. He enjoyed my singing and our evening musicales at our home. But, I must admit to losing my temper over his delay in deciding on a wedding. Still, I desired to earn his esteem even as I pressed him to give up his reluctance to marry. I even suggested when he returned to his post in the Netherlands, that I go with my father to The Hague where we could marry. John Quincy objected to this arrangement because of the appearance to the public, to which I replied that I was perfectly satisfied with my proposal's appearance to the world.

ABIGAIL: He kept the plans for his wedding to himself and even hinted that he might give up a public career and write for the rest of his life. I was sure he had blundered badly in his choice for a wife yet a person married is in it for better or for worse. I reminded John Quincy that he must put aside dawdling and be in earnest about success. Great things were expected of him.

LOUISA: Soon following our elaborate wedding at my family's home in London, we sailed to Berlin where John Quincy has been posted as American minister to Prussia. His father, now President Adams, appointed him because of his need to have a loyal friend in the post, one in whom he could have complete confidence.

JOHN: In Berlin, I fell ill from worry about Louisa's miscarriages. Even as she felt the full measure of sorrow because of our losses, she still nursed my sadness with all the tenderness and affection that only women can display and which she possesses in a degree so eminent even among her own sex.

ABIGAIL: John Quincy's posting to Berlin meant he could not readily bring his wife to America. I was shocked and saddened when he wrote me about his wife's four miscarriages. Other friends who met her told me my daughter-in-law's frame was so slender and her constitution so delicate that her years may well be of short duration. Still, my son assured me that his wife had displayed admirable strength.

John Quincy wrote me of how proud he was of his wife who finally bore him a son despite the mishandling at birth by a drunken midwife.

How I wish she had confided in me. It would have been better to have had their child in America.

JOHN: Would you know, so taken by Louisa's spirit and charm, the King and Queen of Prussia banned all traffic from the street where we lived so that Louisa would not be disturbed during her recovery.

LOUISA: Despite my illnesses, we were expected to attend all the diplomatic parties given quite regularly in Berlin. My knowledge of French learned at the school I attended in France, aided me among the diplomats. My reading and musical gifts drew them to me and to my husband. Even as we made a good impression, John Quincy was well aware of his unnecessary harshness and severity of character as I learned that he would bow to no woman's will.

JOHN: You know, I was aware that I had a bleak presence and appeared a bumbler around women. I attribute this to my mother who urged me as a boy to keep quiet in company lest I blurt some comment which might embarrass my family.

LOUISA: I remember one night in Berlin as we were going to a ball, he removed the rouge on my cheeks before going out. It was common for European women, he said, but not for an American. But when he attempted to do so the next night, I refused and he went to the party without me. *(Laughs)* Still, I attended the party alone with my rouged face.

Now ladies, I did not need to depend upon John Quincy as a dancing partner. His brother Thomas who was his secretary, liked nothing better than to look after his sister-in-law. We danced gaily at parties while John Quincy spent time talking politics with the various diplomats. He had cautioned me that women have nothing to do with politics. So be it! *(Laughs, sips tea)*

JOHN: When my father recalled me from Berlin after he lost his re-election bid to Thomas Jefferson, it was the first time my relatives in Quincy would meet Louisa and our child, George Washington Adams.

ABIGAIL: My dear daughter-in-law, I fear, did not have the same interest in her husband's political career as I did in his father's public service. Politics has been a traditional and expected part of the Adams' family life. I admit, though, she has proved to be a good mother and a stabilizing influence on John Quincy, often softening his tendency to be an over-strict father.

JOHN: As some of you remember, friends urged me to take the Massachusetts' appointment as senator to represent my native state in Washington. With this service and teaching at Harvard, my life seemed fulfilled, especially with the birth of two more sons, John Quincy Jr. and Charles Francis. When in Washington, Louisa enjoyed the company of her family where they had come after suffering financial distress in London. Louisa enjoyed the life in the city as she did in Boston.

However, my tenure as Senator was not an easy one because my fellow Federalists in Massachusetts did not take kindly to my support of President Jefferson's purchase of the Louisiana territory from the French. Unlike most New England people, I had always believed in expansion of the American frontier and the building of roads and canals to connect the various parts of the country. This was a desire promulgated by Jefferson and his fellow Republicans and I believed such ideas were beyond party loyalties.

LOUISA: Following the example set by his father, John Quincy declared himself not to care what independent devotion to principle might cost him personally.

JOHN: But, my friends in Massachusetts did not agree and so my first term as senator was cut short when a replacement was chosen. This was possible, you know, because the state legislature voted for senators and not the people. They had chosen a replacement for the next election. But when the Massachusetts' legislature demanded that I vote for repeal of the embargo act which kept the United States free of involvement of foreign wars, I could not agree and so I resigned. I suffered indescribable pain as even my mother appeared suspicious of what seemed collusion on the part of her son with Jefferson, my father's political enemy.

ABIGAIL: When John Quincy accepted Jefferson's request that he serve as America's emissary in Russia, I disapproved vehemently considering the terrible things Jefferson's allies said against my husband in his presidential campaign. A man of my son's worth to his country ought not be permitted to leave his native land.

When it was determined that he would take the position, I urged him to leave his two oldest sons in Massachusetts where they could continue their education and maintain close ties to their own culture. Their Quincy family would provide the proper discipline for the young boys.

LOUISA: As I did not want to be separated from my husband and yet not wanting to leave my two older boys, I was in a terrible quandary. Still, it was insisted that I go with John Quincy to St. Petersburg. The leaving of our sons, George and John, in the Quincy household for almost six years filled me with a succession of agonies that will cease only when my very existence ceases. We took only our youngest son, Charles. I left George and John at the expense of every feeling of my soul and of the sweetest affections of my heart. I found it difficult to forgive John Quincy for an enforced betrayal of my responsibilities as a parent.

JOHN: Louisa again suffered a miscarriage in St. Petersburg but in the summer of 1811, she gave birth to a lovely daughter, Louisa Catherine. *(Laughs)* I told my mother that I think this will convince her that the climate of St. Petersburg was not too cold to produce an American..

ABIGAIL: Louisa's letter from St. Petersburg telling of her young daughter's death from dysentery also related that her heart was broken, her health gone, and her peace of mind forever destroyed. I understood her anguish for at the same time I too had suffered the loss of my dear daughter, Nabby, at age 48 of the cancer of the breast.

Louisa's saddened condition brought me to write President Madison to ask him to bring my son and his family home. Indeed, the president offered John Quincy a place on the Supreme Court but my son refused and continued to serve in Europe.

JOHN: My dear Louisa suffered no less than our dear daughter as she sat beside the bed of our dying child. So often I have seen Louisa deal with tragedy with resignation and fortitude. I was deeply grateful for her comforting efforts on my behalf as we buried the child on a knoll in the Russian capital's English cemetery.

LOUISA: I undertook to comfort my grieving husband who soon turned his love to our remaining child, dear Charles Francis. In my silent grief, I thought of suicide so I could lie beside my dead daughter. Still, releasing my emotions in my diary helped me mute my guilty emotions for weaning the child too soon that made her susceptible to the disease which claimed her young life.

ABIGAIL: Louisa had anguish also because the Baltic Sea froze each winter for half a year which meant there could be no word from her sons for six months. From other friends familiar with Russia, the women there were described as cold and haughtily repulsive in their manners but wholly unrestrained in their relationships with men. Sensual lavish living abounded around the court, they said.

JOHN: I found myself impressed with the Russian peasants who were recruited to withstand Napoleon's siege at the gates of Moscow.

The French troops were forced to retreat through the bitter Russian winter. Napoleon could not believe that the Russians could gather a citizen army disciplined enough to defeat the greatest professional force in the world. As America's emissary to the Russian court, I kept the president informed of the calamity that had befallen the French nation.

ABIGAIL: With the end of our war with England in 1814, John Quincy was told to travel to Paris to meet with the English ministers to conclude a peace treaty between our two nations. He traveled there with haste, urging Louisa to stay in Moscow until he knew better how long he would be in negotiations.

LOUISA: While still in St. Petersburg, death claimed my sister Nancy, our mother and my brother-in-law in America. Then my unmarried sister, Kitty, who was in Russia as my companion, became enamored with William Steuben Smith, Nabby's son and Abigail's grandson who was sent to Russia to be John Quincy's secretary. Kitty became pregnant as young Billy had become quite comfortable in Russian gambling casinos and, apparently, in my sister's bed.

ABIGAIL: The only comfort I could take from the report that Nabby's son had made Louisa's sister pregnant was the knowledge that my grandson was forced to marry an older woman who might curb his wanton ways.

LOUISA: When word reached me from Paris that John Quincy wanted me to come to him, I had to sell our furniture, pack for the trip with my son, Charles Francis, hire a sled and take four servants across the vast snow- covered Russian plains. It took 40 anxious days of travel to Paris, often past battlefields strewn with dead French soldiers. When we neared the French capital, the servants quit, fearing they would be recruited for military service. As the coach we obtained in Berlin moved closer to Paris with only my son and our loyal coachman, the French army stragglers along the road became more menacing. To prevent harm, I informed them that I was Napoleon's sister traveling to meet him. This fabrication of relationship to the French general provided a pathway to safety.

JOHN: The harrowing trip by Louisa to Berlin and then Paris where now the diplomats met gave me pause for having her take on such a burden. Her tale of the pillaging troops heightened my respect for her and made me fear that I could have lost her and our son in that vast winter wasteland.

ABIGAIL: Following the signing of the peace treaty with Britain, John Quincy was sent to London as American minister. Now, he and Louisa could be parents again to their family. John Quincy Jr. and George joined their parents in the English capital until all could return in 1817 when President Monroe appointed my son as Secretary of State. The family lived in Washington, close to members of Louisa's family and vacationed in Quincy during the summer months.

LOUISA: The summer of 1818 was appalling in Quincy where unprecedented heat fostered the growth of disease. My mother-in-law took ill in October and declined through the month. On October 31, she died with none of her family at her bedside as she simply fell into final sleep. Unable to reach Quincy from Washington in time, we could only read the newspaper accounts of her death and burial beside her beloved daughter, Nabby.

JOHN: I remember my mother's habit of rising with the dawn and laboring until night, a routine I have tried to emulate all my life. I will always remember her delicate sense of propriety and her love of politics.

LOUISA: Abigail Adams was the guiding planet around which all revolved. *(recites)* "Depart thou sainted spirit/wing thy happy flight/ to the bright realms of everlasting light."

ABIGAIL: *(Bathed in blue light)* Would John Quincy and Louisa attain that which his father and I did, a true partnership built on love and respect. He has greatness in him and she has the spirit to help him to this greatness. I pray that they will be true partners in life.

JOHN: I found that even after being appointed as Secretary of State by President Monroe, our family finances would not permit us to have homes in both Washington and Quincy. I chose that the family live in Quincy but Louisa was stubborn as to her choice. She wished to stay in Washington near family members and friends. Besides, she did not like Quincy's cold winters.

LOUISA: For a time, we were both stubborn until our loneliness for each other forced us to relent. John Quincy's letters to me sent a thousand kisses to the boys and twice the number to me.

JOHN: When I planned to return to Louisa in Washington, I was emboldened to copy part of a John Donne poem to send her: "To teach thee, I am naked first; why then what needst thou have more covering than a man."

ABIGAIL: It would seem that John Quincy spent too much time in Europe's salons amidst sensual men and women.

LOUISA: John Quincy abhorred the practice of cabinet officers going about Washington visiting Congressmen and senators. President Monroe agreed that it was not a good custom. Instead, we planned a ball for 300 people so all these officials and their wives could gather with us. It was a wonderful success and my husband agreed that I should plan more such events. Soon my parties rivaled anything done by Dolly Madison with whom I became a great friend. I admired her vitality and sense of humor.

JOHN: It was the custom that the Secretary of State would run for the presidency once the president's term was completed. I was hoping that I would be nominated without any opposition because I did not like the dirty game of politics, especially like that practiced against my father.

LOUISA: Despite his protests of being above politics, I knew that John Quincy looked upon the presidency as a capstone of his ambitions. To help him, I visited many friends and officials urging them to support my husband for that illustrious post even as I urged John Quincy to greet the people with a pleasant countenance.

ABIGAIL: Seeking the presidency is a noble ambition and most certainly John Quincy was a man worthy and qualified for this post.

But I fear that there is an abundance of greed and sensuality and corruption that will soon rule and ruin American politics.

JOHN: Even as my father admonished me when I was a young man that I had too honest a heart, too independent a spirit, and too many brilliant talents for a political career, I believed that I should run for president to continue the good which my predecessors established. As Secretary of State I had advised President Monroe that a statement had to be made to keep foreign nations from annexing countries in the Western Hemisphere. He agreed and the decree he handed down became known as the "Monroe Doctrine" whereby all nations from the west and the east should not attempt to annex countries in South America and North America. As a result, Spain retreated from its adventures in South America and Russia gave up attempting to annex parts of the West Coast and Alaska.

LOUISA: The election of 1824 was the most complicated in our young nation's existence. John Quincy competed with General Andrew Jackson, William H. Crawford and Henry Clay. The famous general appeared as the favorite although he failed to get a majority of the electoral votes. As a result, Congress was called upon to choose the president and they chose my husband when Henry Clay gave his support to John Quincy. Even as I was elated and proud of his victory, my husband dreaded the inertia a minority president may face in trying to bring together disparate factions for the greater good.

JOHN: My status as a president without majority support made me an incomplete man, a president unable to move legislation through the Congress. And, I suffered vicious criticism when I appointed Henry Clay as my secretary of state. My opponents viewed the appointment as compensation to Henry for turning his votes to me so I may win the office of president. Although it had that appearance, I defended my choice because he was a good man and a brilliant negotiator worthy to represent our country.

Still, I understood my dear father's dilemma as president succeeding General Washington. Politics had divided the nation then as it appears to have happened now. I more fully respected his tireless efforts to elevate the country's stature in the eyes of the world while suffering division among those who believed more in the pettiness of domestic politics. My life as president found me buffeted by the storms of scorn even as I had hoped to bring the nation to new and expansive horizons.

It makes me weary to think of it. *(Sighs, sips his wine)*

Now gentlemen, if you excuse me for a brief time, I must retire to where I can find release from the sumptuous meal and plentiful wine. You may take the same opportunity if you wish. But, I implore you to return so we can continue to remember our times together.

(He exits as lights dim on John's area, Louisa's room and Abigail's position while curtain falls)

End of Act One

ACT TWO

(At curtain rise, all three characters return to their original areas. It is shortly after end of first act. John continues to talk to the men in the audience and Louisa talks to the women. Abigail talks to whole audience)

JOHN: *(Standing, sips wine)* As you well know, my loss of the presidential election in 1828 to Andrew Jackson left a bitter taste. The severe partisanship exhibited by my enemies was similar as happened to my father before me. He too was denied a second term by the vitriolic slander spread about him. My opponents were as severe in their unwarranted criticism. I determined not to attend the inauguration of my successor to the White House. Jackson's election had been so bitter that conventional gestures would have been ridiculous.

ABIGAIL: John Quincy's father felt the same way about the bitter election when Jefferson turned his scandalous dogs upon him to win the presidency. Even if my husband had decided to attend the inauguration, I would not have set foot at the affair.

LOUISA: All Washington could only wince when they saw the hordes of Jackson's muddy-booted admirers crowd into the White House after his inauguration. The beauty of that venerable building was tarnished by the destructive antics of these followers of the new president.

ABIGAIL: My son was right in upholding the good name of Adams against the calumny which destroyed his presidency.

JOHN: It was time then to write a document defending my good name first tarnished by the New England Federalists who believed that I had betrayed them and all my Massachusetts friends by joining the Jefferson camp during 1807 when serving as senator. They could not believe then or when I was president that national interest, not partisan loyalty, was uppermost in my mind.

LOUISA: How I wished my husband had minimized the slander against him by simply ignoring it. But, it is not his nature so he promised friends and foe alike that he would spend the rest of his life defending and vindicating his own reputation.

JOHN: In examining the journals of the 1808 legislative session, I found little that I did for which to be censured, certainly nothing that I intended. The criticism was based on lies, all lies, as was the criticism during my presidency.

LOUISA: As many of you know, tragedy struck us both even as my husband finished his manuscript in defense of his administration. Our son George died when he drowned in the Long Island Sound. Witnesses have said that he leaped into the water from a steamer taking him to his father.

JOHN: Was I the cause of this death of my son? Did he fear my stern demeanor or was it the life he led, avoiding work as he gambled and drank, even impregnating a young employee of our kinfolk, the Welsh family.

LOUISA: It was a month before we were able to recover our son's body after it washed up on the shore. Were we destined to suffer the long line of fate of the Adams' family?

ABIGAIL: Quincy had lost two brothers to the demons of alcohol and now he has lost a son, so dear to our hearts. The scourge of our family continued to visit tragedy upon those who had come after us.

JOHN: Had I pushed my son harder than the young man could sustain? I implored mercy on my dear boy's pathetic soul and viewed my future life with a broken and contrite spirit.

ABIGAIL: *(Upstage)* I added my prayers that this tragic event would not deter John Quincy's quest for the greatness that was to be his destiny.

LOUISA: Even as we were burying our unfortunate son in Quincy, we were threatened by persons in Boston prepared to exhort money and favors to keep the story of the illegitimate child and other mischief by our dead George from the public. With the help of his brother, Charles, this mortifying notoriety soon faded from public notice.

JOHN: After the chill of that cold November burial service, the spring and summer brought some balm to my punishment of losing both a son and the presidency. At the behest of my son Charles I began to assemble my father's papers to write a biographical memoir that might defend my father's legacy against his enemies, many of them now mine.

ABIGAIL: It is right that the son should defend his father and we all wished that John Quincy would be conscientious about writing the history of my husband's life and its impact on this wonderful country.

JOHN: Now, I wondered, why had I saved the writings of Voltaire? His book on Joan of Arc was a vicious burlesque, fit only to be read in a brothel. Gross and immoral, it represented Voltaire's rancor against Christianity. The French heroine was not to be a subject of ridicule; rather, she deserved reverence.

ABIGAIL: I had cautioned John Quincy as a young man to be wary of the immorality of Europeans, particularly the French. It is easy to see that it was not advice he followed.

LOUISA: We had a joyous occasion in September of 1829 when our Charles Francis married Abigail Brown Brooks, the sister-in-law of Edward Everett, a man who moved from legislator to governor, then Harvard president and well-praised orator.

JOHN: The wedding was a shining moment for us and since then in the past 18 years, this joining of hearts has brought many blessings to the couple and to their families. Charles has been a bulwark to the family, proving to be a success as a lawyer and a man who handles finances fairly and wisely.

ABIGAIL: It was good that another Abigail moved into the family to remind everyone of those of us who came before her.

LOUISA: That Thanksgiving, John Quincy and I moved into our son John's new home located across the square from the White House. It was here we spent the winter, close to the home we had shared for four years.

JOHN: Yes, aching for an activity to keep my mind alert and busy, I undertook the writing of the history of the Russo-Turkish War, my first attempt to compose a history. By April, 1830 I was proud to be able to deliver the manuscript although quite a bit longer than the 40 pages requested. The extra verbiage was a result of my desire to suggest to the minds of European diplomats the value of negotiation.

LOUISA: That summer, John Quincy and I took a vacation throughout New England but we returned home sick and exhausted, mainly because of fear and trembling over worry about our son John who seemed to be soon another victim of the family scourge, alcohol.

JOHN: Not even reading Cicero could spark the interest it once did. This was true even though his writings encouraged those who wrote our Declaration of Independence. Charles urged me again to write my father's biography; I assume he wished me to have a task to keep me busy. I was so overpowered by the project that I took to having two-hour naps each day.

LOUISA: I had wished John Quincy would put away his thoughts of Cicero, an ancient who wrote so vividly of awaiting his own death. My husband admitted to me that he had no plausible motive for wishing to live.

JOHN: My depression was leading into dejection, despondency and idleness. What changed me, you may ask? Why, a charming, delightful bundle of feminine charm, our new granddaughter named Fanny, the second child of our son John and his wife, Mary.

LOUISA: When the doctor failed to appear, I was pressed into serving as midwife and Mary had a very safe delivery, a fact that brought added joy to our family.

ABIGAIL: My grandson John produced girls with alacrity but they may well benefit in life by the promise of equality of sexes urged by those Adams' women before them.

JOHN: The happiness of Fanny's birth was followed by an invitation to me to attend the bicentennial commemoration of the founding of Boston. Two marshals had been designated to escort me into the Old South Church where my cousin, Joshua Quincy, delivered the oration. Excitement ruled the day when at the close of his remarks, a bench broke upstairs and the audience ran fearing the gallery was falling on them. Calm was restored and the program was completed with the singing of Handel's "Hallelujah Chorus" and a glorious display of fireworks on the Common.

LOUISA: The honor given my husband at the bicentennial celebration exhilarated him, even to the point where he accepted the offers of old enemies to shake hands.

ABIGAIL: Perhaps, it was best to shake the hands of enemies so they may not stab you in the back. Still, it was too soon to forget the vituperation of these men while my son served his country so well.

JOHN: It came as a surprise when the editor of the Boston Patriot, John David, and the Quincy district's congressman, the Reverend Joseph Richardson, indicated they wanted to meet with me. Both had been loyal supporters of me in the past so they were most welcome.

LOUISA: When these fine gentlemen sought to meet with John Quincy I had trepidations. The editor of the Boston Courier had written an editorial a few weeks before the meeting urging that the people of Quincy send my husband to Congress. Still, that support was suspect.

JOHN: I learned that Reverend Richardson had been urged by his congregation to quit his Congressional post because of the mixture of politics and religion. As a result, both he and John David believed I would be the man to take the seat in Congress. The fact that the Courier also supported my candidacy raised the question of whether that editor who had long supported Henry Clay, might want me to be sit safely in Congress and not run against Clay for the presidency in 1832.

ABIGAIL: The acceptance of a congressional candidacy would be unseemly to a man who had served as president. I had hoped wiser heads would dissuade John Quincy.

LOUISA: Thoughts of John Quincy returning to politics gave me cold shivers. I had hoped that after the presidency, he would stay with his plan of retirement. I made it plain to him that if he returned to Washington, I would not go with him.

JOHN: An angry commotion surrounded my thoughts of going to Congress, not only Louisa's protests but also those of my son Charles who questioned my vow to lead a life of scholarship, particularly in preparing a biography of my father. He felt that taking a seat in Congress would be a loss of dignity and set a precedent. Most of all, it would give new opportunities for assaults by my enemies.

ABIGAIL: My grandson spoke wisely about providing a chance for old enemies to attack his father as they had done through all the four years of his presidency.

LOUISA: The die was cast when John Quincy was nominated unanimously by the Republican convention. He remained convinced that this majority gave him a place of dignity from which he could strive once again to benefit mankind.

JOHN: Now all sorrow can be set aside. No election or appointment conferred upon me ever gave me such pleasure. Being elected to Congress gave me more satisfaction than being elected president.

LOUISA: Even as I had no sympathy for this new status in my husband's life, I was forced to relent because I realized once again that I could not live separate from him.

JOHN: We both gained renewed spirit in Washington even as I suffered from inflamed eyes and a severe cough. I soon realized both afflictions were due to the smoke from the burning coal in the Capitol's fireplaces.

LOUISA: It was soon that the merriment of social events took over our lives. On New Year's Day, 1831 we had 300 callers at our home, a situation which gave John Quincy a fine opportunity to meet and get to know his fellow congressmen.

JOHN: On our April trip to Quincy following the Congressional session, we stopped in New York to visit the dying James Monroe. Then, I overruled Louisa and booked passage for both of us on the steamer to Providence through the Long Island Sound. A rising nor'easter was a storm that made me question my boast of fearlessness on water. As the sea battered the bow of the boat, I had sufficient time to think twice about my obstinacy of resisting Louisa's good advice.

LOUISA: Even as we arrived safely in Quincy with our lives intact, John Quincy soon became involved with the Anti-Masonic Party, and at its convention it considered him as a candidate for president to run against Andrew Jackson, a well-known Mason. It was our good fortune that the party turned instead to our great friend William Wirt as it candidate. Our son Charles knew that this political activity by his father gave him another reason to delay research on his father's papers. As for me, I began to write my own autobiography: "Adventures of a Nobody."

JOHN: The invitation to me to deliver the Fourth of July address in Quincy gave me an opportunity to rebuke South Carolina's contention that a state had a right to declare a federal law null and void. This doctrine of nullification was a theory espoused by Vice-President John Calhoun in order to combat the restraint on slavery's expansion.

ABIGAIL: It was known also as his father's wish that slavery would be contained to the states that practiced it before the Revolutionary War.

JOHN: I urged independence and union forever and warned that South Carolina's claim of sovereign statehood was a hallucination that could lead to a war against the federal government. When praise for this speech came from other parts of the nation, I knew I had struck the right chord.

71

LOUISA: John Quincy was almost immediately called upon to deliver a tribute to James Monroe who died on July 4, the same date as did his father and Thomas Jefferson some seven years earlier.

JOHN: Tribute to James Monroe as one of the Founding Fathers of our nation gained my deep interest in that my tribute would include testimony to the late president's urging Congress to make a system of internal improvements. Yet, Congress, in its so-called wisdom, believed that a nation celebrated the world over, was still incompetent to build roads, dig canals and institute seminaries of learning. Even as I had tried when I succeeded James Monroe as president, Congress would not hear of such developments.

ABIGAIL: What would one expect of people who would permit the federal capital in Washington to remain the dirtiest hole I ever saw for a place of any trade or respectability of its inhabitants.

JOHN: As sessions of Congress moved along, I determined to fill every moment of my time with some action to contribute to the pleasure or the improvement of my fellow citizens. The move by Congress to lower tariff rates and to maintain the life of the national bank was supported by my actions among my colleagues. The creation of a tariff would encourage economic growth and be less threatening to the plantation states. Yet again, South Carolina refused to be calmed.

LOUISA: We were confronted once again with the family sorrow of knowing that our son John was succumbing to the agonies brought on by alcohol. The family curse was closing in on us.

JOHN: At this time of close family worry, we received word that my brother Tom had died, also paying the price of abuse of alcohol. This news was a deep affliction for me because Tom had been, not only a dear brother, but also a close, wonderful and affectionate friend throughout our lives together.

ABIGAIL: Oh! This woeful curse has become almost the very fiber of our family's sinew.

LOUISA: John Quincy took on the task of caring for Tom's widow Nancy, and their young children. This effort would be helped by our son Charles who advised his father on how to extend the limited family funds to include those left in the will of the first President Adams to take care of his descendents.

JOHN: It was too incomprehensible to realize that my cousin, Joshua Quincy, now president of Harvard, had joined with the college's board to bestow an honorary degree on Andrew Jackson, a man wholly unworthy of this great honor. So sick of heart was I that I determined to be pruning my trees in Quincy during the ceremonies. But, because of Jackson's illness and fatigue, he was unable to take part in the Harvard ceremonies or a public meeting at Bunker Hill. There, Edward Everett made a suitable oration and gave the president two cannon balls as mementoes. I had thorough disgust for the ceremony as I had seen the original battle as a child standing on a nearby hill. It was a battle to be held sacred for the men who fought there and not an excuse to honor a pretender to greatness.

LOUISA: As time moved on, John Quincy suffered ill health to the point where he anticipated death. Yet, as he reached depths of despair, almost praying for death to relieve him of the infirmities of old age, the Anti-Masonic Party nominated him for governor of Massachusetts. This cheered him but he was able to urge his followers to chose another man for this honor.

JOHN: We were blessed with the birth of our first grandson when Charles' wife Abigail, gave birth to John Quincy Adams 2nd. The birth of this wonderful child and the baptism ceremony gave me more comfort than I had for some years.

LOUISA: The joy of the grandson's birth was almost lost in tragedy when John Quincy returned to Washington on a train which derailed in New Jersey. He recalled that men, women and children, dying and injured, were scattered along the road beside the tracks. I gave thanks for his escape from death and injury. Still, he remained fascinated with the railroad development and was a passenger at every opportunity.

JOHN: From that experience, I determined to gain a significant shift in outlook. After all, much in my success in life occurred before inauguration as president in 1824. It was only then that I suffered decline in health and spirit. Why should I fret if I never recover the good will of my countrymen. Forget public applause I told myself and move ahead.

LOUISA: This switch to an attitude of self-righteousness was a welcome elixir for John Quincy although his peers in Congress might not think so. He became argumentative and seemed to enjoy the attacks by his enemies.

JOHN: With renewed vigor, I set about debating national banking and the questionable behavior of the executive branch. Still, I was considered as the only man to be invited by Congress to deliver the memorial address on the death of Lafayette.

ABIGAIL: It was appropriate that John Quincy make this memorial. The great French general was close to our family since the Revolution. Well do I remember his special effort to visit me in Quincy upon a trip to this country when he brought news of my husband in France.

LOUISA: What joy John Quincy may have received from his new vigor in Congress was diminished with the news that our son John was deathly sick in Washington. I was too ill to travel but his father hastened to his side.

JOHN: When I reached my son's sickbed, he was already in a coma and failed to recognize me. As I kissed his lifeless brow, I submitted to overpowering grief when he died the next morning at age 31 from what his brother Charles said was the scourge of intemperance.

ABIGAIL: Oh! What a taint to our family that is carried forward.

LOUISA: Again, John Quincy assured John's widow, Mary that she and her two daughters would have a home with us. It was found that they had been left $15,000 in debt by John's waywardness. When we gathered again in Washington, Charles Francis and his father planned to gain enough funds for that liability and enough to pay our expenses during the winter.

JOHN: The stratagems urged by Charles to make financial recovery included selling much of our original family property in Quincy. I could not permit this even as we were financially insecure. This I stated in no uncertain terms often at the top of my voice. As a result, Charles prepared to take his leave back to Boston when it appeared that I would not compromise. At this news, I gained my self-control and relented. I agreed he should manage our family's resources as he deemed appropriate.

LOUISA: I was overjoyed at John Quincy's decision. Charles was a wonderful lawyer and estate trustee while also writing political pamphlets. In temperament, too, he was his father's son. Soon after he took over our finances, John Quincy was able to relax from these domestic and personal afflictions.

JOHN: All our hopes of our future now rest upon the shoulders of our last son.

LOUISA: It was a strange set of events in Congress whereby my husband stood with the hated President Jackson to contest the efforts of Daniel Webster and John Calhoun to limit the powers of the executive and give more to the Congress.

JOHN: As Calhoun had quit as vice-president to serve solely in the Senate, I drew on my full vigor in writing to my son Charles of the attempts to change the balance of government. I knew he would distribute my letters among like-minded people in Boston who were aware my sense of duty gave me the tenacity to continue as a public man intent upon remaining in the field of politics.

ABIGAIL: Despite his father's admonitions, John Quincy had found his life's work with all its faults, foibles and failures. Still, a man unwilling to risk failure will never know success. So it is with my son.

LOUISA: Tenderness became part of John Quincy's life when he acted as a father to our dead son's two young daughters, Fanny and Mary Louisa. He became teacher for John's children and brought them to church. And, he had a rousing good time when he took the little girls to a circus where he commented on the skill of the trainer although the lion appeared to behave like a lapdog. He noted that the trainer did not seem fit to associate with the white bear or the tiger.

JOHN: Through the kind invitation of the Atlas Insurance Company of Boston, a fine fishing party was organized where we anchored below the harbor's lighthouse. The group included Edward Everett and other community leaders from whom the company was interested in gaining favor. No matter; in two hours we caught some fifty fish. My contribution was three fine cod.

Our hosts were determined we not go hungry or dry. With fine cold beef we had excellent wines but the greatest success of the day was lemonade. I remembered the recipe: a gallon of water, a bottle of Jamaica rum, a bottle of cognac, a bottle of champagne and a pound of sugar. Oh, yes! The recipe also suggested a pint of lemon juice.

LOUISA: One unusual visitor to our house was Mrs. Philadelphia Cook, a leading temperance advocate. She read to John Quincy from a bundle of literature that recounted the evils of alcohol. She asked him to make a confession about drinking and he admitted that usually he had two glasses of wine with dinner. I am afraid that despite the deaths of two brothers and two sons because of alcohol, he never took seriously the possibility that he too might be as vulnerable. Perhaps it was the long morning walks he continued to take and his daily swimming in the Potomac that preserved his constitution.

ABIGAIL: May his walks be straight and true and not unsteady due to his consumption of the beverages that have destroyed so many!

JOHN: Prepared to face the fury of the storm of the new Congress, I was bound to cleanse the temple of evildoers, those men who had developed base and dirty tricks to thwart my progress in life and destroy my character. It was now that I would raise the challenge of combating slavery which appeared to be a permanent painful presence in the republic.

LOUISA: To combat John Quincy, his enemies in Congress adopted a new parliamentary procedure known as the "gag" rule.

JOHN: I vehemently opposed the attempts to contain any discussion of slavery by the institution of the "gag" rule which provided that any petitions even remotely dealing with slavery were to be tabled without printing, discussion or referral to committee. This rule was instigated by Southern congressmen who saw petitions flooding into Congress calling for the end of slavery.

LOUISA: John Quincy had found the fight of his lifetime, one for which you would think he had prayed. With this battle he may leave a legacy to posterity and awaken men of this nation to record his name as one of the fairest among all men. Even our son Charles conceded that calming his father was hopeless. John Quincy scoffed at his physician's advice to seek a quiet existence.

JOHN: Equal to my fight to abolish the "gag" rule was the effort to keep Congress from wasting the bequest of John Smithson. He was the illegitimate son of the first Duke of Northumberland and he left his entire estate of more than 500,000 dollars in gold to enable the United State to increase knowledge among its citizens. I did battle to deny wily members of Congress from attempting to divert the funds for personal projects. My suggestion as president to use the funds to build a national astronomical observatory was hooted down by Congress. They considered the idea a lighthouse of the skies. I then suggested a national repository for significant inventions and literary merit was an excellent use of the money.

ABIGAIL: Perhaps, such an idea might be one where my husband's papers would finally be researched and published.

LOUISA: John Quincy's zealous pursuit of his mission seemed all consuming. While I truly admired his goals, I wondered if he were not wasting his fine mind on people who do not appreciate or understand his talents.

JOHN: Even though weary from an exhausting session in Congress, I accepted the invitation of the city of Boston to deliver an eulogy for James Madison who died in June, 1836. The eulogy was set for

September and I spent the summer writing it, certain I wanted to picture the Union's growth from the Continental Congress to the adoption of the Constitution. While honoring the late President Madison, a leader among our founding fathers, I also wished to taunt the Southern States about their ideas of nullification.

LOUISA: At a dinner with Governor Edward Everett, the woman who prepared a sumptuous feast informed us that her mother had prepared the wonderful feast for our wedding in London. What a happy coincidence; one that the governor was proud and pleased to have brought to fruition. He also pleased and delighted John Quincy by asking for a list of his publications with the prospect of publishing them. It was a grand evening.

JOHN: Once again, the Anti-Masonic party nominated me for Congress and I was overwhelmingly approved but in this session, such was the enmity caused by my ruses for circumventing the "gag" rule, that walking into Congress was like entering a fiery furnace. I had found methods to speak on innocuous petitions and maneuvering my discussions to the slavery questions. This so inflamed the southern representatives that they called for my expulsion from Congress but to no avail.

LOUISA: As a respite from the tiring session of Congress, I urged John Quincy to pose for sculptor Hiram Powers who wished to use clay gathered around Washington, said to be the best in the land. My husband agreed grudgingly.

JOHN: In my lifetime, I have posed for sixteen painters, five sculptors and one medallist. The first painting was when I was 16 and the last was when I was 70. They show who I was and what I am.

ABIGAIL: Even as that boy of 16, he showed the promise that has come to full glory.

LOUISA: It was pleasant again to be back in Washington where the diplomatic corps treated John Quincy with the respect they would give their fathers. And, the social activities were pleasant again especially when Dolly Madison, now a widow, moved into the house next to ours. Her charm remains legendary and her appearance belies her years. It gave me an opportunity too to continue my writing of poetry and plays for my family and friends. Translating classical Greek literature from the French was also a marvelous diversion.

JOHN: While at first I declined the invitation to deliver the principal address at the New York Historical Society's celebration of the 50th anniversary of General Washington's inauguration, I finally decided to undertake this momentous task at this point of my life. The two-hour speech was well received. In it, I stated that the decision of our founding fathers to create a union based on the self-evident truths of the Declaration of Independence was the basis of our greatness. The word "union" should be the cry throughout the land, I said.

LOUISA: In his humble moments, John Quincy said he felt his only means of benefiting future generations was to plant trees, a favorite past-time for many years. Still, the courage shown in his congressional battles brought many letters from the public to which he had to answer personally since Congress did not supply secretarial help. Recipients of his letters often passed them on to newspapers.

JOHN: The practice of answering constituents' letters became irksome since I never could be sure which would be published. As a result, I had to be cautious to write nothing unfit for publication. It constrained my writing style.

ABIGAIL: Persons receiving letters from John Quincy knew that publishing his letters gave them a link to the aura of his celebrity.

JOHN: Having fought for so long for causes unpopular in the minds of many Bostonians, I disliked admitting that the city's attitude towards me may be changing. *(Wryly)* Their enthusiasm in wishing to see and hear me was like the passion of a crowd to see an execution.

LOUISA: When we moved from our daughter-in-law's home to the house we had when John Quincy was President Monroe's secretary of state, his happiness was complete because he felt his service in Monroe's cabinet was the height of his career.

ABIGAIL: He may well be remembered as this country's finest diplomat deserving of the full honors befitting his achievements.

JOHN: Again, my family urged me to write my father's biography. Even, my friend George Bancroft, a fine historian, encouraged me to get secretarial help. Such help only cost 50 cents a day, so I had no excuse.

LOUISA: I could not help being stern with my husband and put my plea in a letter to him. Could he not honor and repay his parents by writing of their important lives? I implored him to commune with his own heart, and do justice to himself as well as to his parents. Writing the biography was too sacred to be trifled with under any pretensions whatever.

JOHN: My wife's letter exhorted me to continue the work, so I determined to set aside an hour a day on the biographical project.

LOUISA: John Quincy resolved to discipline himself in the writing but, as his nature, he became involved with the genealogical aspect of the family. Soon, he was immersed in reading of family members who lived many years before the birth of his father. He even found that at an early 17th century wedding ceremony in his father's family, an elderly aunt dropped dead and was laid to rest in the bridal chamber.

JOHN: It was important to accept the requests to talk about national affairs at the Smithsonian lectures in Boston which honored the use of the Smithson bequest for a national establishment to preserve the best of scientific and artistic endeavors in the country. It was also possible within this speech to detail the evils of slavery and I also made full use to argue against a war with Mexico to bring Texas into the Union as a slave state.

LOUISA: Even as John Quincy was being honored throughout the country for these lectures, we were crushed by the death of our nine-year old granddaughter Fanny who succumbed to diphtheria, a terrible blow to both of us. John Quincy gave little Fanny a last kiss on her still warm cheek and then left the room in uncontrollable tears. After the funeral we watched the little white coffin carried to the Quincy burial place where it was placed upon her father's casket in the Adams' vault.

ABIGAIL: Now my grandson John would receive eternal comfort close to his young daughter.

JOHN: As the convening of the new Congress, I determined to place our family on a strict budget so we might live within our means. I gave up horses and a carriage and walked to the Capital each day in any weather.

LOUISA: I could not believe that he would walk to work in a heavy snowfall. The terrible idea of a quarter of a dollar for a hack induced him to risk his bones. No persuasion could induce him to spare himself.

JOHN: Despite my family's pleas to discontinue my walking, I did very well. However, in the late spring a misplaced roll of matting on the Capital's floor caused me to trip and dislocate a shoulder.

LOUISA: We were able to keep him home for at least two weeks to recuperate when we also hoped he might return to his father's biography. No matter, he began a correspondence with our nation's leading actor, James Hackett, well known for his portrayal of Hamlet.

JOHN: Shakespeare's creation of "Hamlet" was the masterpiece of the human mind. These letters with Hackett were a delight to read and write. But, my euphoria was soon grounded when before leaving for Quincy, I stopped at the Treasury Building to receive my congressional remuneration and expenses... a total of $2,241 for the session.

LOUISA: As the Christmas holidays of 1840 brought good cheer among our friends, it permitted the legislators, John Quincy among them, to celebrate New Year's more as schoolboys on a holiday than gray-bearded statesmen.

JOHN: The start of the New Year was spent in my preparation to appear before the Supreme Court on behalf of the 39 Africans who were threatened with return to the slave-owners from Cuba. These owners suffered the loss of their ship when the Africans revolted and took over the ship. I readily accepted the invitation of Lewis Tappan to plead before the Supreme Court to gain their freedom. Tappan was one of the founders of the American Anti-Slavery Society and saw the plight of the Africans as a powerful weapon for his cause.

LOUISA: I had never seen John Quincy more prepared and determined to take up the cause of the Africans. It was also a time when he took extreme care to denounce President Van Buren for his efforts to whisk the Africans out of the country and back into slavery.

JOHN: The justices' decision in favor of the Africans was the high point of my career, gaining for me the esteem of the nation north of the Mason-Dixon Line. More than that, it made me determined to complete my life as a legislator for such service was as much necessary to me as breathing atmospheric air. The world will retire from me before I retire from the world.

LOUISA: I could not deny him his wish even as I had wished for a retired life. Still, his need and his ability to redeem his name were finally more important to me.

JOHN: *(Looks at his pocket watch, rises)* Gentlemen, I do think that the mention of retiring reminds me that this has been a long and wonderful day, one which will be more glorious with a sound sleep.

LOUISA: *(Looks stage right)* It appears the men are getting ready to leave. Let me thank you again ladies, for your most pleasant company tonight.

JOHN: So, I now take leave of you and wish you and your ladies a safe trip home.

Thank you, again, for the wonderful celebration. Good night to all!

(John Quincy exits as lights dim, permitting Louisa and Abigail to exit while curtain falls)

THE END

"Dolly Madison: Hostess to History"

The reflections of a president's wife
By Margaret M. Kelly

Performed in the first production of the play at Whitehall NY

Dolly Madison..............................Carol King

Note from the Author

When I was a schoolgirl, my mother, a history teacher, introduced me to a biography of Dolly Madison. My reaction to the book was one of inspiration and I remembered my admiration for this 19th century woman through my adult years.

Here was a woman who rose to become a confidant to many of the men who helped shape our country's future by their work in creating the Declaration of Independence and the Constitution.

But, more than that, Dolly Madison was a survivor, recovering from the untimely deaths of her young husband and a son while attempting to raise an older son. With her meeting of James Madison, however, the die was cast for future greatness.

Madison was a man who brought her into the world of American politics. She became the White House hostess for her husband's dear friend, the widowed Thomas Jefferson, and then became even more renowned when she became the First Lady as her husband was elected the fourth president of the young United States.

Dolly's bravery during the War of 1812 when, with the help of a few White House servants, she saved records from the burning building as the British army moved into the capital city. This action strikes deep into our hearts as the epitome of valor in the face of national tragedy.

Originally, I envisioned this story as a musical because of its wide-ranging events and the numerous important people in her life.

But, then I decided that it would be better to concentrate on the woman herself and to let her tell her own story in the structure of a one-woman play.

Even as I find myself ever more admiring of this marvelous woman, I am also so thankful and appreciative that my mother introduced me to her as I was learning the power of reading.

MARGARET M. KELLY
April 2010

"Dolly Madison: Hostess To History" is dedicated to my mother, the late Margaret Ashman Kelly

ACT ONE

(The curtain rises on James Madison's study at Montpelier. It is summer, 1836, the day after his funeral. The room is dominated by a large desk covered with books and pamphlets, that are also piled up everywhere, on every available table and chair.

Dolly enters, carrying some letters and papers, and her favorite possession, a music box. She is not wearing the colorful outfits and bright turbans usually associated with her, but a plain gray "Quaker" outfit and small, close-fitting white cap of Quaker style.

Dolly is a sincere, friendly woman, very popular, with a retentive memory that never forgets names and faces. But at this time, she is very alone, having just lost her dear companion of 40 years. The friends gathered are her neighbors of the surrounding Virginian community)

DOLLY: *(Entering)*

Good afternoon! It was so good of you to come!

(Shows music box to her visitors, the audience)

Here is the music box I have always treasured. James gave it to me after he proposed marriage. I was so surprised and overcome that my sister Lucy said I should come to her house to think it over! James arranged my travel to her house at Harewood and when Congress adjourned on June 30th, he joined us on July 1.

(Chuckles)

No, James swore he had not caused Congress to adjourn the day before my departure.

(Places music box on stack of papers)

Oh, these papers! I must fulfill my duty now that my beloved James is dead. The publication of his papers must be completed with no delay, so the world may see the important Constitutional debates!

(Sits)

I have asked my dear son Payne to approach a New York publisher, but no offer has been made. A friend advised me to offer the work to the patronage of Congress. President Jackson recommended to Congress, the acquisition of the Madison papers.

(Caught up in emotion)

Excuse me! I will strive to keep my composure.

(After a moment)

Look, here is George Tucker's biography of Jefferson, which he dedicated to James. My dear husband's last dictation to me was a letter of thanks.

Oh, I have never understood why this great man sought my hand in marriage. These documents he wrote created a nation!

(To members of gathering)

You wonder why I am wearing these Quaker clothes? You see, I was born a simple Quaker. The Revolution broke out when I was seven years old. My father's firm Quaker beliefs did not allow him to fight. He had more personal concerns—my family had freed our slaves from our farm. Then my father suffered business reverses and we had to sell our plantation at Scotchtown.

(As if recalling a memory)

Ah, those childhood summers in North Carolina when we had visitors like my cousin Patrick Henry who read bedtime stories to us. On my father's side, we were related to Martha Washington. Often I spent summers with my maternal grandparents, the Coles. From my grandmother I acquired a fascination with cooking and appreciation of fabrics and styles of clothes.

(Laughs lightly, adjusts her cap)

And I so loved the transparent silken cap my grandmother wore!

(Soberly)

But my father thought the plantation was no longer profitable, and he and my mother and I traveled to Philadelphia to find a new home.

(With wonder)

That city was the largest in the Colonies, and the capital of our new country. I was amazed at the number of people, the beautiful shops, and all the activity!

At our home in Philadelphia, we had frequent guests. Thomas Jefferson was among them, as the Constitutional Convention was convened.

James was a member, and he also drafted the Constitution, the Bill of Rights, and the Federalist Papers. He and Thomas had many political discourses in our home.

(To audience)

My friend Elizabeth was a great comfort to me after my first husband died. I remember the day I was in my "widow's weeds" and we went shopping together, walking along the Philadelphia streets. She teased me with "Look, Dolly, gentlemen station themselves where they can see you pass. Really you must hide your face, there are so many staring at you!"

Yes! Even James came to pay his respects "expressing condolences in my bereavement."

(To audience)

You did not know my first husband, John. After my father's business failed and my mother became ill, I took over the household duties. I was the eldest girl and my sister Lucy and I cooked, sewed our clothes, and kept house. Our plain Quaker dresses had to be modest, but

(Smiles conspiratorially)

I bought scraps of dark velvets for our collars and trims.

(Serious)

I was nineteen when John Todd, a promising young lawyer of means and a good Quaker, proposed to me! But, my parents were both sick, my father near death, so I told John I was "never meant to marry!" But father called me to his bedside and told me he wished me to marry John, of whom he had the highest opinion. John had shown my father great kindness in his trouble. I obeyed in the best possible grace.

(Pleasantly)

In 1790, I was wed in a proper Quaker wedding and we moved into John's house on Chestnut Street. Father passed away soon after, and then John and I were blessed with our dear son Payne.

Oh! There was no other infant like him in all the world! I can still hear John teasing our son: "I hope my sweet little Payne can lisp "Mama" in a stronger voice than when his Papa last heard him!"

Soon after, I bore John a second son, dear little William! Oh, it was the happiest of time. But soon afterward, John came home with alarming news! He told me people in Philadelphia were coming down with a deadly fever.

(To audience)

Do some of you remember? Well, John made me stay indoors. Then he made arrangements for me to take the babies to his cousin's home at Gray's Ferry. My mother stayed with me. I heard nothing from John. He remained behind to care for his parents.

(To audience)

Many people fled Philadelphia every day, the dead numbered in the hundreds! Only the Quakers would assist the poor afflicted! John had told me his duty was to his people.

(Pauses to gain control)

Then one day, I head a knock at the door and my mother spoke to someone. Then John's voice cried out: "I feel the fever in my veins, but I must see her once more!" I ran to him as he collapsed in my arms and breathed his last.

(Pauses, closes her eyes, then darker voice)

When I recovered from my fever, Mama told me I had been sick for awhile. Then she had to tell me of William's passing! My dear baby!

(She seems to collapse in a chair, but regains control)

But, I still had my little Payne! His tiny voice crying "Mama" pulled me back to life.

(Pauses - Picks up a letter)

After that, I wrote my friend Elizabeth a letter and I have kept it as a memento.

(Reads)

"Dear friend, thou must come to me. Aaron Burr says that the 'great little Madison' has asked to be brought to see me this evening"

(To audience)

Yes, we were both perplexed. Why would he wish to court a widow of less than a year's standing? Aaron had been an acquaintance of mine, but James asked him to make a formal introduction! When Elizabeth opened the door, there stood that flamboyant Mr. Burr in a blue velvet suit, rose-pink waistcoat, white silk stockings and silver-buckled shoes...

(Laughs)

...introducing drab Mr. Madison all in sober black!

(Laughs lightly)

I saw them before they saw me. While Elizabeth met them and poured the tea, I peeked in before I entered in my mulberry satin gown. Elizabeth had told me to abandon my widow's weeds for this special occasion.

I found Elizabeth and Aaron chatting merrily! Poor Mr. Madison could not get a word in until I asked him how his Constitutional debates were proceeding.

(Laughs)

Then, he waxed poetic. "We the people of the United States in order to form a more perfect union..."

(Explains to audience)

...he was courting me!

After Elizabeth and Aaron—two very clever conspirators—took away the tea things together, I asked James about his lovely ancestral estate.

Ah! He loved this place so!

(Gestures around the room and to the window)

I shall never forget his response: "Ah, Montpelier! You should see the view! The Blue Ridge Mountains thirty miles away across the broad expanse of green meadows and sweeping forests, long undulating miles of them! All changing in color and shadings every hour! One could watch them for years on end, and they would never be the same. Enough food for the spirit for a lifetime!"

(Seems lost in reverie)

Then he asked me to marry him—and we have had food for the spirit for a lifetime—together!

I was so unsure at that time. Reverend Balmaine arrived as the wedding approached. I heard the guests gathering in the parlor below and then James arrived to the sounds of fiddle music and much chatter about his Mechlin lace ruffles on his shirt. I sat alone upstairs writing to Elizabeth. I was only 25 and James was forty—what did this great man see in me? I had been "read out of meeting" by the Quakers because James was Episcopalian. My son Payne would have a generous and tender protector, and James was the man who of all others I most admired...

(Pauses)

...but did I love him?

(Pauses)

I put on the crown of white flowers, wore a wedding gown of silvery satin, and slowly descended the stairs. "My lovely beauty," James whispered to me as he placed a necklace of exquisite gold coins about my neck.

(Remembers)

As the country dancing began, I ended that letter to Elizabeth. "... Evening—Dolly MADISON! Alas!" I do not understand why I wrote that way, now that I have lost my dearest husband.

(She grips Madison's papers tightly to her breast)

Adieu, my beloved, our hearts understand each other.

(Pause)

Elizabeth was right. I had no doubts of my love for James at his first inaugural to the presidency!

My sister Anna accompanied me as our family sat in the gallery with the Justices and diplomats in the House of Representatives for James' swearing-in. Anna said to me: "Why, Dolly, they say you are the first President's wife to attend an inauguration! Your presence creates a stir!" I told my sister I could not be away from my dearest James on this important day.

(Laughs)

I believe what really caused a stir was my bonnet of purple velvet trimmed in white satin with two white plumes and my long white wool cloak, edged in purple! Madame Pichon, the French diplomat's wife, always showed me everything she had.

She decorated herself according to the French ideas and urged me to do the same. She always used to ask for Anna, calling her my "belle soeur."

(Laughs – then lets it subside. Mood darkens)

Elizabeth asked me about Payne. We have not heard from him much lately. Elizabeth has been my life-long friend and knows how much my sister, Anna, worries now that my dear son has spent his own fortune, he is wasting my resources also.

His eccentric plantation at "Toddsbirth" and strange attempts at silkworm farming were disasters. Anna fears he will mismanage the operation at Montpelier and we will lose it.

I tell Anna we must forgive his eccentricities, for his heart is right, my poor Payne. I know Anna believes each of Payne's trips to New York about these papers is merely an excuse for frequent and long stays in the taverns there.

(Embarrassed)

His drinking, you know!

(To audience)

You have seen all the sculpture, metalwork, and paintings around this estate.

(Drifts into a memory)

…Ah, when the peace delegation returned in 1814 after the war, Payne had been shipping crates to us from Paris! Daily, my faithful servant, French John, was opening crates and Sukey, my maid, was bringing me messages from Payne that he was coming. James had sent Payne to work with our peace delegation in Paris, and Payne filled our house with his art purchases. I tried not to be disappointed about his absence.

(Reflective)

Payne returned to us by a long route! After the delegation finished its work, Payne used the opportunity to tour to St. Petersburg. From there he took the Swedish route, by way of Copenhagen, and on to Paris. Then he took off for London! His ship, the Neptune, put in to Harve de Grace, but Payne was not there! Only his baggage! I asked the Captain to send on Payne's clothes and artwork he had collected. But I pined for my dear son.

Indeed, Anna and I have been finding strange papers!

As we have been sorting James' papers, we have been finding letters Payne sent to my dear husband, asking for loans.

(Still unbelieving)

It appears Payne had serious gambling debts. From what I have found...

(Indicates another sack of papers on the desk)

...James gave Payne expense money and believed it was adequate for his six-month sojourn in Europe. Ah, indeed James did not wish to worry me about Payne, but...

(Lifts a paper)

...here is a report from Treasury Secretary Gallatin to James. Payne owed a loan, for which Mr. Gallatin co-signed and asked James to remit the sum immediately. James told Mr. Gallatin he was prepared for a heavy demand for the expenses of Payne! But James never told me that he was covering Payne's debts. Still, I remind Anna how happy we were that summer here at Montpelier when Payne finally arrived.

(To audience)

He told wondrous stories: His audience with Louis the 13th at the Tuileries, the great performances at the Opera Comique and the Theatre Francais. And, there was the visit to the State Museum to see the famous Apollo, the Venus de Medici, and Raphael's Transfiguration. Why, once, Payne was seated near the great Napoleon at the theater!

(With motherly indulgence)

I remember his comments about women. "The City of Ghent was a poor substitute for Paris—beautiful spires, but ugly women!" he said.

(Chuckles)

Payne once told me he was interested in diplomacy!

(Her voice trails off as she drifts over to a window and looks out)

My, my, the roses and tiger lilies are doing well this summer, although Anna has had to make the daily cutting lately. The past few days, with James' death and all the funeral arrangements, have been most trying! You see my Cape Jasmine? Why, even my gardener has complimented me, the dear fellow.

(Back from the window)

I remember when James and I returned to Montpelier, after the inaugural ceremony for President Monroe. James embraced his new life as the gentleman tobacco farmer! Each morning, James would ride out to oversee the tobacco crop and our livestock. Some mornings, I would join him for a ride through the fields. James was in constant communication with Thomas Jefferson, who would invite James to ride over to see some new threshing machine, or to discuss the tolerable weather for the wheat crop.

(To audience)

We always enjoyed the visitors who came to call. We kept that telescope you noticed on the portico to scan our winding country roads, often spying carriages bringing friends, and sometimes even tourists who wished to pay their respects to James and me. We welcomed them all!

(Animated)

I remember the visit of General Lafayette! It was his last visit to our country, in 1825, I believe. The general had become a marquis by then, and he and James would converse for hours about the old days, first with Thomas at Monticello, then here at Montpelier.

James would talk about a trip they took to a parley with the Six Nations Indians, remarking on the head winds on the Hudson, the rich loams of the Mohawk Valley.

When here at Montpelier, I would take the Marquis down to the cabins occupied by the field hands. He loved meeting Granny Milly who was 104 years old. He would stroll down to the "Walnut Grove" for a little chat, coming back with a fresh egg or nosegay that had been presented to him.

On that visit, the Marquis had brought with him Miss Frances Wright who was researching and writing a plan for the abolition of slavery. Many in our family had made an experiment of freeing our slaves.

James had considered the abolition of slavery when he was drafting the Bill of Rights. However, the social and economic structure here in Virginia was built on the institution. Yet, James opposed slavery in all his written works.

(Explains further)

Due to the meager government salaries, and the fact that James and the other founders had to set up the American Treasury with their own money, we all had to continue to live plantation life or risk bankruptcy. We have strived to treat our field hands with compassion, building houses for them, providing liberal food, clothing and medicines.

(Points out to the hall)

That is a Gilbert Stuart painting, one of my sister, Anna. While James was Secretary of State, Stuart was one of Anna's many beaux! He had made portraits of the country's leaders and their wives during the winter, and painted portraits of James and me.

Anna asked for his portrait and Stuart played a little trick on her. The curtain behind her in her portrait was his jesting answer to her. Those of us who know Anna's portrait also know the curtain was shaped like his profile!

(Laughs)

I do recall how Stuart was all the rage, and worked to death. He told wonderful anecdotes to divert his sitters. I wore my dark dress with white ruching, a shawl, and an exotic turban with tassels and sat quietly while he painted me. When we presented Elizabeth with the oil portraits that Joseph Wood painted of us, she said the likeness of James almost breathed. In short, it was himself. But my painting was not satisfactory to Elizabeth. She said it lacked expression of my eyes, which spoke from and to the heart.

While I was finishing the Presidential Mansion with my decorator Benjamin Latrobe, we placed Stuart's painting of George Washington in the dining room. What a majestic portrait! Full-length, with George wearing a lace-flattered black velvet suit!

(Sighs, assures audience)

It is quite alright now. I have put the memories of that dreadful night behind me.

(Pauses)

They were such difficult times. Those years just before the War of 1812! James was troubled by the embargo which threatened our trade. I was so concerned for James, that I pressed our cousin Edward Coles to be his private secretary. Advisors and cabinet members came to James constantly! He slept little and rose frequently in the night to read or write. I kept a candle burning for him.

One day when I came to James for our late breakfast at noon, I overheard such dreadful talk!

Some advisors were telling James that he risked war with Napoleon because he had opened trade to England, but closed it to France. Another was arguing with James about a new British envoy, Francis James Jackson, who was known as "Copenhagen Jackson" for his bullying threats to blow up Copenhagen if that city did not capitulate to his demands. It was all so frightening.

(Explaining further)

There was such factionalism in our beautiful new country....James was hated by both the New England Federalists and the Southern Republican War Hawks.

(Explains)

The New England Federalists did not want to challenge the British Orders in Council and said the Southerners were bloodthirsty and wanted to start "Mr. Madison's War." The Southerners struck back with a horrible accusation that the New Englanders only cared for their shipping and would sell out their country and secede from the Union.

(Exasperated)

James wanted a 60-day embargo but the Foreign Affairs Committee reported Britain had just seized 18 more American ships and recommended war!

(Throwing up her hands and with irony in her voice)

In the midst of all this, James was being nominated for a second term as President by a vote of 82 to zero!

(Finds paper in stack – reads it)

Here is James' message to Congress. I still have it!

"On this, the first day of June, in the year of our Lord, 1812, I hereby declare that countless times on that highway of nations, the sea, the British have violated the American flag, kidnapped American sailors, plundered American property, violated American harbors, and spilled American blood. Hoping to avoid war, the United States had laid an embargo. At any time, Britain could have repealed the unjust Orders in Council but she refused. Anxious for peace, Americans have met injuries with unexampled forbearance and conciliation. A war is being waged against these United States. Shall we meet it with war? The decision is up to you...the Congress!"

(She slumps in a chair)

Only years later, we discovered that on the 17th day of June, 1812, when the Senate concurred with the House and declared war, that very same day, the British Cabinet announced the hated Orders in Council were repealed!

(Throws her hand to her head)

Oh, what a waste! A totally unnecessary war! If only we could have communicated with them!

(She becomes trance-like)

Be comforted, the memories of that night come often but I remind myself my dear James was safe.

(She paces, mutters)

That night, that night!

(From this point until the end of the act, Dolly's agitation slowly increases as she acts out what she describes)

As I had nursed James for three weeks, he was much too indisposed to see the Committee of the Senate. All of Washington was in alarms. A British frigate was at the mouth of the Potomac. The fort was being repaired, five hundred militia were stationed on the Green. Though a Quaker, I have always been an advocate for fighting when assailed. I therefore kept the old Tunisian saber within reach.

(Even as she is older now, she appears to have a saber in her hand, but has difficulty lifting it so drags it as she speaks)

One of our generals had discovered a plan of the British. In the night they would be on hand to burn the President's House and offices! I did not tremble at this…

(Still dragging the saber, paces to the other side of the room)

…but felt hurt that the admiral should send me word that he would make his bow at my drawing room soon.

(Drops saber, paces to other side of room)

Even the people of Washington made exclamations and threats, saying if James attempted to move from the President's House, in case of attack, they would stop him and then he would fall with it! But the British force on the bay did not venture nearer than 23 miles…

(Pauses, then darkly)

…until that night, that night.

(Almost like a chant)

…that night, that night.

(Dolly is in constant agitated movement now)

James had to leave to join General Winder. He inquired anxiously whether I had courage or firmness to remain in the President's House until his return on the morrow, or succeeding day…and on my assurance that I had no fear but for him and the success of our army, he left, beseeching me to take care of myself and of the Cabinet papers, public and private. Later I received two alarming dispatches from him. He desired I should be ready at a moment's warning to enter my carriage and leave the city.

(Dolly acts out the following)

I got ready—pressing as many Cabinet papers into trunks as to fill one carriage. Our private property had to be sacrificed as it was impossible to procure wagons for its transportation. Disaffection stalked around us! My friends and acquaintances—all gone! Even the Colonel with his hundred guards—gone!

French John, my ever faithful servant, with his usual activity and resolution, offered to spike the cannon at the gate, and lay a train of powder, which would blow up the British should they enter the house. I positively objected, without being able to make him understand why all advantages in war may not be taken.

Two messengers, covered with dust, came to bid me fly—but I meant to wait for James!

At a late hour, a wagon was procured, and I had it filled with plates and the most valuable portable articles belonging to the house. Whether it would reach its destination, the Bank of Maryland, or fall into the hands of the British soldiers—I had no idea!

(She becomes more frantic)

The fires started—that night, that night! The British had arrived that night...that night!

(She stretches out her hands to stop the British)

Our kind friend, Mr. Carroll, came to hasten my departure, but I insisted on waiting until the large picture of General Washington is secured...

(She points to a picture on the wall)

...and it requires to be unscrewed from the wall.

(She looks at the flames racing toward her from both ends of the President's House—she 'mimes' that the heat is overcoming her)

I ordered the frame to be broken.

(She mimes pulling the picture from the wall)

...and the canvas was taken out.

(She mimes that she carries a rolled-up canvas under her arm.)

It is done—and the precious portrait in safekeeping! Where I will be tomorrow...

(She turns to look once more at the flames consuming the house)

...I cannot tell!

(Cries out to her maid)

Sukey! Sukey! Come quickly now!

(Suddenly, she is silent. Dolly is looking to left and right as she regains her composure. Then with accustomed dignity)

I have been so remiss in my duties as hostess. Sukey, please prepare some refreshments for my guests.

(Dolly exits.)

End of Act One

ACT TWO

(The audience is gathered in a sitting room at Dolly Madison's Washington D. C. home. Before Dolly appears, waltz music is heard.

After a few moments, Dolly appears. This is a different Dolly from the person in the first act, all bubbling, outgoing, friendly, light steps and smiling face. She is decked out in a bright colored gown with her trademark Empire waistline and one of her famous turbans. She carries a fan.)

DOLLY: *(To the audience)*

Oh! No need to get up! I just want to rest a bit. I hope Sukey has taken care of you.

(Sits)

My niece, Anna, is having a wonderful time upstairs with her friends, her young friends, but ah—it is refreshing to rest a moment.

It was wise to take the advice of Anthony Morris, my dear friend. Those five weeks at White Sulphur Springs restored my spirit and healed my tired eyes!

Little did I know my fine nephew, Richard Cutts, would find me this house on Lafayette Square. I am so glad to be back in Washington! It was such a pleasure to return here and welcome all my old friends.

(Taking audience into her confidence)

I fear I could not conform to the formal rules of visiting you now here in Washington. I would disgrace myself by rushing about among my friends at all hours.

(Laughs)

John Quincy Adams just greeted me a few moments ago: "Let me be the first, dear lady, to welcome you back to our city!"

Indeed I shall return to my custom of hosting receptions on New Year's Day and the Fourth of July.

(Listens at door, waltz music is heard, She sways a moment)

Ah! That is some new music, Strauss, I believe. Anna will know all about it.

(She returns from door, picks up book and sits)

I have been reading a book from Dr. Sewell. *(Flips pages)* It is about Phrenology. I was about to give it to Anthony Morris for his opinion.

(Listens to the music again)

Anna was showing me a new dance.

(She demonstrates)

It's called a waltz!

(She is out of breath)

We never danced much as young people…it was a Quaker prohibition, you know!

(She sits)

Ah! To be back in Washington! When we first arrived it was called "Federal City" during Thomas's presidency.

(Laughs)

It was a muddy swamp! It was filled with half built buildings, only two general stores, dirt roads, and boarding houses sleeping eight men to a room! Not a single tavern, restaurant, school, hospital or public meeting place. Thomas and his dear daughters were enduring the partially built, half-furnished "President's Palace," as we called it then.

(As if answering a guest's question)

Oh, no! It was only renamed the "White House" when we had it white-washed to hide the burn marks after the War of 1812.

Poor Thomas seemed out of place in the "President's Palace!" He wandered about, clad in his carpet slippers, down at the heels and even received official visitors that way.

(With pride, she chuckles)

Thomas always said I served his administration as a magnificent hostess! Diplomats arrived every day. Thomas' daughters were young and did not know what to do. I was happy to host diplomatic parties, whether at our little home on F Street or at his "Palace."

(Chuckles)

James told me a story when he was Thomas' Secretary of State. It seems an office-seeker dropped by the State Department one day to ask for the governorship of a Western territory. James told him he was sorry, but other applicants had stronger claims. The man then asked about a collectorship. Unfortunately, James said, they had all been taken. Well, continued the man, how about a post office?

James told him that it was out of the question. Finally, the man said, did James have any old clothes he can spare?

(She laughs)

Anna did not think that it was funny!

So, I told her about Ambassador Mellimelli.

I had arranged a party for Thomas with two delegations coming to call. On one side, Ambassador Mellimelli of Turkey in his crimson robe and 20 yards of white turban, and his 11-man retinue in Turkish costume and a pipe-bearer carrying a four-foot pipe.

On the other side, there was a large party of Indians.

We had Creeks wearing blue coats with red collars, gold-laced hats and beaded moccasins. The other tribes—Osage, Missouri, Sioux, Pawnee, Cherokee--some came in traditional Indian dress, some naked to the waist with only face paint on!

I was in my dressing room adjusting my turban that evening when, in the mirror, appeared an Indian all in war paint, staring at me! He did startle me! But I remained calm and rang my bell for French John and he came and gently persuaded the Indian to return to his group.

When I welcomed Mellimelli, I expressed my hope that our meal contained no dish to offend his Muslim sensibilities.

During the evening, I noticed James had serious discussions with Thomas and they were trying to calm Treasury Secretary Gallatin. There was some financial problem.

When Ambassador Mellimelli presented me with a heavy scarlet velvet caftan, I staggered under its weight and discovered it was laden down with 30 pounds of gold bullion! James rushed over and made a comment that I did not understand at the time, that it would solve our financial problems with the Ambassador.

It seemed the Ambassador's entourage of 12 was running up quite a bill week after week at Stella's boarding house! Mr. Jefferson and James had been considering another solution—Thomas wanted to take the three fine Arabian stallions that Mellimelli had brought to him and mate them with local mares to see how much money they could earn. The groom refused till he received a Presidential order to mate American mares to Turkish stallions.

I found out also, even though Thomas and James tried to keep it from me, that Mellimilli had asked especially for concubines...

(Giggles)

..and James suggested a local 'lady'---Georgia-a-Greek! And I later found a State Department financial statement, listing her fee under "Appropriations to foreign intercourse!"

(Feigns shock)

I will never forget the way that evening ended—or how we almost lost a fine servant woman. It seems when she entered to serve the coffee to our guests, Mellimelli suddenly rushed to her, threw his arms around her generous frame, and cried out: "You are the handsomest woman in America! You look like one of my wives, the high-priced one—she cost me a whole camel!"

The whole party broke up laughing!

(Outraged)

It took me hours to get the poor woman calmed down!

(Dolly calms herself and walks to other part of the room, sees a flag folded)

What is this doing here? Why, the letter is still attached!

(Opens the letter)

This flag was presented to me from the British warship "The Macedonia" accompanied by a letter from the Postmaster of New Orleans who had witnessed the battle.

(Dolly reads)

"Madam—the American army in Louisiana has gained immortal glory. It was on the morning of January 8 when the British attempted to storm our lines. They were permitted to approach within twenty yards of our batteries, at which moment our musketry opened on them. The ground was strewn with their dead and dying. The loss of the enemy exceeded two thousand. The city is saved. Your obedient and admiring servant, Thomas B. Johnson, Postmaster of New Orleans"

(To audience)

My sister Sally saw a messenger run in during the presentation of this flag, and next we heard her jubilant cry from the upstairs balcony: "PEACE, PEACE!"

She had seen the messenger approach James and his Cabinet, meeting upstairs in the Round Room, and James followed Sally down to make the formal announcement of the Treaty of Ghent.

(Folding letter and flag together)

The battle described in this letter took place 14 days after the Treaty was signed. Again, communication would have spared lives.

Our government had to convene in all sorts of buildings since most of the public buildings were completely razed during the war. All was confusion when Sukey and I fled in that carriage after the President's House was set afire.

(Gathers herself)

I can talk about it now. General Mason and Attorney General Rush took James into the forest outside Washington. A fierce hurricane had blown up with much thunder and lightning. Messengers had brought me word of safe havens that James had arranged for me.

But, there was something I never told James! The inn where Sukey and I were supposed to sleep that night—ah, how could James have known? The innkeeper's wife shrieked at us: "Your husband has got mine out fighting, and damn you, you shan't stay in my house!"

Yes! It was awful, but I know all citizens did not favor the war. But, poor Sukey, she was terrified and did not comprehend. I gathered her in my arms and we concealed ourselves with our capes, and stumbled through the awful night, searching for James.

It was important that James and I could not be found together that night. The British troops would gladly have paraded us through London to our execution.

(Enjoying a loving memory)

James and I did meet for a few precious moments that night in the woods near Mrs. Minor's house, until news was brought that British were in the area, and General Mason again took James to safety.

Our disguises were good as Sukey and I were almost denied passage the next morning by the bargeman. I could not remain on the Virginia soil and had to cross in his ferry. He said: "No Madam, I dare not let an unknown woman into the city." I threw back my hood and he gasped: "Why, Mrs. Madison, for you, of course!"

Sukey was exhausted by then, but she overheard my cry: "Oh! God, they have burned my city" and she wailed helplessly.

(Gathers strength)

When James and I saw the wreckage the next day, he was desolate, muttering about the charred walls of the President's House, the hundreds of citizens impoverished, and even the dead horses on the Capitol lawn! Mrs. Smith, with her ever-present diary, recorded that she doubted that the seat of government ever again be organized.

(To audience)

It was then a messenger from the City of Philadelphia did approach James to say that they were inviting the Federal government to return there.

(Emphatic)

It was the shock James needed! He immediately resolved to rebuild Washington—we had built the city once from swamp and we would prevail! Oh, but such confusion after the war! Secretary Gallatin lost his home! Then Secretary Monroe brought news that Secretary Armstrong had resigned as Secretary of War, and James made Monroe Secretary of both State and War! They convened a Cabinet meeting at the F. Street house. The undamaged Post Office building was used to convene the House of Representatives and the Senate used the Patent Office.

We were offered the Octagon House by French Minister Serurier. It was owned by Mr. and Mrs. Tayloe. Mrs. Tayloe had beseeched him to preserve her husband's winter home before the invasion. So Minster Serurier moved into it and protected the house with his country's flag. That was the house where the news of peace was brought on the day I was presented this flag.

(Dolly replaces the flag)

James and I had lived in many houses which served as the President's House. During his two terms, I was always pleased to have my dear sisters and their families join us. While I was decorating the President's House, Anna and Lucy were with us. Lucy loved the parties and enjoyed our distinguished guests: Washington Irving, Robert Fulton, Charles Wilson Peale, and even the actor George F. Cooke.

It cheered her so, after the death of her dear husband during his trip through North Carolina.

I did introduce Lucy to her second husband, Judge Todd, a fine widower with his own children to raise. In spite of our massive preparations for war, I resolved to give my dear sister Lucy a beautiful wedding in the President's House. James escorted her and gave her away to the distinguished Supreme Court Justice Thomas Todd of Kentucky, a man of most estimable character. He took Lucy to his home at Lexington, where there was fine society.

(Composes herself)

It broke my heart to find myself left far from my sister, but I rejoiced at her new husband—and I had acquired a fine brother!

My sisters loved James! I remember a summer at Lucy's home at Harewood, when I was considering James' proposal of marriage, my friend Elizabeth came to visit and gossiped right along with Lucy and Anna.

They enjoyed his clumsy attempts at love letters! But, oh! James could write towering prose when drafting a Constitution but his words of love were stilted.

James would visit me daily to drop off books for me and toys for Payne. I told Lucy that I needed to come to Harewood to think things over. James was being distressingly blunt! It was plain that marriage was his object.

And James had very powerful people assisting him. I recall the day Martha Washington and I were conversing and she said her husband had great esteem and friendship for James and they would all wish me to be happy. Then, George rushed in to me and praised James, telling me some day James would marry and I would be the most fortunate woman on earth.

Yes, even my good friend Thomas Jefferson told me I would achieve my greatest contentment in life if I married James. Even my sister Anna told me she found James a charming man and was half in love with him herself.

(Pause)

My sisters and I worked together to sponsor worthy charities which I hope we can do again. I recall the time we outfitted Captain Lewis and Captain Clark for their expedition. Some Cabinet wives and Senators' wives helped me support many fine causes, including purchasing provisions for their expedition west.

Thomas Jefferson had announced in 1803 that he wanted the two Army Captains to explore the Missouri River, with the hope the brave captains would discover the best route to the Pacific Ocean.

I clearly remember how much we feared they might never return from the distant, uncharted lands!

The expedition was announced during the party we had for Ambassador and Mrs. Merry. Oh, we had such a breach of diplomatic protocol at that party, caused by Thomas' beliefs in the equality of man.

What a night that was!

James and I were helping Thomas with another diplomatic party. This was a very important one, as he was in the midst of difficult negotiations with Spain and France over the purchase of Louisiana. Then Thomas had to deal with England on the unjust impressments of our sailors on the open seas. This party was to welcome the new British minister, Mr. Merry, and to improve relations.

(Significant pause)

And, we also had to learn how to deal with Mrs. Merry! What a woman! It did not help that Thomas made it clear that he mingled with all persons equally, and expected at state dinners, a perfect equality among the guests composing the company.

(Pause)

It was a very democratic idea but it made chaos at a diplomatic function. Mrs. Merry was –ah—"difficult". She had passed some years in Paris and Madrid and was a lady of fashion.

It was overheard that Mr. Merry had anticipated a more "rural" life-style and had brought along with his family, his entire ménage, all his furniture, down to the last pot and kettle!

Mr. Merry told his wife that this was a thousand times worse than the worst parts of Spain! And Mrs. Merry declared: "she would bear up stoutly against difficulties." So, she arrived with a gown of white satin with long train, blue crepe over the dress. A shawl of blue crepe put over her head. Her hair bound tight to her head with a diamond crescent, comb, earrings and necklace.

My dear friend Hannah, Treasury Secretary Gallatin's wife, described our menu to Mrs. Merry: the round of beef with a soup called "bouil-li", and a rich gravy. The dish of cabbage, much boiled and cut in strips, in the middle, a large ham. The dessert—apple pie!

I did hear Mrs. Merry's remark that the splendors of the Secretary of State's table were more like "a harvest home supper!" But I did not take offense. The profusion that was so repugnant to foreign customs arose from the abundance and prosperity of our country. I preferred more liberal fashion of Virginia, abundance over delicacy.

(With a sly look)

I thought that was very diplomatic!

(Pauses)

But, when dinner was announced, Thomas insisted on escorting me, in spite of my protests that he should escort Mrs. Merry, according to protocol. I found myself seated first, and James had to placate Mrs. Merry the rest of the evening.

We were never sure whether it was that night or a political dispute that caused them to complain of bad treatment to their government, but they were soon recalled to England.

(Pauses, then somber)

But, James and I remained dear friends with Thomas to his dying days.

(Lost in memory)

I shall never forget how somber James was, the day he returned from Monticello, after discussing further plans for the founding of the university. James and Thomas were working closely on the founding of the University of Virginia. They would spend hours together, planning. I sat with James and asked him why he looked so concerned. He told me Thomas was deteriorating swiftly. His financial affairs were declining. To raise money to hold back his creditors, Thomas held a lottery to sell the lands of his plantation. It was not successful.

(Explains further)

To add to his misery, Thomas also had taken a severe fall, and was not able to ride his horse. General Lafayette sent him medicines from France, but they did no good.

(Softly)

The last time James saw Thomas alive, Thomas asked him to take care of him when he died. On the Fourth of July, the 50th anniversary of the Declaration of Independence, Thomas Jefferson died.

(Picks up a paper)

I have kept the speech that James gave at Thomas' funeral.

(Reads)

"I have never doubted that the last scene of our illustrious friend would be worthy of the life it closed...But we are more than consoled for the loss, by the gain to him, and by the assurance that he lives and will live, in the memory and gratitude of the wise and good. I have known him for 50 years during which there was not an interruption of mutual confidence and cordial friendship for a single moment"

(Folds paper, pauses)

James suffered such sorrow to lose his dearest friend.

(Pauses, then with a start)

Oh, dear! I forgot to tell you - today my niece Anna and I are invited to the Capitol to see Samuel Morse demonstrate his newest invention! He calls it the electric telegraph. Messages will travel in minutes, rather than days, they say!

(With wonder in her voice)

Today they hope to send and receive messages between Washington and Baltimore! Anna told me earlier that she heard that they may ask me to dictate a message.

(Pause)

My friend Mrs. Wethered will be in the group in Baltimore watching this experiment. Perhaps, I shall say: "Message from Mrs. Madison. She sends her love to Mrs. Wethered!"

(To audience, waltz music is heard)

I wish you could all accompany me to see it happen yourselves. I am sorry I have to leave you now and the party upstairs. It was so pleasant sharing my memories with you.

(Starts out, then turns back)

Do try the waltz before the music ends!

(Dolly waltzes out the door)

THE END

"Fall From Grace"

Benedict Arnold: Hero and Traitor
A Two-Act Play

By Martin P. Kelly

Note from the Author

A dozen years ago, I visited Whitehall NY in search of a venue where my touring theater troupe might perform. It was the first time I had ever been in this village.

Following the visit to the village, I realized that this was the site of one of the great periods in American history. Since I was a school boy reading about American history, I often wondered about the dichotomy of a man who could be a great hero at one point in his life and then be considered a despised traitor to his country and its cause almost six years later.

In 1776, Benedict Arnold had led a flotilla of 18 ships north on Lake Champlain to intercept a large British fleet that was bringing troops towards Whitehall, then called Skenesborough, in order to have General John Burgoyne's army march into New York territory and split the colonies.

A veteran ship captain and a recognized heroic soldier because of his previous exploits in battles in Canada and at Boston against the British, General Arnold was able to maneuver and outwit the British fleet of more than 600 vessels, so that while losing his ships but saving many of their crews, he was able to delay the British invasion sufficiently so that the arrival of winter weather forced the invaders to return to Canada.

This feat is one that so impressed me as I researched that battle that I found it difficult to consider the man as a traitor. Yet, eventually he was!

I wrote a play at that time ("Victory In Defeat") relating the effects of his Lake Champlain "victory" on the American Revolution even as I tried to divine reasons for his future treachery.

As a result of further research, I imagined in this present play ("Fall From Grace") the influences on Arnold to bring about his break with his fellow Americans. As the first act once again celebrates his "victory" on Lake Champlain, the second act attempts to reveal the reasons for his later actions.

This second act letter is pure fiction but still based on events and revelations in Arnold's life filtered through the mind of one who still finds admiration for the man who was so instrumental in keeping the American cause alive in the most perilous of times for the founding of this country.

MARTIN P. KELLY
April 30, 2009

ACT ONE

"Victory in Defeat"

The Cast

Silas Perkins............*Colin Thompson*

Molly Sampson........*Susan Ingerson*

Benedict Arnold.......*John Noble*

The Place: A tavern in Skenesborough, New York

The Time: October, 1776

(Lights come up with Molly Sampson sweeping her floor. There are several tables in the old tavern she owns and manages. In a few moments, Silas Perkins comes up the aisle and on stage to admonish her.)

PERKINS: Feed this mob before the general arrives!

SAMPSON: Don't be telling me about how to care for m'guests.

PERKINS: We'll want to be hearing the news of the battle when he arrives and not have people still chewing their grub while he speaks.

SAMPSON: Don't I want to hear what he has to say, too?

PERKINS: I should have been with him these past weeks as I was when we went to help out the Boston militiamen last year.

SAMPSON: So you were with the general, were you?

PERKINS: I've told you that before.

SAMPSON: I pay little attention to your ramblings.

PERKINS: They were no ramblings, I tell ya. It was a Saturday morning April last year, only days after the massacre at Concord. The general, only a captain then, marched us through Hartford and then New Haven buying food from his own money as we moved towards Boston.

SAMPSON: He was rich then?

PERKINS: Rich I don't know but he had a good business where we worked, unloading his ships that sailed to the Caribbean and the southern colonies.

SAMPSON: He ran the blockade, then?

PERKINS: And, he rode these parts here in Ticonderoga for almost 20 years, first as a 14-year old militiaman fighting off the French and Indians at Fort William Henry.

SAMPSON: Fourteen, he was!

PERKINS: Yes, a feisty lad! Later, he supplied the British army during the war with the French in Canada back in '58, He brought supplies by ship up the St. Lawrence to Montreal and Quebec where the British army took those towns.

SAMPSON: A busy man if what you say is true.

PERKINS: It's true, I tell you! Didn't I sail with him?

SAMPSON: He must have dealt in black magic to run a business and still sail on his ship.

PERKINS: No, woman! He was no magician. His sister, Hannah, a good maiden lady moved into his house, collected money owed to him, paid his bills and kept good records. She still runs his shop even as he fights on the lake above us.

SAMPSON: Then, he's a fortunate man. I know his sister's tasks since I do all myself here with no man to help, or woman either.

PERKINS: You had a man but his heart stopped one night because of your overwrought affection.

SAMPSON: He was not a well man but I did my best to nurse him to health.

PERKINS: You nursed him into eternity and was paid well too. He left you this inn by a scrap of paper with his hand on it. And you not even his wife.

SAMPSON: His will was judged good and sound.

PERKINS: So be it, I'll not be your judge. Now, feed your guests.

SAMPSON: What further news have you?

PERKINS: Only that the fighting has stopped. Our troops still hold Ticonderoga.

SAMPSON: The general's ships are still afloat?

PERKINS: I fear not from what news drifts south.

SAMPSON: It was a pitiful fleet he did sail out of here.

PERKINS: Support for the general's invasion of Canada last year did not come fully. There was mixed opinion in Congress and lack of sufficient supplies from those who did support the general

SAMPSON: But there's no question the British are intent to come through here.

PERKINS: It was not obvious to every one. With the lack of support General Arnold knew that it was only a defensive fight he can wage with his few ships against all that England can muster in Canada.

SAMPSON: Then, he has enemies?

PERKINS: Ay! There are others seeking command who envy him his success and his military bearing and sense of discipline.

SAMPSON: Ethan Allen was such a man!

PERKINS: When he failed to take over this command, Allen took his troops to the Green Mountains to fight his own war and taking booty in battle. A land pirate, he is!

SAMPSON: They are renegades! Even my man saw battle not so much as patriotic but as a business. It was our constant quarrel.

PERKINS: Even as General Arnold returned last year from his sailing into Canada and destroying the forts on the Richelieu River, he was not rewarded. They reduced him from colonel of the Massachusetts command to captain of his Connecticut troops.

SAMPSON: That was a glove across the face, for sure!

PERKINS: But, even as he was needed at home with his children and a sister working night and day to keep his business afloat, the general persisted.

SAMPSON: I'm told he went to Philadelphia to plead his case.

PERKINS: He did that after reporting to General Schuyler in Albany about the need to fortify Ticonderoga and all the lake forts, including Lake George. With Schuyler's blessing, he went to Philadelphia.

SAMPSON: It would appear he found allies.

PERKINS: He first made his acquaintance with General Washington when he brought reinforcements to the general in Boston a year ago last spring.

SAMPSON: I hear tell his wife died while he was fighting in Boston.

PERKINS: She did! That is when his sister took over care of his children.

SAMPSON: What happened when he went to Philadelphia?

PERKINS: When Washington heard Colonel Arnold's information, he formed an army of Northern New York with General Schuyler in command.

SAMPSON: But, what of Arnold?

PERKINS: Schuyler named Arnold his adjutant, a general in charge of the defense of Lake Champlain.

SAMPSON: From all reports, he took his command seriously. I see no British in sight.

PERKINS: We'll soon know from his own lips.

(A cry from the back of the meeting hall: "The general has arrived!!")

PERKINS: *(Steps forward)* Ah! Good people of Skenesborough. Let's give welcome to General Benedict Arnold!

(He leads applause and huzzahs as Arnold walks around the room greeting townspeople)

SAMPSON: A sight you are, General! You look like you've ridden with the wind.

PERKINS: He brings news to all of us who have supported him these two years in his battles with the British.

ARNOLD: Thank you, Silas Perkins. And Mistress Molly, it is good to be in the warmth of your inn again. And I greet all of you and thank you for your support these last weeks.

SAMPSON: It's good to know you're safe.

ARNOLD: Safe, perhaps, for the moment!

PERKINS: Are we in danger, General?

ARNOLD: There's a chance, but only a chance, sir! The troops at Ticonderoga with General Gates are our only defense.

SAMPSON: With you to lead our men, we'll be safe. You kept the British army away from us last year and they're not here now.

PERKINS: But, what of the battle, general?

ARNOLD: Two weeks ago, I sent a report to General Philip Schuyler on the battle of Valcour Island.

PERKINS: Read it to us, General!

SAMPSON: Yes, let us know of our men's valor.

ARNOLD: *(Takes his place behind a podium, opens portfolio and takes out papers.)*

This is a draft of my letter! I wrote: "My dear General Schuyler:..

"'I am writing this from Fort Ticonderoga, October 15, the year of Our Lord 1776. At four o'clock yesterday morning, I reached this place extremely fatigued and unwell, having been without sleep or refreshment for near three days. After fighting two battles on the lake and rowing for two days, we walked the last 20 miles, carrying our wounded in slings made of our sails.

'We made Crown Point yesterday, only hours before the first British landing parties.

"I ordered the troops, almost 150 men worn by battle, to burn barracks, warehouses, docks and the blockhouse before we left for Ticonderoga, where I write you now.

"Crown Point will give little succor to the English now. As I wrote General Horatio Gates a month ago, we kept two small schooners continually cruising above our fleet's base on Isle La Motte awaiting the first action by the English coming out of the Richeleu River. Our scouts had informed me that Sir Guy Carleton, the governor of Quebec, was taking command himself. He understood the value of controlling Lake Champlain, a strategy I told you I shared strongly."

PERKINS: Didn't I tell you, general?

ARNOLD: *(Nods to him. Points to rest of townspeople)*

But now, the rest of your neighbors need to know!

VOICE AMONG TOWNSPEOPLE: General! Continue! Let us hear of the battle.

ARNOLD: I continue then!

"Disappointed that not one sailor was sent from New York and that only three of eight row galleys had been completed, I prepared for the English fleet. Since half of my fleet was unfinished and I did not have sufficient numbers of seaman, I could not attack the British fleet on the Richelieu River or destroy the large fleet that was under construction.

"I was forced to assume a defensive position, hoping to trap the English fleet when it came down the lake in open waters.

"Tis a good harbor, Valcour is. We could have the advantage over the enemy. If they are too many for us, we can move down further in the lake towards Crown Point but I meant to make my stand at Valcour. I had hoped Carleton would expect to find my fleet farther north and would expect me to meet him in the open lake where their faster fleet would surround our frail ships and pound them with lethal broadsides.

"No, my dear general, I was not going to let that happen. Our duty and our plan was to delay this British fleet from reaching Ticonderoga where the superior numbers of English soldiers could move south and link up with the British troops coming north to Albany from New York City. By all means, this could not happen."

SAMPSON: Oh, that is for sure!

PERKINS: Oh, woman! Can you keep from interfering?

ARNOLD: *(Annoyed but continues)*

"As I indicated, general, in previous reports, in May 1775, I had found Valcour Island while sailing to Canada and sailed past it twice this summer. I knew it well and decided now to place my ships in an arc facing south between the island and the New York shore as the British fleet moved in the open lake on the other side of the island with Vermont to their port side.

"As I placed 16 of my 18 ships in a crescent, facing south, provisions from General Gates reached us. I was able to supply the vessels so the men could eat and restock our ships' stores.

"Now, General, as you know, I was not equipped to defeat this armada coming down the lake but I could try to delay it and reduce its force so it would have to return to Canada. Then with enough men and animals, we can bring the lumber across the frozen lake to Skenesborough in February and rebuild our navy for the offensive the British will be sure to wage in the spring."

PERKINS: They'll not find comfort coming down here again, I should say.

SAMPSON: Our men will find comfort in this port for the winter.

PERKINS: *(Laughs)* There's many's the one that'll find a haven in your snug harbor!

SAMPSON: You can be sure, it'll not be your little dinghy.

PERKINS: Tell us more of the battle, general!

ARNOLD: *(Annoyed, looks at the papers)*

"We were as well-prepared for the enemy as our circumstances would allow. They would not have it in their power to surprise us. My men were daily trained in the exercise of their guns. Still the drills were fewer than I wished as we had not sufficient ammunition.

"Now, I had two guard boats on the north of Valcour Island and on the morning of October 11, the Liberty came racing south and at the tip of Valcour Island, fired a signal shot. When the captain boarded my ship, he told me that the first elements of the British fleet were at Grand Isle, just seven miles from our refuge.

"After Liberty had delivered the alarm, she joined the arc of ships prepared to spring the trap on the British.

"We had learned also that Lord Carleton was carrying Hessian troops while training the English to fight Indian style and not in the European manner where whole regiments of troops would march in open columns into battle. But, the fleet carried regular English troops who were not accustomed to fighting in the woods as the Indians did and which our troops had proved so able to do.

"I warn you, general, our scouts report that the Hessian troops include many German hunters and woodsmen with short, lightweight rifles with far greater accuracy than the regular British Brown Bess rifle.

"General, as the British fleet and troop barges left the Richeleu River, our scouts counted more than 600 ships, including boats carrying artillery and long canoes filled with Indians.

PERKINS: Six hundred ships! My Gawd!

ARNOLD: "Burgoyne's redcoats were being held in reserve it would seem until Carleton felt he had swept the lake of our fleet. "The English fleet left the Richeleu on the morning of October 10, an armada which left our scouts shaken as they reported."

"I had a plan which I kept from my ship's captains until close to battle. When I explained it to my second-in-command, General Waterbury, he urged me to sail quickly to Ticonderoga to protect Gates' army.

"Since we knew we could not fight in the open lake and that an armada the size of Carleton's would reduce Crown Point and overrun Ticonderoga, I had no choice but to try to trap the British into fighting where we had the advantage.

"I had confidence in my captains, including my trusted Connecticut sea captain David Hawley whom I placed in command of our largest ship, the Royal Savage...."

SAMPSON: David Hawley! Another man of strong back who'll protect us all!

ARNOLD: *(Deliberately)*

"...And Seth Warner who had arrived in Skenesborough by oxcart from Connecticut this past spring with skilled mariners, supervised construction of the eighty foot, ten-gun Trumbull, which he now commands. It is the smallest of our row galleys.

"My plan was simple but dangerous. As the British ships passed Valcour island on the lake side and the main fleet was fully past the southern point, two of my smaller ships would lure them back into the area where we lay, between the island and the New York shore.

Any British ship approaching us would be met with the full crossfire from my 16 ships."

SAMPSON: Oh, the slaughter!

ARNOLD: "We would protect ourselves from boarding parties by using grape shot that at 100 yards could tear apart boatloads of men as they approached. It would be daunting even to the most seasoned British sailor.

"As larger British ships approached the arc, my plan was to have our galleys rowed out to fire their cannons all the while being protected by fire from our other ships. Once the galleys fired, they would be towed back to reload.

"Our scouts reported that Burgoyne's scouting parties may have discovered our hiding place near Valcour Island. But, if Carleton had been told, he did not act as if he had known, coming straight down the lake on the other side of Valcour, moving into our trap."

PERKINS: *(Let's out a whoop)* The lake will be full of English dead to feed the fish we'll catch next spring

SAMPSON: They'll soon wash ashore all bloated and bereft of fight.

ARNOLD: *(Takes control again)* "Three of my ships -- the Trumbull, Congress and Washington--sailed a good five miles south of Valcour Island where three British men-of-war were. The impression we gave was to slip past Windmill Point. When we were spotted by British sentries aboard the Inflexible, battle flags about the British warships were run up the masts, signaling "Engage"!

PERKINS: Now, we have it! A battle for sure!

ARNOLD: "Our decoys dashed straight into Valcour Bay as the British ships prepared to fire. When the first English ships entered the bay, they saw the trap which awaited them and the volley of fire that engulfed them. But the captain aboard the Inflexible, the largest of Carleton's ships, bore down on Hawley's Royal Savage. As Hawley rounded the southern tip of Valcour Island, he ran aground and was hit by a broadside from the Inflexible.

"At least three men were killed outright and as the explosion ripped the main mast, Hawley lowered a boat to get his men off the ship.

"Hawley then tried to pull the Royal Savage off the reef but the Hessian gunners aboard the Inflexible hit his small boat with shot and shell and his men were soon in the water, swimming for the island.

"With this diversion, I was able to turn the Congress broadside and use the swivel guns and heavy cannon to rake the Inflexible.

"The fighting became fierce as British sailors fell dead in the water and our decks became awash with blood shed by British cannon fire.

SAMPSON: This is madness you describe!

PERKINS: Madness imported from across the sea, woman!

ARNOLD: "The British frigate Maria was next to try to test our line of ships. Carleton was in command aboard this ship, the flagship of the British fleet. One of our cannon shots reached the Maria's bridge and disabled the officers there, including Lord Carleton.

"We learned later from a British sailor we rescued from the Maria that when wounded in the battle, Carleton, the royal governor, withdrew the ship despite his captain's desire to stay and fight.

"By quitting the fight, we gained heart as I'm sure the British officers and men lost fervor.

"Still, others in the English fleet were not as timid. The gunboats with Hessian artillerymen aboard fought their way into our line. By now, this naval battle was in full fury.

"With pride, I speak of our gunners who hit magazines aboard British ships, blowing some of them out of the water.

PERKINS: Shots heard in London soon enough!

ARNOLD: "What we had succeeded in doing was to permit only one British man-of-war to confront us at a time.

"It finally wound down to the last British ship of size, the Carleton, which fought valiantly to close to hit us broadside. But, our ships, arrayed in an arc, would rake the ship's decks, killing and wounding the ships officers. We learned later, that a 19-year old midshipman had to assume command.

"Yet, aboard the Congress, we could not rest. I ordered the crew of the Congress to raise anchor and close on the Carleton.

"For almost three hours, we slammed hundreds of pounds of shot and shell into the stubborn Carleton. Most all of the crew members were dead aboard the British ship.

(Perkins and Sampson make ad lib comments to each other)

VOICE FROM CROWD: For Gawd's sake! Let the general continue!

ARNOLD: "For our part, we too took severe damage. We counted more than 20 holes in our hull, mostly above the waterline.

"Those of our ships closer to the shore were being hit by Indian snipers who were challenged by our marine sharpshooters tied to our masts.

"Again, the Inflexible came up the lake to challenge us and with her heavy guns, raked our ships from out of our range to retaliate until darkness.

"A British party of marines boarded the Royal Savage, once my flag-ship, and before setting it afire, they took my papers, journals and letters. Many of our men were killed trying to save it. The loss of letters and documents has troubled me.

"Throughout the night, we could see the flickering light from the fires on the Royal Savage and hear the moans of our wounded aboard the stricken ship.

"During the evening, my captains and I assessed the damage of the day. We had lost 60 men killed and three-fourths of our gunpowder was gone. Every one of our ships had been badly damaged. All officers on the Lee had been killed. I tried to rally the officers gathered with me and they were attentive as I explained the plan to escape Carleton's navy.

"I urged that we sail through the British fleet in darkness. After a brief objection by General Waterbury, all agreed we should attempt it.

"Seth Warner aboard the Trumbull led the way with only a hooded lantern on his fantail. Each of the ships did the same and kept the oars moving silently in the water. We were fortunate that Carleton had ordered his ship captains to spread out over the lake which gave us room to sneak past them.

"By seven o'clock the next morning, October 12, we were seven miles south of the closest British ship. At Schuyler Island, we scuttled the badly damaged Providence, the New York and the Jersey.

"Meanwhile, I wrote a dispatch to Gates and put it aboard the Liberty which carried it and the wounded to Crown Point.

"We suffered mightily from the superior number of British ships. However, I learned only hours ago that Carleton could not believe we had slipped through his fleet and sent his ships to the north of the island, believing we were trying to come around the island to escape down the center of the lake. It would have been foolhardy of us but our English friend had been foolish in withdrawing his fleet on the night of the 11th. It permitted us to slip past him.

"If he had kept us contained in Valcour Bay, we would now be prisoners or dead men on the bottom of the lake. We were fortunate too that Carletton did not notice our escape until midday on the 12th and had difficulty following us because the wind was against him.

"Still we only covered 12 miles rowing the ships overnight and were only at Willsboro where it was still possible for the British to get between us and Crown Point.

"I sent the slower ships ahead with orders to keep going until they reached that post.

"I had the Congress stand with the Washington to block the British men-of-war coming upon us.

"The Washington was too damaged to take flight and Waterbury ordered Hawley to strike colors. Only 16 of the Washington's crew of 122 escaped.

"We on the Congress fought off the three British warships for five hours as we took 12 shots below the waterline.

"We were attacked broadside with musket shot from the shore. They kept up incessant firing on us for these five hours with round and grapeshot which we returned as briskly as we could. Our sails, rigging and hull all were shattered and in pieces.

"We were surrounded by seven British ships finally and we had lost 27 of our 70 officers and crewmen. Our ammunition was gone and Crown Point was still 10 miles away.

"I ordered my small ships to run aground on shore and set up snipers to fire upon the English ships. Then I maneuvered the Congress into the shallow cover where I knew from soundings months before the British ships could not follow. We made sure that British marines could not board the Congress to salvage by raking all British gondolas with rifle fire.

"That night, as Burgoyne's Indians searched for us, we took a secret path and walked the last 20 miles, all 150 survivors and our wounded carried in our ship's sails.

'We burned all of Crown Point before marching to Ticonderoga so the English army will have to live in tents as the snows from Canada and the Vermont mountains begin to swirl about them.

"I rest now in Ticonderoga, dear general, awaiting word of what I should do next.

"Yours sincerely, Benedict Arnold"

PERKINS: They are there still, are they general?

ARNOLD: They were yesterday when I left to proceed to Albany to urge strengthening our defenses at Ticonderoga.

SAMPSON: And defend us here at Skenesborough. I'll not want to defend my good name from Englishmen.

ARNOLD: Madam, we have no intent that the English army should capture New York although I imagine his forces are moving into Crown Point at this moment. We will need to fight every foot from Ticonderoga to here to Saratoga if need be but he cannot be permitted to split our colonies. We must stay unified!

PERKINS: *(Rushing in with a letter)* This just arrived by courier from Ticonderoga.

ARNOLD: *(Opens letter and reads)* Great God! It is from General Gates. He reports that Lord Carleton is leaving Crown Point and returning with his fleet north to Canada.

We have been given the chance to breathe new life. We'll be able to build a new navy here in Skenesborough through the winter and resist any invasion next spring. The fight we fought was not in vain, the losses we suffered have borne fruit.

PERKINS: Carleton turned tail, wise man that he is.

ARNOLD: *(Turns to assembled townspeople)* To you, my faithful friends, I thank you for your support. My men served well and bravely because of the knowledge that their fight was your fight. I promise you, we will persevere!

(As Arnold takes his exit, Sampson and Perkins lead the group in singing: "My Country 'Tis of Thee." All join in the cheers for Arnold as he exits door)

End of Act One

ACT TWO

Benedict Arnold's
"Pro Vita Sua"

Cast

Benedict Arnold.............................. John Noble

(A British general officer is seated at a desk in his modest home in the English countryside. He is in his shirtsleeves. A uniform coat is hanging on a coat rack behind him. It is a simple room, dark with just a small flickering oil lamp on the desk. It is General Benedict Arnold editing his memoirs. The date is early June, 1801)

ARNOLD: My dear comrades and friends who bore arms with me in the search for the liberty and freedom we so long sought in America, give me your solace. That I fought by your side with such great love of this freedom is well known. But, that service has since been despised because I found it judicious to reconcile the differences we had with our British kin, our fellow subjects of the king .

I reach what does now seem my final days here in England, my adopted home. With full realization that it may be too late to change the minds of you with whom I shared the great love of what we sought together under arms some 25 years ago, I have undertaken this writing.

Having fought by your side when the love of our country animated our arms, I shall expect from you the justice and candor of a fair hearing of my later actions. It is a hearing that those who did deceive you with more art and less honesty, dared not give me. Often have I declared that when I quit domestic happiness and left my family for the perils of the battlefield, I conceived the rights of my country, our native land, a new nation near birth, in peril. Duty and honor called me to her defense. It was honorable to seek redress of grievances.

(Writes and reads)

And, this redress of grievances was my only object. No man can declare that I did not fight with full vigor for the defense of the land of my birth. No man can deny that I gave full measure of my material wealth and my spiritual being. A wife who died while her husband was at battle is a memory which has been a lifelong torment. Even as I later enjoyed the affection of another dear wife who came to me in my depths of despair, I cannot dismiss the thought of a woman who was a casualty of war as much as one who would suffer death on a field of battle.

In what seemed a denial of all I held dear in our days of comradeship, I say to you that my body and soul joined yours at peril when faced by British armies some 25 years ago.

Yet now I know that I am a despised man in that country of my birth as I prepare to reach my final rest here in the land which gave our ancestors their birth and proved a refuge for me these final years.

I acquiesced in the Year of Our Lord 1776 when the Declaration of Independence was written by Congress and signed by its members to state the needs and dreams of our country. This signing was coupled with force of arms which I supported fully. Still, these same signers of this declaration did not seem fit to heed my calls for direct and swift action or acknowledge my contributions to the fight for this same independence.

Supplies were denied me, bills I paid were not reimbursed, others were promoted before me. Vicious rumors accused me of using private property for my own welfare when all that was done was for the good of the fight for liberty. Farmers' wagons were needed to haul captured cannon to Washington's troops in Boston. Petty men do not see the greater good! Even more, men who were not prepared to place the full measure of fortune or life at risk for the common good and ultimate victory were given command above me.

As I sailed north on Lake Champlain in the fall of 1776 to face a massive British fleet sailing to invade the New York colony, it was obvious that full support of the Congress was not forthcoming. I moved north with a meager force of 18 ships, the result of limited supplies of lumber and men from our leaders in Philadelphia. We were able to delay the British invasion with its 600 ships and many thousands of soldiers even at the expense of our full fleet and the loss of many brave men.

Despite my urgent appeals, I did not get the supplies to build a new fleet to do battle when the next invasion from Canada was mounted in the spring of 1777. As a result, it was necessary for us to retreat south, fighting all the way in ferocious rearguard action. We took our stand at Saratoga where despite timid leadership, the heroism of many brave soldiers preserved the colonial cause. It was my full conviction that when we faced General John Burgoyne at Saratoga, we could, with convincing result, stop this invasion of our land and demonstrate once and for all to the British sovereign that our redresses were honorable and worthy. Then I prayed that the king would accede to our petitions for redress from the laws and actions which caused revolt in the first place.

Yet, men in Congress saw fit to deny the facts those of us in the field brought to them. Even as General Washington sought to place me in my rightful position in battle, my enemies in Congress thwarted his desires and replaced General Phillip Schuyler with General Horatio Gates.

Gates and his friends in Congress denied me the title of major general. I protested vehemently because my leadership experience was greater than those who were selected ahead of me. Headstrong and willful are words they used to describe me. If determination to lead in a just cause is willful, so be it. It was with full vigor that I sought to overcome these slights, even at the risk of insubordination.

The bravery of those soldiers, Continentals and Militia alike, at Saratoga inspired those of us who led them. Force of arms forged a common spirit as we advanced before those who would invade our land, savages and hired troops among them.

Comrades in arms told of families destroyed, women murdered, all this gave us a zeal for the fight. Yet, even then, I full well knew that common blood to ours flowed in the veins of those British troops which faced us in the field. Soon the blood of both sides would form a common pool as we battled on at Freeman's Farm.

No more could I stand and watch the utter knavery of a man who would not take advantage of the turn in battle. Gates did not deserve the charge given him by Congress. He sought to wait for Burgoyne to attack when all good sense indicated that we should force the action. Strike hard and fast was my cry as I attempted to rally the dispirited American troops.

My wounds in the battle were of grievous nature: A horse shot beneath me, similar to what happened to me earlier that year in Ridgefield and a leg shattered where it once received wounds at Quebec in our attack in 1775. Still, the intense pain I suffered as they carried me from the field of battle, did not deter me from making a call to continue the fight to crush Burgoyne and end this revolt so that we could gain from the British king those rights due us.

Still, those in command at Saratoga gained less than they should from Burgoyne. The British general appeared the victor as Gates permitted the defeated troops to march to Boston for a return to England.

I was helpless to argue this action as I fought off doctors for months in Albany who wanted to separate me from my wounded leg.

Even as Burgoyne agreed that he or his troops would never return to the American continent, full well did we know that they would re-place troops fighting in France who would then be sent to do battle with us. Congress gave little heed to those of us who knew that swift course of action and negotiation were needed to end this rebellion.

But, Congress sought instead to seek an alliance with France whose monarchy still desired to gain control of this American continent to grind down our culture and good Protestant religion. What folly was this that we should fight to gain redress from those of our own blood, only to give up our freedom once again to another king who was at the same time denying freedom to his own subjects.

These French allies so quickly sought by our weak leaders in Philadelphia would seek to govern us with even harsher measures than our forebears, and would soon enslave us with their alien culture and religion.

In Philadelphia, they deemed me crippled and unable to command in the field so General Washington gained for me an appointment to defend the city. Here, I observed the actions by Congress which left me beset by doubts of the righteousness of the rebellion. I was assured by emissaries that Lord North would still grant the liberal terms he first offered and were rejected in 1778.

What folly to continue! Lord North was offering all the rights we had demanded of the English king in 1775, before Congress declared independence. The continued fighting was draining the fervor of liberty which could very well be lost if we did not act swiftly. We could see each day Continental Army officers were quitting their commissions, tired of the machinations of those in Congress who purported to led us.

Faced with the realization that my country's worst enemies were in her own bosom, and the terrible suffering for those still following Washington, I would consider active reconciliation with our blood brothers in England. Else would a victory by England tempt harsh critics to heap further indignities upon the colonies. And, would not we suffer more under French domination?

I ask these questions as I asked myself another. Did not General George Monck of years ago help bind the conflict of a divided England by helping to restore Charles 2nd to his rightful throne? With such honor I have received and respect from my British opponents in the field, would I not be a logical conciliator between the two sides? If I conspired with those considered our enemies, did you not also suffer anguish in raising arms against a brother, those men and women of similar blood, culture and history?

We fought this war as one of defense. I lamented therefore the tyranny and injustice which, with a sovereign contempt of the people of America, was waged upon us.

Yet, I also lamented the same tyranny and injustice towards the people of America shown by the contempt of our supposed leaders in Congress when dealing with proposals from the British to end this conflict with the redressing of prior grievances.

With this end attained, all strife should have ceased.

But, no! With the entrance of the French army and fleet, the separation of this part of the British Empire was complete. No longer could we remain British citizens to enjoy those rights known to our brethren in England.

No! We would now face dominance by an alien monarchy.

No longer could I stomach this deception as I held command of the fort guarding the upper Hudson River. It was not an easy decision to prepare to hand over West Point to General Clinton who headed the British garrison in New York. Still, I would have it force my American brothers to think more kindly of the redress offered by Lord North on behalf of the British king.

Money given me at this time served to redress the great financial losses I suffered during my service when I used personal funds to buy supplies and feed my troops, even as my sister Hannah and my children faced financial ruin.

My mission to place West Point in British hands failed with the capture of Major John Andre while carrying my letter to General Clinton.It was then that I sought and received a commission in the British army where I might repel the French invaders, foreign to our spiritual and cultural history. Still, I hoped for reconciliation between the monarchy and the colonies with terms which respected the rights of all. I swear that with all honor within me that even as I now live in a land not of my birth, I long to be there where I once fought for the liberties due all men and for which I paid the full measure.

For a brief time when the king gave me a large grant of land in New Foundland where my sons and I worked as merchants sending goods to Europe and elsewhere in the world, I was denied an opportunity to visit my native land, now the United States of America.

Even as I knew there were men who might engage in a plot within my native land to capture me and bring me back to the former colonies for trial and execution, I could not permit that possibility to rule my life.

As a man truly without a country, despised by men from both lands of my birth and heritage, I must take comfort in knowing that I did all in my power to gain the liberties now enjoyed by my native land, a bountiful land I would long to see again but know that it is not to be.

(Rises, waves his cane as a sword)

If I were to live my life again, I would still persist in keeping our peoples as one but with the liberty and justice due all men.

I am prepared to quit this life, knowing that I wanted only what was right and just for all men. This I swear even with my final breath.

(He slowly collapses into his chair and rests head on desk.)

THE END

"Champlain Onward"

A brief history of four hundred years
of Lake Champlain and 250 years
of Whitehall, in four acts

By Martin P. Kelly

Note from the Author

Some five years ago the Bridge Theater's board of directors was discussing plays and/or musical revues that I was contemplating for the next summer. One board member, Whitehall town historian Carol Senecal, urged that a play be done about the history of Skenesborough that eventually became Whitehall. The suggestion was duly noted but no action was taken at that time. Still, the idea stayed in my mind. Several months later, I sat with Ms. Senecal as she began revealing a wealth of research that had been done about the town of Whitehall during the past two centuries. It was a treasure chest of information.

When I began reading through this research, I became enthused and also amazed at the depth of Whitehall's involvement in the history of America.

Once I had determined a manner of presentation, story theater with music. I began writing and was captivated by the flow of history that evolved.

I was also introduced to the work of Kenneth Bartholomew, a Whitehall resident who has devoted himself to putting much of this research on computer discs for use by the Whitehall library and future researchers. From this research sprung the script for 'Whither Whitehall," a progression of life in the history of Whitehall.

Then in 2008, the Bridge Theater's board of directors decided to participate in the Champlain Quadricentennial, dedicated to Samuel de Champlain's discovery of this great lake. From that suggestion and the fact that two previous plays I had written, "Fall From Grace" and "Whither Whitehall" could be incorporated into a 400-year history that became "Champlain Onward," I assembled a script, writing a section on Colonel Philip Skene and his family and, of course, the opening act about Samuel de Champlain, the discoverer of Lake Champlain.

Indebtedness is extended to Ms. Senecal and Mr. Bartholomew as well as the members of the board of the Bridge Theater for their determination to raise funds to present this play.

Finally, I was the beneficiary of the work of the actors and technicians who participated in putting this script on stage even after the loss of the theater on the 12th Street Bridge when New York State engineers found that the structure itself had deteriorated and was unsuited to support the building erected 10 years previously as The Bridge Theater.

Amid all that had happened, I was fully appreciative of the wonderful reaction of the audiences who attended this play and the reviewers who wrote such insightful pieces about the work.

MARTIN P. KELLY
April 30, 2010

ACT ONE

"Discovery of Lake"
Scene One

Cast

Jeannette...........Carol Jones

Jacques.............Richard Harte

(Prior to curtain there is music, the lights go down, and different music is heard as lights come up on a man and woman. They are on a mountain top overlooking Lake Champlain. It is 1621)

JEANNETTE: It is quiet now, is it not? Quiet and peaceful! The water appears smooth as silk!

JACQUES: Quiet, you say, smooth as silk! Hah! It will never be quiet to me, this lake!

JEANNETTE: Why not? It seems so now!

JACQUES: It did not seem so 12 years ago when we followed Commander Champlain from Quebec. It was the largest body of water we had seen since we arrived in this new land.

JEANNETTE: It appears like an ocean. But not the rough seas I traveled for eight weeks this past year from France to this new land.

JACQUES: Surely, our trip here in 1609 on this lake was rough enough and dangerous! I did not trust our native allies to guide us. We feared we were traveling into a trap? The Six Nations' tribes from the south and the west of us were killing our trappers and burning the villages of our native allies, the Montagnais, Hurons, and Algonquins. These tribal allies were thirsting for revenge!

JEANNETTE: But your commander was looking for peace, I'm told! Was peace possible with revenge in the air? I heard terrible tales back home in my village in Brittany.

JACQUES: I believed victory was still not certain even when many warriors from our Indian allies joined us. And, when we reached the Chambly rapids on the Sorel River, I felt a cold fear. Commander Champlain sent back the boats and we proceeded in canoes to row down this big lake that we were seeing for the first time.

JEANNETTE: I shudder to think of it! Did the lake have a name?

JACQUES: Then and there, the commander gave it his name, Lake Champlain, one he wrote on maps sent to our then King Henry Fourth in France.

JEANETTE: He named it for himself?

JACQUES: (Laughs) And, why not? Was he going to name it after me? Hah, he was drawing the maps! (Jeannette laughs) No matter! Our commander would not retreat. The expedition appeared fool-hardy!

JEANNETTE: The commander would seem foolish to continue, then?

JACQUES: And were not we as foolish? There were just two of us, his countrymen who remained with him. And, many of our native allies deserted us as we neared Iroquois country.

JEANNETTE: Oh! To think you might not be with me now! Why did you not flee also?

JACQUES: In my heart, I could not desert our leader. But, I did fear for our lives when we paddled south to the place known to the Indians as Ticonderoga, the Five Nations country where the Mohawks lived. Their warriors' were fierce fighters…

JEANNETTE: Fierce you say?

JACQUES: ... when they took captives, native or white man, they burned and tortured them and sometimes made a feast of them.

JEANNETTE: I turn cold thinking of such burning of captives..... and torture!

How awful! Dear Jacques, how were you not afraid?

JACQUES: My Jeannette, I still shudder at my thoughts then but Champlain pressed on.

JEANNETTE: But, why?

JACQUES: He believed this lake could be the passage to India.

JEANNETTE: Oh, many people back home still talk of finding India and riches. It is a foolish dream, I think!

JACQUES: Maybe so, but our commander carried on. And, then we faced the Mohawk tribe's war party in many canoes near where a great falls entered the lake from another large body of water many leagues west of us. It was then certain there would be a battle.

JEANNETTE: But did you not fear for your lives?

JACQUES: I confess I did! But our commander did not flinch! He believed our weapons could win the battle and made us believe on that hot summer day, early July...

JEANNETTE: And did you believe, too, ...facing that large force of Mohawks.

JACQUES: ...at least two hundred all in war paint!

JEANNETTE: I don't think I want to hear of it!

JACQUES: (Continues)...The Mohawks beached their canoes on shore and built a barricade. Our commander had us do the same. The time for battle was upon us. It seemed impossible! Our commander had just two of us with about 60 of our Indian allies to face hundreds of Mohawks.

JEANNETTE: I would have had prayers on my lips the whole time.

JACQUES: So, too, did I when the Mohawk warriors approached in regular formation with their shields and body armor made of wood. Our Indian allies also moved towards the enemy as our commander loaded his arguebus with powder and four lead balls and told the two of us to do the same. He then ordered us into the woods out of sight of the approaching warriors.

JEANNETTE: *(Shudders)* It all sounds so fearsome!

JACQUES: As the Mohawk warriors approached, one of our native allies told the commander to fire at the warriors wearing elaborate headdress. As the Mohawks lifted their bows, Commander Champlain had our allies part their ranks and he stood alone facing the approaching horde. He fired his arguebus and the iron balls killed two Mohawk chiefs and mortally wounded a nearby warrior.

JEANNETTE: *(Shocked)* Oh! 'Tis a terrible thing!

JACQUES: *(Continues)* The rest of the enemy froze at the sight of their fallen chiefs and when we two stepped out of the woods and fired our arguebuses, they fled in a rout, fearing the fire from our guns.

JEANNETTE: You won the battle then?

JACQUES: Yes! But, the Six Nations tribes have been our mortal enemies since that day. Still, in these past 11 years, our colonists and traders continued their fur trade with our Indian allies knowing that the Iroquois nation feared the French guns we carried.

JEANNETTE: Then your battle on Lake Champlain was a victory!

JACQUES: Yes, and as a result, Commander Champlain explored lakes and rivers to the west of the province still believing they would lead to a passage to India. But, all he found were two more bodies of water, some say larger than the one named for him.

JEANNETTE: *(Laughs)* More Lake Champlains?

JACQUES: No, one the Indians called Ontario and the other was Lake Huron, named after one of our allies' tribes! His comrades with him then tell us he also found a great falls many leagues west of here that seemed to form a horseshoe of rushing water from the north.

JEANNETTE: But what of the colonists back at Quebec?

JACQUES: During his travels, Commander Champlain had the colonists at Quebec erect houses, sow grain and conduct the fur trade while he went back to France each winter. And, to establish a firm colony, he asked that colonists be sent from France, particularly women such as you.

JEANNETTE: *(Coquetishly)* To find husbands…

JACQUES: Ay! To find husbands and to warm our beds the cold winter nights!

JEANNETTE: Yes! And, we found husbands…of our choice!

JACQUES: Yes! And, I chose you!

JEANNETTE: I did let you think so!

JACQUES: No matter! Champlain has brought wealth in furs to our native land, and gave the king his many maps marking his travels.

JEANNETTE: Maps, you say? He was an artist also?

JACQUES: Artist enough to help ship captains! *(Explains to Jennette)* Many of his earlier maps were drawn 20 or more years ago when as a young man he captained a ship bringing Spanish soldiers to the West Indies in New Spain.

JENNETTE: Were they soldiers of the Spanish army who joined with France during the long war?

JACQUES: Yes! His familiarity with the Spanish language and ships was learned as a boy with his ship captain uncle on voyages to Spain. These experiences prepared him to sail with the Spanish to their colonies of the West Indies.

JEANNETTE: What happened to his quest to find a passage to India?

JACQUES: It is said that he told our King Henri it could be a sure and easy way to reach India if a canal were cut across the narrow isthmus south of Mexico? Champlain even suggested that France could charge a fee for each ship sailing through such a canal.

JEANNETTE: Hah! A merchant's mind! A canal with tolls has merit!

JACQUES: 'Twould shorten the trip to the South Seas by 1800 leagues or more, he told the king.

JEANNETTE: But, I have heard of no such canal being built!

JACQUES: The king's advisors laughed in our commander's face when he told them of his idea!

JEANNETTE: Even when so great a soldier and ship captain urged it?

JACQUES: Yes! But the king awarded Champlain with a pension and made him his representative here in New France.

JEANNETTE: Was that such an honor?

JACQUES: It was an honor that made many wonder how a man born of low degree could become the confidant of the king, a man of the same station as our fathers and brothers!

JEANNETTE: One would wonder! There are stories, you know, of why he was close to the king. I have heard them, even in my small village.

JACQUES: Yes! Our commander served with the king in the religious wars. They were warriors as young men, both king and navigator? They joined with their Spanish allies to keep peace among the Huguenots and the Catholics.

They grew extremely close.

JEANNETTE: But did you not hear of the rumor that your Commander Champlain was one of the king's many bastard children?

JACQUES: 'Tis untrue!

JEANNETTE: Still, the young king Henri had affairs of the heart with many young women who bore new citizens of France.

JACQUES: A fable made up by his enemies!

JEANNETTE: Why then did the king favor Samuel Champlain and gave opportunities to him that no one else received?

JACQUES: These are wild rumors we have all heard but there is no proof of them. Our commander's mother claimed he was the true son of her husband, M. Champlain

JEANNETTE: Proof is in the telling!

JACQUES: No matter! The king joined with our commander in seeking peace and religious understanding in Europe as here in New France. Commander Champlain seeks also to bring religion to the natives along with peace between them and us.

JEANNETTE: We are well aware of that fact. There were priests among us to counsel the women when we came across the sea to marry with the colonists and fur traders. But, did M. Champlain find a woman like us as you did?

JACQUES: Oh, he knew many women from his travels.

JEANNETTE: Sailors do, I hear tell! Hah! But, did he marry!

JACQUES: Yes, on a trip back to France to nurse his wounds from a fight with the Mohawks, he met a young girl named Helene Boulle, the 12-year old daughter of a wealthy man in Paris.

JEANNETTE: So young, it seems! 'Tis a legal age to marry, is true?

JACQUES: Ah, she was old enough to marry according to church and state law and with the king's blessing and her father's urging our commander married her.

JEANETTE: Oh! So young to marry a man of such age!

JACQUES: We did hear that it was a marriage ordained to give our commander a fine dowry by her father, a close friend, to continue his work in New France.

JEANNETTE: And, the girl had no say in the contract?

JACQUES: Do they ever under such circumstances!

JEANNETTE: My father had no such dowry to give, so I have no experience in that matter. But, to have no say in such a marriage…it would not be my wish!

JACQUES: She protested mightily, I heard! So, there was a compromise. Even though the marriage was legal for a girl of twelve to marry, to appease her, the parents urged Champlain not to cohabit with her until she was fourteen.

JEANNETTE: And what age was he at this time?

JACQUES: A few years past forty, almost thirty years difference in their ages.

JEANNETTE: We are more fortunate, you and me, say you so? Our ages are more compatible, n'est pas?

JACQUES: I would believe so! Our commander honored her parents' request by returning here to New France without her.

JEANNETTE: *(Mocking)* Poor man! Has she ever come to this land as his wife?

JACQUES: Yes! He returned from a trip to France this spring and brought his young wife to Quebec. He visited her in Paris each winter since they married.

JEANNETTE: *(Again mocking)* So soon?

JACQUES: It was nine years since he wed. But, we wonder, can this sheltered woman of 21 years stand the rigors of this land?

JEANNETTE: Have we not survived these many months?

JACQUES: Aye! But, you are of sterner stock that the fragile young Parisian!

JEANNETTE: You do know it!

JACQUES: They say, though, that she has become well adjusted despite living in a place no better than the animal sheds on her father's estate. To be sure, she no longer lives among the high and mighty!

JEANNETTE: *(Struts, chiding the man)* Hah! Not like we do!

(Jeannette laughs as she exits with Jacques with blackout and music coming up)

Scene Two

Samuel de Champlain......Ted DeBonis

Helene Boulle..................Danielle Ingerson

(Music subsides as lights come up. It is 1622. Champlain and Helene stroll along the river)

HELENE: My husband, this is such a beautiful but fearful country…yet so vast and so desolate of people of our culture! I find no comfort here even as I have tried to bring our ways to the Indian women and their children! But, I am ever mindful of the danger that exists with the threats of war among the tribes.

CHAMPLAIN: My dear Helene, you have been most gracious to all who meet you and sincerely helpful to our native brethren. There is no need to fear! We have a great duty to develop this land and encourage many more settlers from France to honor the glory of God and our king.

HELENE: Yet, I still fear the natives of this land! I have never seen such fearsome people in their dress and customs!

CHAMPLAIN: You should have no fear of those among us. They are friends and partners in the fur trade we carry on for the good of our people here and those of our native France.

HELENE: I have dared not write to my parents about these natives. They would worry every day for my safety even as I am concerned about their health. I am so far away from their home….my home.

CHAMPLAIN: Our experience with these tribes who live among us is one of trust in our dealings with them even as we encourage justice to each other. Their acceptance of our priests binds us to them.

HELENE: Still my parents and friends in Paris worry!

CHAMPLAIN: I have given my word of honor that I will protect you and care for you as my wife… and their daughter.

HELENE: Oh, how I do miss people of learning, the parties, dances and the shopping with friends in our dear city, the greatest in France and Europe.

CHAMPLAIN: My dear Helene, some day we will have education and the culture of Europe among our colonists here who will have great parties and enjoy fine shopping that will remind you of home.

HELENE: Oh! You have traveled the world, seen such great things and have met people of all kinds, rich and poor. You are much honored by our French citizens and the king.

CHAMPLAIN: True, I am humbled by such honors even as I grew up in a village as this one here appears now. We are but an outpost of our dear France now but one day this Quebec will be a great city that we would be proud to have founded.

HELENE: My dear husband, I will need you to assure me of that regularly or else I shall die pining for my homeland.

CHAMPLAIN: Dear Helene, I will keep you safe and will comfort you as your loving husband, be assured.

(Lights dim to blackout and music comes up revealing a study with a fireside. The music then subsides)

Scene Three

Samuel de Champlain.........Ted DeBonis

Jacques...........................Richard Harte

(Champlain sits at table with Jacques from scene one. It is 1623)

CHAMPLAIN: Now that our patron M. de Guast has received the privilege and right to oversee the fur trade through the king's patent, we may continue our work.

JACQUES: Ah! The death of M. Aymar de Clermont has opened New France once again as a strong beacon of the king's authority and yours, my dear Champlain, with a strong hand on this vast territory.

CHAMPLAIN: Yes, it does!

JACQUES: It means that you, Governor Champlain and we will be able to develop this land we first found in 1598 under the patronage of M. de Guast,

CHAMPLAIN: It has been my fortune to establish a settlement here at the mouth of the St. Lawrence River on the site of what the Indians call Quebec.

JACQUES: Ah, yes! It does command the hill above the meeting of two rivers.

But, what of Mont Royal?

CHAMPLAIN: I have been charged with establishing a settlement up the St. Lawrence River here in New France. I have urged my friend Francois Pontgrave to establish a fur trading post there! He and I first sailed the rivers of this land to where we are now, Quebec.

JACQUES: M. Pongrave has been your partner in these trips, no?

CHAMPLAIN: We have attempted to find an ocean passageway to India. When we first came to this new world 20 years ago, our sailings took us south along the coast and found only settlements by the English but no water passage to take us to the Far East.

JACQUES: Then, it is here that France must make its fortune, is it not?

CHAMPLAIN: Yes, France will find its glory in this new land and we will share in it.

JACQUES: Riches will come to us, too!

CHAMPLAIN: There are riches, and there are riches! Fur trading will bring us gold to establish a colony for our King. But, he implores us also to blend the colonists with the natives, the Indian tribes who have been on this land for many, many years. We must cohabit this land with these Indian tribes and treat them fairly as we wish them to do with us.

JACQUES: And, this is the king's wish?

CHAMPLAIN: Yes! He read my reports of trips with the Spanish fleet to the West Indies where the natives of those islands are slaves to the Spanish colonists. They are forced to work the fields all day with little rest and less food. Often, natives of these islands are burned at the stake as heretics when they did not accept the religion of the Spaniards. These indecencies the King will not permit in this New France!

JACQUES: He must feel strongly about this peaceful settlement and cohabitation?

CHAMPLAIN: Yes! Nor does he favor the English method of chasing the natives from the colonies they establish. He believes in sharing the land with those who were first living here.

JACQUES: But, he cannot dictate to other European nations or else we will be in new wars?

CHAMPLAIN: You are right! Both King Henri, a Bourbon by birth, and I were born in the midst of the terrible religious wars of the past century. I was much honored to serve as an officer in the battles that the king led to end these wars once and for all. The great battle of 1598 established peace in Europe where we defended toleration of the Protestant reformers.

JACQUES: But the King Henri was Catholic as you are still!

CHAMPLAIN: I was born Huguenot but converted before the last great battle. I agree with the king that no religion should be persecuted.

JACQUES: That can be difficult, commander!

CHAMPLAIN: Yes, but King Henri and now King Louis, his son, has pledged to uphold this toleration of all religions in Europe and wishes that a similar policy be carried out here in New France with the natives of this land.

JACQUES: Even before our arrival. French priests traveled throughout this new land seeking to convert the natives to our religion. Jacques Cartier and the Jesuits with him spent years converting the natives.

CHAMPLAIN: But they did not threaten to burn the natives at the stake if they did not accept Catholicism.

JACQUES: And yet, many of our priests have suffered terrible deaths because of their missionary work with the natives.

CHAMPLAIN: They will be the saints for future generations to honor. But, we cannot reply in kind even though there will be temptation to do so.

JACQUES: This toleration of cruelty is a difficult thing that you ask of us.

CHAMPLAIN: King Henri and I fought in a brutal war in Europe where brave soldiers understood duty, honor and loyalty to their cause, but we still hated war for its cruelty, destruction and terrible waste. King Henri dedicated his life to peace and was martyred by a religious zealot for it. I vowed to continue his mission.

JACQUES: My dear Champlain, we also will join you in this mission!

CHAMPLAIN: So be it!

(Music comes up as scene goes black, then lights come up as music diminishes)

Scene Four

Champlain.....Ted DeBonis

Helene...........Danielle Ingerson

(Scene is at a dock. Champlain is boarding the ship to return to New France. The year is 1624.)

HELENE: My dear husband, understand that I must remain at my parents' home!

CHAMPLAIN: I am heartsick at your decision but I will not demand that you come back to me to New France.

HELENE: I am grateful for your kindness in not exerting the power you have as a husband.

CHAMPLAIN: I could not and would not. I desire you to return with me but only if you wish. There is no other way.

HELENE: Know that the life there has been a great hardship for me. There are those who say that I am strong-willed and selfish because of my decision. Yet, I tell you that I have tried but cannot be comfortable with that life.

CHAMPLAIN: I am your champion in acknowledging that you have tried.

HELENE: You know also the stillborn loss of two babies has been a terrible thing for me to experience. My mind and heart will never forget that my body could not bring you children.

CHAMPLAIN: I, too, felt the loss deeply for the suffering you experienced. I take heart that you are still a young woman, only 25 years. You have a life to live.

HELENE: As you do!

CHAMPLAIN: My dear, I am an old man, really! The sum of 57 years takes its toll! You have kept me young in spirit, in ambition and health. I cherish every moment we have spent together. We may never meet again in this world as I am bound to complete my life and my mission in that far off country.

HELENE: We will write often and I will pray for you every day between your future visits to our home here.

CHAMPLAIN: As an old soldier knows, his life is not always measured in years. When you hear word of my death, grieve for me but then seek a new life with a man of your choice who will care for you and love you as I have.

HELENE: Should your soul precede me to heaven and I still have life within me, I will marry again but I will marry into the church. I will enter a nunnery and become one who will minister to the sick as I devote my life to God.

CHAMPLAIN: I am overwhelmed at your thought. I take comfort that I will have someone praying for me in a cloister built on eternal love. I do promise to name the island near Mont Royal in your honor so that you will always be close to me.

HELENE: We will then share our prayers with each other.

CHAMPLAIN: I miss you now as I will always!

HELENE: Goodbye, my dear Samuel! I wish you safe voyage and a good life

(They embrace and he crosses the dock and walks to ship as music comes up. as stage goes black. Music then subsides as lights come up on next segment).

End of Act One

ACT TWO

"The Land of Skene"
Scene One

<u>Cast</u>

Philip Skene......Richard Harte

Elizabeth.........Janet Stasio

(Elizabeth Skene stands on a hill looking to the harbor. Philip Skene, her brother, joins her on the hill)

PHILIP: Ah! The ship is approaching. My young lady will soon be home.

ELIZABETH: Yes! I do hope as a daughter of a British army colonel, Kathi behaved on her journey. The French have corrupted Montreal!

PHILIP: Now Elizabeth! I'm sure Mary, as her older sister, was a good influence on our dear Kathi. Since Mary is in Montreal still, I know you will remain the good influence you have been since her mother's death.

ELIZABETH: I do hope so! Kathi has all the high spirits of her poor dead mother.

PHILIP: Yes! She does often remind me of my dear Katherine. Kathi and Mary are blessed to have you as aunt and surrogate mother.

ELIZABETH: Mother, indeed! If I were more than an aunt, they would not be so frivolous.

PHILIP: Now Mary is not frivolous or flighty. *(Boastful)* She is her father's daughter! It is for that reason, I permitted her to stay in Montreal to aid John Watson to purchase supplies for our estate.

ELIZABETH: If you are sure you can trust Mr. Watson. Young girls bear watching when near an attractive man!

PHILIP: Yes, Elizabeth but I feel confident that her uncle, Lord Hamilton, will keep a sharp eye on Mary until she returns.

ELIZABETH: I do hope so, although I do trust Mr. Watson to respect your daughter and care for her as you would yourself.

PHILIP: As I am confident you will also, particularly during the next coming months while I am in England.

ELIZABETH: The girls will be upset to know that you cannot bring their mother's body back to her native Ireland for a fitting burial. They abhor the fact that she lies in a vault in the cellar even as it is in a private area and well protected.

PHILIP: You will help me in that matter, I trust. It is important that I get to England as soon as possible and present the petition to the King to make this whole area a new province.

ELIZABETH: And you should be named governor of this new province with Crown Point as its capital. Or, perhaps Skenesborough would be a better site from which to govern. It is well named for so honored a man, dear brother!

PHILIP: You are a dear sister to think so. The New York authorities have issued their own grants for this land and friends locally have urged me to take their plea to the king to protect these Hampshire grants from the governor in Albany as soon as possible.

ELIZABETH: For certain, there are those who covet the land given you for your service in Canada during the war with the French.

PHILIP: I cannot argue that fact! Willful men do willful things.

ELIZABETH: Why should they receive land that was given you by the king for your courageous service as a major, leading brave English infantry against the walls of Quebec.

PHILIP: I agree! And since the king's grant, my purchases of other lands nearby have made me owner of more than 50,000 acres at this southernmost point of Lake Champlain. Almost half of this acquired property is at Crown Point. It is not land to be granted to others by the New York governor.

ELIZABETH: Be assured, all of your tenants and workers in your sawmills and shipyard here in Skenesborough are prepared to defend this land and your manor with cannon, firearms and their lives if need be.

PHILIP: They will be much rewarded for their loyalty. I wish that the king permit me to raise an army of fellow loyalists to combat the rising rebellion of the New England colonists.

ELIZABETH: And, you would lead them brilliantly as you did those fine soldiers who followed you some 20 years ago in Canada. It could not be so too soon! Those New England rebels are making threatening moves towards this region.

PHILIP: Yes! We must crush this rising rebellion. So, I ask you to take care in my absence for your own life and the lives of our people here in Skenesborough.

ELIZABETH: I will work with your superintendent John Watson to do that when he returns from Montreal! And I will protect your daughters with my life.

PHILIP: You are dear to me and I love you for your loyalty. Now, come! We must greet our daughter and Lady Hamilton when they arrive.

(They exit as lights come down and music rises)

Scene Two

Kathi Skene.........*Danielle Ingerson*

Lady Hamilton......*Susan Ingerson*

Sarah, a maid.......*Brittany Hurlburt*

Elizabeth Skene.....*Janet Stasio*

Philip Skene.........*Richard Harte*

(Music subsides as lights come up and a young woman walks along with an older woman on a dock. The two women are accompanied by a young maid.)

KATHI: *(To Lady Hamilton)* Where is my father to greet us, Lady Hamilton?

LADY HAMILTON: My dear Kathi, I am sure he has been been atop the hill up there waiting for our ship to sail into port from its Canadian voyage.

KATHI: Do you think so?

LADY HAMILTON: Be assured your father is only too anxious to greet you!

KATHI: Yes! I know he will be here soon and I do want him to meet us, and to hear about Lieutenant Frederick de Piquet.

LADY HAMILTON: Now, there will be none of your talk of flirtations, you young one!

KATHI: *(Laughing)* Oh, no, Lady Hamilton! I would not think of it!

LADY HAMILTON: Be wary of your youthful exuberance, young lady! *(To maid)* And you Sarah are cautioned also. Remember your position as Miss Skene's maid *(Points to Kathi)*. I don't want to hear of you frolicking with the local farm boys!

SARAH: *(Curtsies to Lady Hamilton)* Oh, no, your Ladyship!

KATHI: *(To maid, lightly)* Yes! We must display delicate decorum.

LADY HAMILTON: And, so well she should!

KATHI: She shall be all my mother taught her to be.

LADY HAMILTON: I should hope so. *(To maid)* All right, take our luggage to the carriage.

(The maid exits as Philip Skene and Elizabeth enter. Philip and Elizabeth cross to Kathi and embrace her)

PHILIP: My dear Kathi! It is so good to see you after such a long absence.

KATHI: Father, it has only been two months!

PHILIP: A day is too long! And, you my dear Lady Hamilton, I am indebted to you for your kindness in escorting my daughters in Montreal.

LADY HAMILTON: You are most welcome my dear colonel. They did nearly exhaust me daily with their shopping and visits to friends.

KATHI: *(Laughs)* Now father, Lady Hamilton doth protest too much. Our dear aunt had many friends to visit and shopping to be done.

LADY HAMILTON: But, I do wish that Mary had come back with us.

PHILIP: You know that she serves as my secretary and will be very helpful in assisting John Watson in selecting supplies. No matter! I am indebted to you, Lady Hamilton.

KATHI: Oh! We had so much fun. Why we attended a ball given by the army commandant! Lady Hamilton received a personal invitation and she took me as her guest.

ELIZABETH: A ball in Montreal!

LADY HAMILTON: It was the high mark of the social season, Elizabeth!

PHILIP: And, I trust Kathi was on her good behavior?

KATHI: I had a wonderful time and danced away the evening.

ELIZABETH: Danced away the evening?

LADY HAMILTON: *(Defensive)* She behaved herself and enjoyed the evening.

KATHI: And, I met this wonderful young lieutenant!

LADY HAMILTON: Kathi!!!!

PHILIP: A young lieutenant, you say?

KATHI: Yes, father! He was a most wonderful dancer....

ELIZABETH: Oh! He was, was he?

KATHI: Yes, father! And he is French!

ELIZABETH: There are too many Frenchmen still in Montreal! What was a French officer doing at an English army ball?

KATHY: Oh, he serves with the English army.

PHILIP: He does?????

LADY HAMILTON: His father served also in the English army before him.

PHIILIP: But, we were fighting the French twenty years ago!!!

LADY HAMILTON: He appeared a most cultured young man, Colonel.

KATHI: And, he speaks so beautifully in French!

PHILIP: Never mind English officers who are French. I had my fill of Frenchmen.

KATHI: Father! That's not fair to say!

PHILIP: I know whereof I speak! Our superior officers warned us of the dangers of Montreal. While it has many churches it also has even more places of temptation within its walls.

LADY HAMILTON: But, your daughter, sir, is as fresh as lovely field flowers wherever she is.

PHILIP: But, she is not ready to be plucked from her father's care! *(Kathi looks chagrined)* It is too soon for one so young and so fair to be swept away by romantic notions.

LADY HAMILTON: She remains as safe as in their dear mother's arms or at your side.

PHILIP: I trust that she remains so! Come ladies, until I depart for England on that schooner at the wharf, let us declare this a time of holiday for all of us.

(They exit)

Scene Three

Kathi...........Danielle Ingerson

Elizabeth........Janet Stasio

(Several weeks later, in a garden)

KATHI: The news that my father is preparing to leave within days is more than I can bear. What are we to do?

ELIZABETH: It must be now or he will not have a chance for more than six months. The long sea trip and the business he must deal with will take at least that long.

KATHI: I worry that the colonist rebels will soon come to us here in Skenesborough and our lives will be changed. Surely, we will be protected from these American rebels by the British army?

ELIZABETH: The main body of the British army is in Canada or in the lower Hudson area, too far from saving this land from rebel occupation on short notice. It is one reason your father is going to England. He seeks a commission to raise an army here in this territory of Loyalists who will defend lower Lake Champlain from the colonists.

KATHI: I know my father will be able to find men to serve in such an army and keep this land secure in England's hands.

ELIZABETH: Still, loyalty has diminished as the king and his advisers have taken a toll on the colonists' patience and endurance. The taxes levied are more than are levied on our people in England and the order to provide shelter for the British troops has proved odious to the colonists.

KATHI: Still, if the rebels come here, I will flee on my trusted horse.

ELIZABETH: Much as I admire most earnestly your horsemanship, I feel you would have to ride far to escape them if they come.

KATHI: I have ridden since childhood, often into the woods with my mother. My father says she seemed born to the saddle as she rode over the Irish countryside of her birth. Yes, Aunt Elizabeth! I learned to ride from my dear mother.

ELIZABETH: Over land that appears to go far beyond the horizon. One day your sister Mary and you will be owners of all of this estate.

KATHI: Do not talk that way, dear aunt! Father will rule here for many years as lord and master.

ELIZABETH: I would pray so! Yet, he would wish you married with a fine husband to help you maintain this land and care for the people who till its soil and minister to our needs.

KATHI: *(Bluntly)* Aunt Elizabeth! I have such a man!

ELIZABETH: *(Surprised)* What is this you say?

KATHI: Since I met Lieutenant de Piquet in Montreal and grew to know him, I see him as my helpmate for the rest of my life.

ELIZABETH: Lieutenant de Piquet! What is this I hear? And, all this happened in so brief a time while you were in Montreal?

KATHI: We met at a military ball when our general invited his officers. Lady Hamilton and I were among those who were the general's guests.

ELIZABETH: You were!

KATHI: Yes! And, when Fred was introduced to me I was taken back by his bearing, charm, polite manner…and wonderful dancing ability.

ELIZABETH: And, those are the reasons you wish to marry? Well, dear girl, you must cool your ardor. Your father will not wish to give his consent to any marriage at this time. He is due to leave for England in days and will not return for many months. Kathi, I will admit to being surprised.

KATHI: But he is as fine a man as I have ever met.

ELIZABETH: No more of this!

(She strides out of the garden)

Scene Four

Lady Hamilton……..Susan Ingerson

Elizabeth Skene………Janet Stasio

(Lady Hamilton and Elizabeth are standing on the veranda)

LADY HAMILTON: I am still struck with the beauty of this wonderful building.

ELIZABETH: The stone facing is of English construction, a design by an English architect brought here for three years by my brother. Soon, much of this building will be covered with ivy, something the colonel remembers from his youth in Scotland. And, the colonel had almost two dozen frame houses built on this estate for the tenants. Many of them work in Phillip's lumber mills and iron works.

LADY HAMILTON: Does he not also own the shipyard?

ELIZABETH: Most certainly! It was one of the first enterprises he established to provide income for the estate.

LADY HAMILTON: He does well then?

ELIZABETH: Oh, yes! The income permits us to live handsomely on this estate.

LADY HAMILTON: But, what of the rebellion that is broiling in the New England colonies? Is that not a threat to your lives here.

ELIZABETH: When Philip returns from England with the king's permission to raise an army, we will have all the protection we need to prevent rebellion here.

LADY HAMILTON: There can be no reasons for rebellion. They can only be considered traitors to take up such an uprising against the king. You did not see any of that sentiment in Montreal!

ELIZABETH: The French natives appear to be most content with British rule. Still, there have been American forces early this year attempting to take Quebec and arouse the French natives to revolt.

LADY HAMILTON: Little did they succeed! Our forces were sufficiently supported to resist the elements of a rebel such as Benedict Arnold. He was forced to retreat from Quebec with his tattered army.

ELIZABETH: But, there is word that Arnold along with Ethan Allen are leading forces through New Hampshire out of Connecticut and Massachusetts to reach this region.

LADY HAMILTON: Well, then Lord Carleton will send English troops to support us. He has General Johnny Burgoyne at his side.

ELIZABETH: We take comfort in our English forces.

(They depart into the house)

Scene Five

> Lady Hamilton...............Susan Ingerson
>
> Philip Skene..................Richard Harte

(Phillip and Lady Hamilton wait at the dock before the colonel's departure)

LADY HAMILTON: You were wise, Colonel, to make your good-byes at dinner last night. I believe Kathi and the servants would be too unsettled to see you leave this early in the morning.

PHILLIP: I place my trust in my family to protect the people in Skenesborough until I return with the full support of our king.

LADY HAMILTON: They pledge their loyalty to you.

PHILLIP: And, to the king? He is my king as he is yours and as he is to those colonists who are now being called rebels. And so they are subjects of the king as our brothers in England.

LADY HAMILTON: Even though the people called rebels protest that they do not have the same representation in parliament as their compatriots in England? They claim they are subject to taxes levied only in America and are forced to house soldiers who patrol their villages. They would that you could carry that message to the king!

PHILLIP: I am a soldier, madam, not a diplomat or a representative of people who would usurp the power reserved for the king. No! I would not and could not carry such a message.

LADY HAMILTON: Again, I promise my husband, Lord Hamilton, will help protect your property and your tenants in your absence. God be with you in your voyage and may you gain every success for which you wish.

PHILLIP: Thank you, Lady Hamilton! I take my leave.

(They shake hands and Phillip walks down the dock to the ship)

Scene Six

Kathi Skene .... *Danielle Ingerson*

Elizabeth Skene...........*Janet Stasio*

Sarah, the maid.........*Brittany Hurlburt*

Lady Hamilton.........*Susan Ingerson*

(It is seven months later. Kathi, Lady Hamilton, Elizabeth and Sarah are at the Skenesborough dock preparing to leave for Montreal)

LADY HAMILTON: Lord Hamilton is convincing the ship's captain to make comfortable arrangements for our passage to Montreal. The ship captain had not prepared for the numbers of people seeking escape to Canada on his ship.

ELIZABETH: An escape made necessary by that dastardly American general Benedict Arnold. In the seven months since my brother left for England, things have become seemingly hopeless..

KATHI: They say Benedict Arnold's troops are a day's march from here.

LADY HAMILTON: So, we must hurry! The ship leaves within the hour. Let's onboard now!

(She goes aboard followed by Sarah, the maid)

KATHI: I cannot bear to leave my home! Who will protect our mother's crypt in the manor? How can we leave her so? Oh Aunt Elizabeth! Why must this be so?

ELIZABETH: John Watson will stay with the manor as he has promised our father. He will see that nothing happens to your mother's resting place.

KATHI: Oh, I cannot bear to even think such a thought.

ELIZABETH: John has made a pledge to my brother who is now a prisoner of the rebel Congress. How could that ship's captain fail to know that Philadelphia was in American hands? We know now that American privateers are boarding and taking British ships captive who seek to land anywhere in New England. Even the New York harbor is not safe for British merchant ships..

KATHI: Our father a prisoner of the rebels is a thought I cannot bear to think of.

ELIZABETH: Be assured he is a valuable prisoner so he will be treated well. The king will surely propose an exchange of your father for American merchants and diplomats who are now captives in England.

KATHI: Is such a thing possible?

ELIZABETH: Such an arrangement is possible but it will help your father to know that his family is safe in Canada. So, we must go now to Montreal. John Watson is now riding about the estate preparing the tenants for an invasion as he keeps his promise to safeguard them and the buildings.

KATHI: We will soon be with Lord Hamilton who will keep us informed about my father's health and well-being.

ELIZABETH: He will keep us informed. And, now safe voyage to us all!

(Kathi and Elizabeth board the boat as lights dim and music comes up.)

End of Act Two

INTERMISSION

ACT THREE

Victory In Defeat

Molly Sampson.............Susan Ingerson

Silas Perkins...............Richard Harte

Benedict Arnold...........Ted DeBonis

Messenger.................Brittany Hurlburt

(Action is set in a Skenesborough tavern. Molly Sampson is the tavern owner. Silas Perkins is a frequent customer who knows everything. It is early November, 1776)

PERKINS: *(To Molly)* Feed this mob before the general arrives.

SAMPSON: Don't be telling me about how to care for m'guests.

PERKINS: We'll be wanting to be hearing the news of the battle when he arrives and not have people still chewing their grub.

SAMPSON: Don't I want to hear what he has to say too?

PERKINS: Oh! I should have been with him these past weeks as when we went to help the Boston militia last year.

SAMPSON: So you were with the general, were you?

PERKINS: Have I not told you that before?

SAMPSON: Go on! I pay little attention to your ramblings.

PERKINS: These are no ramblings, woman! It was a Saturday, April of last year, only days after that Concord massacre. The general, only a captain then, marched us through Hartford and then New

175

Haven buying food from his own money for us as we moved toward Boston.

SAMPSON: He was rich then?

PERKINS: Rich I know not but he had a good business where I worked with him, unloading his ships that sailed to the Caribbean and the southern colonies

SAMPSON: He ran the blockade, then?

PERKINS: Aye, and he rode these parts here in Ticonderoga for almost 20 years, first as a 14-year old militiaman fighting off the French and Indians at Fort William Henry. Later, he supplied the British army during the war with the French in Canada back in '58. He brought supplies by ship up the St. Lawrence to Montreal and Quebec where the British army took those cities.

SAMPSON: He must have dealt in black magic to run a business and still sail on his ship to Canada.

PERKINS: No, woman, he was no magician. His sister, Hannah, a good, maiden lady, moved into his house, collected money owed to him, paid his bills and kept good records. She still runs his shop even as he fights on the lake above us.

SAMPSON: Oh! I know his sister's tasks since I do all myself here with no man to help, or woman either.

PERKINS: You had a man but his heart stopped one night because of your overwrought affection.

SAMPSON: He was not a well man but I did my best to nurse him to health.

PERKINS: You nursed him into eternity and were paid well too. He left you this inn by a scrap of paper with his hand on it. And you not even his wife.

SAMPSON: He has enemies in Philadelphia then?

PERKINS: Ay! There are others seeking command who envy him his bravery, his military bearing and sense of discipline.

SAMPSON: Oh, yes! Ethan Allen was such a man! When the general took command here, Allen went back to the Green Mountains to fight his own war of taking booty in battle. A land pirate, he is! Even my husband saw battle not so much patriotic as it was a business. It was our constant quarrel.

SAMPSON: His will was judged good and sound. Now! What further news have you?

PERKINS: Only that the fighting has stopped. Our troops still hold Ticonderoga.

SAMPSON: The general's ships are still afloat?

PERKINS: I fear not from what news drifts south.

SAMPSON: It was a pitiful fleet he did sail out of here.

PERKINS: The general's invasion of Canada last year did not have enough men and supplies, even from those few in Congress who did support the general.

PERKINS: When General Arnold returned last year from his sailing into Canada and destroying the forts on the Richeliu River, he was not rewarded. They reduced him from colonel of the Massachusetts command to captain of his Connecticut troops.

SAMPSON: Ahh! A glove across the face, for sure! But there's no question the British are intent to come through here?

PERKINS: General Arnold will continue to fight even as he knows that it is only a defensive fight he can wage with his few ships against all that England can muster in Canada.

SAMPSON: That he will!

PERKINS: Even as he is needed at home with his children and a sister working night and day to keep his business afloat, the general fights on!

SAMPSON: But, has he no allies?

PERKINS: He became a friend of General Washington when he brought reinforcements to Boston a year ago last spring. When Washington heard Colonel Arnold's tale of his battles, he formed an army of Northern New York with General Schuyler in command.

SAMPSON: But, what of Arnold?

PERKINS: Schuyler named Arnold his adjutant, the general in charge of the defense of Lake Champlain.

SAMPSON: And, he has taken his command seriously! But, will he succeed?

PERKINS: We'll soon know from his own lips.

(A cry from the back of the meeting hall: "The general has arrived!")

PERKINS: Ah! My neighbors of Skenesborough welcome you, General Arnold.

(He leads applause and huzzahs as Arnold walks around the room greeting townspeople)

SAMPSON: A sight you are, General! You look like you have ridden with the wind.

PERKINS: Give us news of your battle with the British on the lake!

ARNOLD: Thank you, Silas Perkins. And, Mistress Molly! It is good to be in the warmth of your inn again with all our friends. I greet all of you and thank you for your support these last weeks.

SAMPSON: It's good to know you're safe.

ARNOLD: Safe, perhaps, for the moment!

PERKINS: Are we in danger, General?

ARNOLD: There's a chance, but only a chance, sir! The troops at Ticonderoga with General Gates are our only defense.

SAMPSON: With you to lead our men, we are safe. You kept the British army away from us last year and they are not here now.

PERKINS: But what about the battle, general?

ARNOLD: Two weeks ago, I sent this report to General Philip Schuyler about the battle of Valcour Island.

PERKINS: Oh, yes! We heard very little! Read it to us, General!

(Arnold takes his place behind a lectern. Takes paper out of leather case, reads)

ARNOLD: "My dear General Schuyler: I am writing this from Fort Ticonderoga, October 15, the year of Our Lord 1776. At four o'clock yesterday morning, we reached this place extremely fatigued and unwell, having been without sleep or refreshment for near three days. After fighting two battles on the lake and rowing for two days, my men and I walked the last 20 miles, carrying our wounded in slings made of our ships sails.

"We made Crown Point yesterday, only hours before the first British landing parties.

"I ordered the troops, almost 150 men worn by battle, to burn barracks, warehouses, docks and the blockhouse before we left for Ticonderoga, where I write you now.

"Crown Point will give little succor to the English now. As I wrote General Horatio Gates a month ago, we kept two small schooners continually cruising above our fleet's base on Isle La Motte awaiting the first action by the English coming out of the Richeleu River. Our scouts had informed me that Sir Guy Carleton, the governor of Quebec, was taking command himself. He understood the value of controlling Lake Champlain, a strategy I told you I shared strongly.

PERKINS: I remember it well! Yes, I do!

ARNOLD: Good that you do! *(To audience)* I continue! "Disappointed that not one sailor was sent from New York and that only three of eight row galleys had been completed by the end of September, I prepared for the English fleet. Since half of my fleet was unfinished and I did not have sufficient numbers of seaman, I could not attack the British fleet on the Richelieu River or destroy the large fleet that was under construction.

"I was forced to assume a defensive position, hoping to trap the English fleet when it came down the lake in open waters.

"Now, 'tis a good harbor, Valcour is. We could have the advantage over them towards Crown Point but I meant to make my stand north at Valcour. I had hoped the enemy would fight us there.

"If there were too many for us, we could move down the lake. Carleton would expect to find my fleet farther north and would expect me to meet him in the open lake where their faster fleet would surround our frail ships and pound them with lethal broadsides.

"No, my dear general, I was not going to let that happen. Our duty and our plan was to delay this British fleet from reaching Ticonderoga where the superior numbers of English soldiers could move south and link up with the British troops coming north to Albany from New York City. By all means, we could not let this happen."

SAMPSON/PERKINS: *(Ad lib to each other)*

ARNOLD: *(Annoyed but continues)* "As I indicated in previous reports, in May 1775, I had found Valcour Island while sailing to Canada and again sailed past it twice this summer. I knew it well and decided now to place my ships in an arc between the island and the New York shore as the British fleet moved in the open lake on the other side of the island with Vermont to their port side.

"I placed 16 of my 18 ships in a crescent, facing south. At about that time, provisions from General Gates reached us. I was able to supply the vessels so the men could eat and restock our ships stores.

"General, as you know, I was not equipped to defeat this armada coming down the lake but I could try to delay it and reduce its force so it would have to return to Canada. Then with enough men and animals, we could bring the lumber across the frozen lake to Skenesborough in February and rebuild our navy for the offensive the British will be sure to wage in the spring."

PERKINS: They'll not find comfort coming down here again, I should say!

SAMPSON: But, our men will find comfort in this port for the winter.

PERKINS: Many's the one'll find a haven in your snug harbor! *(Laughs)*

SAMPSON: You can be sure, it will not be your little dinghy.

(A voice in the audience): "Tell us more of the battle, general.'"

ARNOLD: *(Looks at the papers)* "We were prepared as circumstances allowed.

They will never have it in their power to surprise us. My men were daily trained in the exercise of their guns. Still the drills were fewer than I wished as we had not sufficient ammunition.

"Now, I had two guard boats on the north of Valcour Island and on the morning of October 11, the Liberty came racing south and at the tip of Valcour Island, fired a signal shot. When the captain boarded my ship, he told me that the first elements of the British fleet were at Grand Isle, just seven miles from our refuge.

"After Liberty had delivered the alarm, she joined the arc of ships prepared to spring the trap on the British. We had learned also that Lord Carleton was carrying Hessian troops. Our scouts, general, report that the Hessian troops included many German hunters and woodsmen with short, lightweight rifles with far greater accuracy than the regular British Brown Bess rifle.

"General, as the British fleet and troop barges left their haven on the Richeleu River, our scouts counted more than 600 craft, including boats carrying artillery and long canoes filled with Indians.

"Burgoyne's redcoats were being held in reserve it would seem until Carleton felt he had swept the lake of our fleet. The English fleet left the Richeleu on the morning of October 10, an impressive armada of 600 ships which left our scouts shaken as they reported."

PERKINS: Six hundred ships! Good gawd!

ARNOLD: I had a plan which I kept from my ship's captains until close to battle. When I explained it to my second-in-command, General Waterbury, he urged me to sail quickly to Ticonderoga to protect Gates' army. Since we knew we could not fight in the open sea and that an armada the size of Carleton would reduce Crown Point and overrun Ticonderoga, I had no choice but to try to trap the British into fighting where we had the advantage.

"I had confidence in my captains, including my trusted Connecticut sea captain David Hawley whom I placed in command of our largest ship, the Royal Savage. Seth Warner..."

SAMPSON: An able man, he is!

PERKINS: But, not for you, m'lady!

ARNOLD: *(Deliberate)* "...And Seth Warner had arrived in Skenesborough by oxcart from Connecticut this past spring with skilled mariners to construct the eighty foot, ten-gun Trumbull, which he now commands. It is the smallest of our row galleys.

"My plan was simple but dangerous. As the British ships passed Valcour Island on the lakeside and the main fleet was fully past the southern point, two of my smaller ships would lure them back into the area where we lay, between the island and the New York shore. Any British ship approaching us would be met with the full crossfire from my 16 ships."

SAMPSON: Oh, the slaughter!

ARNOLD: "We would protect ourselves from boarding parties by using grape shot that at 100 yards could tear apart boatloads of men as they approached. It would be daunting even to the most seasoned British sailor.

"As larger British ships approached the arc, my plan was to have our galleys rowed out to fire their cannons all the while being protected by fire from our other ships. Once the galleys fired, they would be towed back to reload.

"Our scouts reported that the British fleet left their anchorage the morning of October 11 and they also informed me that Burgoyne's scouting parties may have discovered our hiding place near Valcour Island.

"As it turned out, if Carleton had been told, he did not act as if he had known, coming straight down the lake on the other side of Valcour, moving into our trap.

"Three of my ships -- the Trumbull, Congress and Washington--- sailed about three miles north of three British men-of-war which were a good five miles south of Valcour Island. The impression we gave was to slip past the British fleet in mid of night to catch unprotected British troops at Windmill Point. When we were spotted by sentries aboard the Inflexible, battle flags about the British warships were run up the masts, signaling "Engage"!

"Our three decoys dashed straight into Valcour Bay as the British ship prepared to fire. When the first English ships entered the bay, they saw the trap which awaited them and the volley of fire that engulfed them. But, the captain aboard the Inflexible, the largest of Carleton's ships, bore down on Hawley's Royal Savage.

"As Hawley rounded the southern tip of Valcour Island, he ran aground and was hit by a broadside from the Inflexible. At least three men were killed outright and as the explosion ripped the main mast, Hawley lowered a boat to get his men off the ship.

"Hawley then tried to pull the Royal Savage off the reef but the Hessian gunners aboard the Inflexible hit his small boat with shot and shell and his men were soon in the water, swimming for the island.

"With this diversion, I was able to turn the Congress broadside and use the swivel guns and heavy cannon to rake the decks of the Inflexible. As it turned out, Carleton did not act as if he had known that coming straight down the lake on the other side of Valcour Island he was moving into our trap.

"Our guns swept the British gunboats now rushing towards our arc of ships.

"Our gondolas emerged from the island's bay, firing rapidly and effectively at the British gunboats. The gondolas would quickly vanish into the bay to reload for another volley into the British boarding ships.

"The fighting became fierce as British sailors fell dead in the water and our decks became awash with blood shed by British cannon fire.

"The British frigate Maria was next to try to test our line of ships. Carleton was in command aboard this flagship of the British fleet. One of our cannon shots reached the Maria's bridge and disabled the officers there, including Lord Carleton.

"We learned later from a wounded British sailor we rescued from the Maria that Carleton, the royal governor, withdrew the ship despite his captain's desire to stay and fight.

"By quitting the fight, we gained heart as I'm sure the British officers and men lost fervor.

"Still, others in the English fleet were not as timid. The gunboats with Hessian artillerymen aboard fought their way into our line. By now, this naval battle was in full fury.

"With pride, I speak of our gunners who hit magazines aboard British ships, blowing some of them out of the water. What we had succeeded in doing was to permit only one British man-of-war to confront us at a time. It finally wound down to the last British ship of size, the Carleton, which fought valiantly to close to hit us broadside. But, our ships, arrayed in an arc, would rake the ship's decks, killing and wounding the ships officers. We learned later, that a 19-year old midshipman had to assume command.

"Yet, aboard the Congress, we could not rest. I ordered the crew of the Congress to raise anchor and close on the Carleton.

"For our part, we too took severe damage. We counted more than 20 holes in our hull, mostly above the waterline.

"Those of our ships closer to the shore were being hit by Indian snipers who were challenged by our marine sharpshooters tied to our masts.

"Again, the Inflexible came up the lake to challenge us until darkness, and with her heavy guns, raked our ships from out of our range to retaliate.

"A British party of marines boarded the Royal Savage, once my flagship, and before setting it afire and killing many of our men trying to save it, they took my papers, journals and letters to General Gates. The loss of letters and documents has troubled me.

"Throughout the night, we could see the flickering light from the fires on the Royal Savage and hear the moans of our wounded aboard the stricken ship.

"During the evening, my captains and I assessed the damage of the day. We had lost 60 men killed and three-fourths of our gunpowder was gone. Every one of our ships had been badly damaged. All officers on the Lee had been killed. I tried to rally the officers gathered with me and they were attentive as I explained the plan to escape Carleton's navy.

"I urged that we sail through the British fleet in darkness and, all agreed we should attempt it.

"Seth Warner aboard the Trumbull, led the way with only a hooded lantern on his fantail. Each of the ships did the same and kept the oars moving silently in the water.

"We were fortunate that Carleton had ordered his ship captains to spread out over the lake which gave us room to sneak past them.

"By seven o'clock the next morning, October 12, we were seven miles south of the closest British ship. At Schuyler Island, we scuttled the badly damaged Providence, the New York and the Jersey.

"Meanwhile, I wrote a dispatch to Gates and put it aboard the Liberty which carried it and the wounded to Crown Point.

"We suffered mightily from the superior number of British ships. However, I learned only hours ago that Carleton could not believe we had slipped through his fleet and sent his ships to the north of the island, believing we were trying to come around the island to escape down the center of the lake. It would have been foolhardy of us but our English friend had been foolish in withdrawing his fleet on the night of the 11th. It permitted us to slip past him.

"We were fortunate that Carleton did not notice our escape until midday on the 12th and had difficulty following us because the wind was against him.

"Still we only covered 12 miles rowing the ships overnight and were only at Willsboro where it was still possible for the British to get between us and Crown Point. I sent the slower ships ahead with orders to keep going until they reach that post. I had the Congress stand with the Washington to block the British men-of-war coming upon us.

"The Washington was too damaged to take flight and Waterbury ordered Hawley to strike colors. Only 16 of the Washington crew of 122 escaped.

"We on the Congress fought off the three British warships for five hours as we took 12 shots below the waterline.

"We were attacked broadside with musket shot from the shore. They kept up incessant firing on us for these five hours with round and grape shot which we returned as briskly as we could. Our sails, rigging and hull all were shattered and in pieces.

'We were surrounded by seven British ships finally and we had lost 27 of our 70 officers and crewmen. Our ammunition was gone and Crown Point was still 10 miles away.

"I ordered my small ships to run aground on shore and set up snipers to fire upon the English ships. Then I maneuvered the Congress into the shallow cover where I knew from soundings months before the British ships could not follow.

"We made sure that British marines could not board the Congress to salvage by raking all British gondolas with rifle fire.

" That night, as Burgoyne's Indians searched for us, we took a secret path and walked to Crown Point, all 150 survivors and our wounded carried in our ship's sails.

'We burned all of Crown Point before marching to Ticonderoga so the English army will have to live in tents as the snows from Canada and the Vermont mountains begin to swirl about them.

"I rest now in Ticonderoga awaiting word of what I should do next.

"Yours, sincerely,

Benedict Arnold"

PERKINS: They are there still, are they general?

ARNOLD: They were yesterday when I left to proceed to Albany to urge strengthening our defenses at Ticonderoga.

SAMPSON: And defend us here at Skenesborough.

(Courier rushes in with a letter and gives it to Perkins)

PERKINS: "This just arrived by courier from Ticonderoga,"

ARNOLD: *(opens letter, reads it)*

Great god! It is from General Gates. He reports that Lord Carleton is leaving Crown Point and returning with his fleet north to Canada.

We have been given the chance to breathe new life into this land! We will now be able to build a new navy here in Skenesborough through the winter and resist any invasion next spring. The fight we fought was not in vain, the losses we suffered have borne fruit.

SAMPSON: Carleton turned tail, wise man that he is.

ARNOLD: I take my leave, good people, as I ride to Albany to report this good news! And to you, my faithful friends, I thank you for your support. My men served well. I promise you, we will persevere!

(Arnold strides upstage, exits)

SAMPSON: God be with you general!

(All join in the cheers!)

(Lights dim out as music rises)

End of Act Three

ACT FOUR

"Whither Whitehall!"

Society Woman............*Janet Stasio*

Biker Girl.................*Danielle Ingerson*

Flapper....................*Carol Jones*

Teacher....................*Susan Ingerson*

Man About Town........*Richard Harte*

Canal Worker............*Ted DeBonis*

Maid.......................*Rie Lee*

News Boy.................*Brittanny Hurlburt*

Butler....................*Gary Hurlburt*

(Scene is tavern seen in previous act with action from 1800 to present. Dialogue is spoken to other characters on stage and members of the audience)

JANET: Now! This here town wasn't always Whitehall. No, it wasn't! You know that from what you've heard earlier.

DANIELLE: Yes, it was originally called Skenesborough when Major Phillip Skene acquired the land in 1759

CAROL: And, it became a town in 1765 but practically completely owned by Major Skene.

JANET: But, he didn't keep it past 1775...

DANIELLE: ...because you know Benedict Arnold made it the birth place of the American Navy. Fought its first battle right here on Lake Champlain...

CAROL: ...but you know that or else you weren't listening to the scene just before this...or got locked in the privy.

JANET: No matter! Now some say, how can you have a navy on a lake? Well, you don't want to be in the middle of this here lake during a storm.

CAROL: It feels just like the ocean, I tell you.

DANIELLE: But, no mind! You see, ol' Benedict took the 'Liberty,' Major Skene's merchant ship, all the way north to Crown Point...

CAROL : ...where he armed it and put aboard sailors and marines for a trip to St. John's in Canada.

JANET: This was in 1775, don't you know! There, they captured a British sloop that they renamed the "Enterprise." That was a full six weeks before the Battle of Bunker Hill, I'll have you know.

CAROL: Yeah! But the United States Naval Department has documents from six other ports that claim to be the birthplace of our national navy.

DANIELLE: *(Points to audience)* Well, tell those folks! Whitehall is the real place where the navy began!

SUE: The folks down in Washington say there are six seaports that played a big role in the American Revolution and they don't want to play favorites.

JANET: Favorites! Hah! Did Beverly or Marblehead in Massachusetts, or for that matter, Salem, stop the British cold in 1775 as they tried to come down the Champlain?

SUE: No m'am! And did any ships from Machias, Maine fight a deadly battle in 1776 at Valcour Island?

CAROL: And, don't tell me Portsmouth, New Hampshire or Philadelphia did any fighting better or earlier to merit the name of "Birthplace of the American Navy."

SUE: *(Shouts)* And don't tell me...!

DICK: My good woman, don't get yourself excited!

SUE: Who's excited? I'm not excited! I'm just plain mad that the government won't agree with historians that Whitehall is the real birthplace of the American Navy.

TED: Well, we have to admit we had to retreat in 1777 because the Continental Congress wouldn't give ol' Benedict money to build new ships here in Skenesborough.

JANET: So when Johnny Burgoyne led his troops down the Champlain again in 1777, he spent four weeks in Whitehall as his men built a road to Fort Ann, about 10 miles south.

DICK: That's right, he did! But our boys fought rearguard actions to slow up the invasion until militias could come from the whole of New England to meet Gentleman Johnny's troops on Bemis Heights in Saratoga.

DANIELLE: And thanks again to General Arnold, the army followed his example and attacked the British despite General Gates orders to sit and wait for Burgoyne to attack.

TED: That's the truth! So, we have every right to be proud of our forefathers here in Whitehall.

CAROL: Oh! Did you know that the oldest soldier to fight in the American Revolution died in Whitehall at the age of 134 years?

SUE: *(Incredulous)* Go on!

DICK: Yes ma'm! Henry Francisco joined the Continental Army in 1777 at the age of 91 and was discharged a little more than a year later. Then he lived another 42 years. He passed away here in Whitehall in 1820, aged 134 years.

SUE: I never heard that one!

TED: Not only that! He outlived two wives and had 21 children *(afterthought)*...the last one was born when he was 80 years old.

CAROL: There's hope for you fellas yet!

DICK: Never you mind! We know that peace was finally signed in 1783 and we were a real nation recognized by the rest of the world.

JANET: And, Major Skene's land, all 50,000 acres of it awarded him in the 1750s by the king, was sold by the State of New York in 1779 to anyone who wanted to buy land.

DICK: It was called an illegal act but New York needed funds and the good colonel and his lawyers were back in England so....

CAROL: ... our citizens took up farming, logging and boat building again here in Skenesborough....

TED: ...and shipped goods north by Lake Champlain and south over land until we reached Fort Edward and a waterway.

DICK: Still, people didn't want any more recognition of Major Skene so they changed it to Whitehall in...in...in....

JANET: I think it was 1788.

DANIELLE: That's close enough!

CAROL: They named it Whitehall. Didn't they say it was because there were two prominent families here, named White and Hall?

BRITTANY: Well, the person named White in the area was a farmer who lived outside of the village....

DANIELLE: ...and the only Hall in town was a seven-year old boy!

TED: It sounds good though, because at first there was a hyphen in the name...

BRITTANY: ...you mean. White...Hall?

DICK: That's it! But I also heard it was named after a common type of rowboat in those years named the Whitehall!

CAROL: That's enough of that! *(Points to audience)* You'll have them all going to the privy again!

DICK: What does it matter? The name's served us well all these years.

SUE: Right! *(To audience)* And, if you don't like it, go to Rutland. *(Derisively)* Now there's a name!

DICK: So, Whitehall folks settled into a whole new free life just like the rest of the country. Why, in 1800 we had about 1,200 people in this here town.

TED: But, we couldn't get away from national problems. Even our freedom caused different troubles.

JANET: Like politics!

DICK: Sure, after Washington refused a third term as president, and definitely didn't want to be king, his vice-president, John Adams became our second president.

TED: And, Thomas Jefferson became his vice-president but they didn't like each other, no sir!

SUE: While John Adams became president in 1800, we here in Whitehall were becoming the Lumber Yard of the region, don't you know.

CAROL: Really!!!

DICK: Sure, all that Skene property was prime woodland and we had trees up and down the mountains around us.

BRITTANY: That's a lotta lumber!

TED: That's right! We had lumberyards all over the town. Every able-bodied man had a job. And, we were using the wood to build ships to carry on trade with Canada down the Champlain.

CAROL: You mean up!!

TED: No, down! You see the water on Lake Champlain is at a lower level than the water south of us so when you sail north on the lake, you're really going down the lake. Understand?

CAROL: Nooooo!

DICK: Forget it! It's one of those strange things that happened here in Whitehall. Like in 1806, we had a blizzard in June with 10 inches of snow and there was ice on the windows on July 4th.

JANET: Many of our farm animals died and we lost most of our crops. But, one of our farmers was smart. He started large fires in the fields and grew the only corn crop in the region that summer.

SUE: I'll bet the people were saying their prayers then!

DANIELLE: Well, they could! The Congregational Church in Whitehall was organized in 1805 and its first real church was built in 1813.

DICK: And General John Williams gave the Reformed Presbyterian Church a building in 1810 to use as a church. Later it was reorganized as the First Presbyterian Church of Whitehall in 1819.

TED: Then came the Methodist Church in 1822, and the Episcopal Church the same year. The Baptists built their first church in 1841.

CAROL: What about the Catholics?

JANET: Well, the Catholics met in private homes and halls until 1841 when their first church, St. Anthony's, was constructed.

TED: They worshipped there until the two language groups, Italian and French, separated in 1868 and built their own parishes.

SUE: That adds up to a lot of prayers no matter what denomination.

DICK: Well, we could use prayers at that time. When 1811 rolled around, Britain was making noises about resuming hostilities with us.

DANIELLE: Yes, they were stopping our commercial ships on the Atlantic and making our sailors join their navy.

TED: In 1812, Whitehall became the scene of military operations. Defensive artillery and barracks were built in Whitehall and ammunition stored to supply the navy on Lake Champlain...

SUE: ...and one of those ammunition storage places is now a restaurant's wine cellar here in the village.

CAROL: Yes, and soon we were building ships here in Whitehall to protect us from any invasion coming up the lake from Canada to Whitehall.

DICK: Commodore Thomas Macdonough sailed his small fleet from Whitehall in 1814 and defeated the British fleet in the Battle of Plattsburgh on Lake Champlain.

TED: Yes, and the commodore's battle prize was the Confiance, the British flagship, and he lived on it in Whitehall for a month after the battle.

JANET: Well, now, you know we won that war and could look to building our little town into a prosperous community.

SUE: In fact, we built a one-room schoolhouse in 1814 and over the next 30 years added a half-dozen more, including the First Academy in 1830.

CAROL: Why, teachers' salaries at that time were reported to be $5.75 a week in winter....

BRITTANY: ...but a dollar less in the summer!

DANIELLE: How come the difference?

DICK: Teachers in the summer term were mostly women while the winter teachers were mainly men. That's why!

CAROL: What?????????????

DICK: Don't "what????" me! That's what I heard!

TED: Never you mind teachers' salaries! Don't forget the canal.... the Champlain Canal. That was the big news around here.

JANET: That's right! The state authorized the canal in 1812 but its construction had to wait until after the war. So, the canal was really started in 1817....

DANIELLE: ... and Governor DeWitt Clinton arrived in Whitehall to officially open the Champlain Canal in 1826.

SUE: It extended the canal from Waterford to Whitehall by way of Wood Creek, Fort Miller Falls and Saratoga Falls, a good 60-mile trip.

TED: Life aboard the packet boats was a wonderful leisurely ride. In calm, sunny weather, passengers would sit upon the cabin roof and view the countryside alongside the canal.

DICK: Right! And, if the destination wasn't reached before sundown, people slept in the cabin with a curtain to provide privacy for the ladies.

CAROL: I should think so!

SUE: You know many of the boatmen were French-Canadian. Most of these boaters stayed in Canada during the winter, but some settled in Whitehall's "Elbow," now known as North Street.

TED: And mules were used to pull the boats through the canal, walking along the towpath. Why, working a 16-hour day, the normal trip from Whitehall to Waterford took 15 days.

DANIELLE: Yeah, but things were different when tugs started working on the canal.

JANET: It's said that a canal boat pulled by tugs in 1876 took 39 hours to get from Whitehall to Waterford, the fastest time up 'til then.

CAROL: Why, during that same year, it was so busy the canal collector's office received $8,240 in tolls.

TED: They kept on the canal in good shape to prevent flooding of the nearby land. Towpath walkers patrolled the canal looking for holes in the canal that might cause leaks.

BRITTANY: But, muskrats would burrow into the canal walls.

SUE: And some of the little critters found themselves in a farmer's field, in a lot of muddy water. Emergency crews had to be called to plug these holes.

DICK: Now, don't forget that Dwight B. LaDue of Whitehall was the engineer who built the Barge Canal Locks. They claim that the barge canal was a more intricate engineering feat than the Panama Canal. So there!!!

JANET: Still, floods in 1927 and 1936 caused extreme damage in Whitehall when the Metowee River and the Barge Canal overflowed because of melting snow and heavy rains.

TED: In one case, the Champlain Spinners Company had 40 inches of water enter its building. But, newly constructed dikes gave employees time to remove much of the material and equipment, saving the company from a total loss.

CAROL: During those floods, many homes in downtown Whitehall had water in the basements causing the loss of heat. Why, people used canoes and rowboats to get around the village.

DICK: But, the success of the Champlain Canal was threatened by the railroad coming into Whitehall in the 1840s. Packet boats lost their passengers to rail lines, such as the Saratoga and Washington Railroad Company that received a charter from New York State to carry passengers.

SUE: But the state didn't permit the railroads to carry freight so as to preserve the state's investment in the canal. But, the railroads hurt passenger travel on the canal.

DANIELLE: And when the Delaware and Hudson coal company decided to form a rail line, it took over the Rutland and Saratoga line and then extended its reach to Plattsburgh by 1875.

TED: And, this permitted the railroad to carry much of the freight once carried by canal boats. It got so bad that by 1897, a fund was raised to help impoverished canal men's families because of the lack of business on the canal.

CAROL: Even so, Whitehall became a thriving community with the transfer of freight from Champlain Lake boats to the railroad cars.

DICK: That's right! In fact, a 600-foot tunnel was built right down the middle of the village so trains could link up with the Champlain Lake shore for a direct connection with the lake steamers.

TED: Right! There were sometimes 40 locomotives waiting in a round house for freight trains to be made up. By the 1920s, the Whitehall D and H Station looked like Times Square with its 24-hour activity.

JANET: But back in the 1840s, some southern politicians in the United States began looking to take over Texas as another state. Of course Mexico didn't think much of that idea and so we moved towards war.

SUE: And, a number of our young men in Whitehall enlisted and traveled several thousand miles to fight the Mexican army when it invaded the Texas territory.

DANIELLE: At that time, too, people in Whitehall became aware that the acquisition of Texas as another southern state heightened another problem, the slavery question.

DICK: And, don't forget, at about the same period we became aware of another tragedy when the people in Ireland suffered the potato famine of 1847.

TED: Thousands were dying of starvation. A great many Irish families fled the famine in the "coffin" ships to Canada. Then, they came through Whitehall on Lake Champlain boats to go to Boston or New York..

BRITTANY: What were "coffin" ships?

DICK: They were the crowded ships that took six weeks to sail from Ireland to Canada. Sometimes almost one-third of the passengers died on these ships. The dead were buried at sea.

CAROL: At the same time, the Freedom Seeker families fled from bounty hunters and bloodhounds to reach the northern states.

JANET: So, we had the Freedom Seekers moving north through Whitehall to escape slavery and find freedom in Canada while the Irish moved south through Whitehall, for their own freedom from starvation.

DICK: As America was torn asunder in 1861 through 1865 by a Civil War that cost hundreds of thousands of lives among the Union and Confederate armies, Whitehall was not immune to the patriotic fervor or the sense of loss.

TED: The numerous cemeteries in Whitehall contain the bodies of soldiers who died in this tragic war. They are buried near men who died in the War of 1812 and the Mexican War of 1848.

DANIELLE: In 1875, many of Whitehall's Civil War veterans and their families attended a lecture by Major General Kilpatrick who commanded local soldiers in the cavalry forces in General Sherman's capture of Atlanta.

SUE: His discussion of this battle was the first time many of the Whitehall families heard of the heroism of their sons, brothers, fathers and husbands.

CAROL: Veterans were certainly not forgotten as, several times a year, full-dress dinners and dances were held in their honor.

JANET: This was not really a new tradition but a carry-over from earlier in the 19th century when these military balls were the social events of the year.

DICK: As the Civil War veterans moved back into the business of life, Whitehall resumed its bustling busy way.

TED: By now, the railroad system had firmly established itself with the Delaware and Hudson Railway making regular runs between Whitehall and New York through Saratoga.

JANET: Ordinary citizens as well as local merchants rode the rail cars all the way to New York to shop. One merchant prided himself in being able to bring back and sell New York City suits for six dollars.

CAROL: The rail cars began competing with boats in moving goods south to their markets.. The local economy was held firm by the pulpwood from Canada that would be carried solely by Champlain canal barges.

BRITTANY: Oh, yes! They were called "paper boats."

SUE: It would be another 70 or more years before canal traffic took a serious downward turn.

TED: Still, business in Whitehall flourished as much as any other town of its size and, in some cases, even more in the period from the Civil War through the turn of the 20th century.

DICK: For example, in 1874, there were three banks in Whitehall, four steam saw and planing mills, two machine shops, one brickyard, one boiler factory, five clothing stores, two jewelry stores, two newspapers, a grist mill, three coal dealers, three billiard parlors....

CAROL: ....one sail loft and rigging shop, two bowling alleys....and 31 liquor stores.

TED: As for occupations and professions in 1874 in Whitehall, there were five doctors, seven lawyers, five dressmakers, two dentists, five pharmacists, five boot makers, three barbers and...one official grave digger.

JANET: And there were four public halls where various visiting and local entertainment was presented. For example, a visiting theater troupe presented Shakespeare's tragedy "Hamlet" and the 19th century melodrama, "East Lynne."

BRITTANY: And, Callender's Georgia Minstrels also came to town.

SUE: Gilbert and Sullivan's operettas were also popular whether performed by visiting professional troupes or by local school children.

DICK: As in other towns throughout the country during the late 19th century, Whitehall's 4,700 citizens in 1876 loved church picnics and county fairs. In fact, they faithfully attended the Washington County Agricultural Fair in Greenwich each year.

TED: This fair had the oldest charter in the northeastern United States. Actually, the first agricultural society was formed in Hudson Falls in 1818 with a goal of protecting its members from horse thieves. It became a county organization in 1819 with Melanction Wheeler signing for Whitehall's membership.

CAROL: And, the first Whitehall town fair was held at Wiswell's Tavern.

DANIELLE: These fairs attracted prominent people, including Horace Greeley, the publisher, and Charles Dickens, the Victorian novelist, in a stopover from his trip around America.

CAROL: Much in the mood of a fair, the local bandstand and park attracted adults and children alike to hear local and visiting musicians and to enjoy life in the sunshine.

DICK: Now, Whitehall was not without its share of tragedy, particularly large fires, especially in the second half of the 19th century. The fact of the matter was that the large factories and buildings were made of wood. A small fire could become a major conflagration in minutes.

TED: This was the case of the Hoit door factory that was completely destroyed with the loss of 2,000 doors in various stages of construction. Insurance didn't cover the owner's losses and 20 men became unemployed.

CAROL: The six volunteer fire companies in town competed by racing to this and other major fires to get to the fire first to be rewarded by the insurance companies.

DANIELLE: In this same period, fires destroyed a Catholic Church, a Baptist Church, the Northern Transportation Line barn area and offices, and the Adirondack Spring Company building.

SUE: Two hotels fell victim to one fire, the largest of the period.

TED: Later, the Grand Opera House was totally destroyed by fire in 1886. However, the biggest fire in Whitehall's history took place in

1860. It destroyed most of the downtown business district, including the newspaper building.

SUE: As a result, much of the historical official town documents were lost.

JANET: Now, fires were not the only disasters to hit the town. We had a hurricane once and two epidemics. In 1849, we had a cholera outbreak that claimed 10 citizens a week.

DICK: Then, our townspeople were among the millions throughout the world in 1918 who were hit by the flu epidemic. So many Whitehall residents were struck by the epidemic that the state armory had to be turned into a makeshift hospital.

TED: Whitehall residents fared better than most of the rest of the state in surviving the disease thanks to the health workers in the town.

CAROL: Resiliency is a characteristic of the people of Whitehall who soon again were attending social events and dances.

JANET: In addition, the five-year period between 1870 and 1875, architect A.P. Hopson designed and built six great buildings, castles with turrets, capturing the majesty of those ancient buildings.

DANIELLE: There was the Griswald Mansion…

CAROL: … the Cook Mansion…

DICK: …Our Lady of Angels rectory….

TED: …the Edwin Hall Mansion…

DANIELLE: … the George Hall Mansion…

SUE: …and Judge Potter's mansion which still survives as Skene Manor.

DICK: With the uplifting of spirits in town, a new industry arrived on the scene. In September, 1887 one Frederick Dale invited the town's citizens to witness the opening of a five-story silk mill. On the following day, 80 employees began working on 3,000 spindles each day.

TED: It was a very successful operation right here next to Lock number 12. The business became world-renowned making good use of the nearby waterfalls that produced its electrical power.

JANET: By the way, Samuel de Champlain called these falls "petit sault"…little falls when he first saw them in 1609.

TED: *(Nods a thank you)* The company became the second largest of its kind in the world by 1901. You know the falls still survive right near us here and produce electric that is sold to the major power company in the state.

SUE: But, Whitehall, as was true of other parts of the country, was never very far from national affairs, especially when wars broke out.

CAROL: Local men joined the army to fight in Cuba and even the Philippines during the Spanish American War at the turn of the 20th century.

DANIELLE: A number of those men were killed in action while following Teddy Roosevelt up San Juan Hill…

SUE…or sailing with Admiral Dewey into Manila Bay. They lie buried among Whitehall's nine cemeteries.

DICK: In the meantime, horses now had to deal with the noise of a new invention…the automobile. Whitehall's citizens kept pace with the rest of the country in buying these new-fangled contraptions.

TED: But, soon war clouds gathered over the country and Whitehall as Europe exploded into a war. When America joined the fight in 1917, local men were caught up with patriotic fervor.

JANET: Until this war, local men were not called upon to serve in Europe, especially in the trenches that dotted the French countryside.

CAROL: Americans were introduced to the sentimental yearnings of wartime. Whitehall families had no less feeling of absence.

JANET: With the returning soldiers after World War One, the "war to end all wars," Whitehall picked up its enthusiasm for peace and industry and also shared tragedies.

CAROL: The "Roaring Twenties" was a troubled but also a carefree time, particularly with the passage of the Volstead Act that introduced Prohibition.

DICK: This produced an industry that involved Canada whose natives made millions shipping illegal liquor down Lake Champlain where it would be picked up by out-of-towners, notably from New York City, to satisfy the thirst of American seekers of alcoholic libations.

TED: Of course, local residents developed a cottage industry of bootleggers, not unique to Whitehall. We just sort of joined the club with an air of carefree nonchalance.

CAROL: Now, midway in the 1920s, Hollywood chose Whitehall to do a story about the Erie Canal. The producer and director saw Whitehall as more like an Erie Canal town than real Erie Canal towns. Go figure!

DANIELLE: Why, the film even had its premiere right here at our local Capital Theater in 1928. It brought happiness back to the community.

DICK: The days didn't stay happy as the 1929 Wall Street crash was heard all the way up to Whitehall.

TED: Our business began to fail as they did all over the country. Still, the indomitable spirit that had repelled the British back in the 18th century and helped the country survive a Civil War in the 19th century, was still here.

BRITTANY: People in Whitehall also found comfort in the Hollywood movie that helped people laugh and smile all over the country.

DANIELLE: Like the ones with Shirley Temple...

BRITTANY... and Mickey Mouse...

CAROL...and, Betty Boop! *(Carol illustrates with hip movement:: "Boop, Boopa Doop")*

DICK: Now, while the Delaware and Hudson railroad and the canal traffic decreased, local people kept faith with the importance of the Canal to its life.

TED: But yet again, as with the rest of the country, we came face to face with another major war in 1941. Soon, Whitehall's men and women were marching towards the battles all over the world that would consume four long and often tragic years.

JANET: And yet, there was still hope in our hearts that peace would come.

DICK: The war ended and millions of men returned to their homes throughout the nation and created a work force that took the country to new technological heights.

TED: While some of these new developments included television and the ability to send men to the moon, they also created a demand for security.

DICK: So soon after the Korean War in the 1950s the cold war developed, in Europe and thousands of miles of Interstate Highways were authorized in 1956 as a defensive measure.

TED: At about the same time, the country was engaged with another conflict in Vietnam. Again, our young men and women served their country with equal valor as their forefathers.

DICK: Even as this conflict continued, the Northway, as part of the Interstate Highway System, was being completed from Albany to the Canadian border.

JANET: As a result, the railways lost business to large trucks and so did barge traffic subside on the canal.

SUE: On Route 22 here in the village, trucks from Canada roll south day and night to join up with the Northway about 20 miles away, From there, they arrive in New York City in four hours.

CAROL: This was the crushing blow to Lake Champlain as a viable industrial waterway and, along with that fact, so too, Whitehall lost its importance.

DANIELLE: As in the past, Whitehall has refused to roll over and play dead. With its marinas and cooperation with the New York State Canal Authority, Whitehall has taken its place as a destination point for pleasure boat travelers from all over the nation and Canada.

DICK: Now, the village and the town are pointing towards attracting visitors who may absorb the past glories of Whitehall when it was Skenesborough fighting to preserve the independence of America.

(Music starts playing over Janet's speech and continues through curtain call, after which cast marches to rear of theater)

JANET: It is a town that has built a history of patriotism, industrial prowess and community-minded stubbornness to rise up from defeat, despair and destruction to face the future with optimism.

TED: And even now, as the country is engaged in battle in far-flung regions of the world, Whitehall's sons and daughters are once again answering the call of their country.

DICK: And their fellow citizens continue to pray and hope for their safe return and a new future for Whitehall and the nation.

(Music ends as cast takes bow)

THE END

"Cases on the Canal"

By Martin P. Kelly

Copyright, 2004

Note from the Author

The Volstead Act enacted by the United States Congress in 1920 completed the prohibition movement which began in 1919 when the 18th Amendment to the Constitution made illegal the distillation, importation and consumption of alcoholic beverages in the United States. Congressman Volstead's bill added beer to the mix of prohibited beverages. This particular legislation set in motion one of the great examples of American ingenuity and innovation.

Whiskey and beer were produced, imported and consumed in greater volume than before the passage of this legislation. The challenge for distilling illegal liquor and beer was met with great vigor by honest and crooked citizens alike. And its transportation to avid consumers was carried out with alacrity.

In all, the Prohibition era (the "Roarin' Twenties"), extending to 1933 when the amendment was repealed, had the greatest number of people breaking the law than at any other time in America's history. Gangsters and upright citizens alike made fortunes even as judges, policemen and legislators received large sums under the table to look the other way.

This play offers the exploits of people in one small community—Whitehall, New York, a village at the southern edge of Lake Champlain, the sixth "great lake" that reaches to the Canadian border.

While working for five years at the Bridge Theater in Whitehall, I heard occasional tales of local hijinks during the Prohibition era as told by people old enough to know and probably contributors to the lore of the period.

The story here is fiction but then again, who's to say it didn't happen.

MARTIN P. KELLY

ACT ONE

Scene One

<u>Cast</u>

Timmy McCoy............*William Hickman*

Sarah Crimmins...........*Susan Ingerson*

Flossie.......................*Janet Stasio*

Colleen Crimmins.........*Danielle Ingerson*

Rev. John Walters..........*Douglas Bates*

Time: October, 1928

(Timmy McCoy comes quickly into the Crimmins' kitchen. Sarah, his sister, is at the stove. He is a dapper, middle-aged dandy, an obvious New Yorker out of place in the late 1920s upstate Whitehall. Sarah is several years younger, more the home grown upstate woman who doesn't cotton to her brother's wiseacre ways.)

TIMMY: Okay! When's dinner! I'm hungry enough to eat your cookin'!

SARAH: You never told me when you were coming. Why didn't you call me?

TIMMY: How can I do that?

SARAH: You just call the Whitehall operator and ask for me. She'll put you through.

TIMMY: Do you think that I want that old blabbermouth knowing all m'business?

SARAH: What business? No, don't tell me. You should have told me you were coming tonight!

TIMMY: Well! I'm tellin' ya now! Besides, I've been back here in Whitehall for two weeks now! That's as permanent as I intend to get around here.

SARAH: Well, go tell it to the squirrels, for all I care.

TIMMY: I've been away on a trip four days and you don't even say you miss me! That's no way to treat your baby brother!

SARAH: Baby brother, my foot! You're ten years older than I am and look it!

TIMMY: Whatever you say, Sarah, m'girl! Now what about some food? I've been drivin' for hours.

SARAH: Get your floozy girlfriend to cook for you!

TIMMY: Com'on, Sarah. Flossie's not built for cookin'! I'd starve to death if she took to the kitchen.

SARAH: Yeah! I forgot, there are no stoves in bedrooms.

TIMMY: Now, Sarah! That's no way to talk about a successful businessman's friend.

SARAH: Some businessman, running booze out of Canada to beat Prohibition. Disgracing the village where you were born!

TIMMY: M'girl! There's thousands of parched throats all up and down the Hudson River lookin' for m'wares! And I take care of the local boys too, you know!

SARAH: Sure, I know you're not the only one in Whitehall pushing the booze. There're families here who haven't had a pot to spit in for years and now they're driving around in big cars without doing a stick of work.

TIMMY: They have their homemade wares and I have my good stuff.

SARAH: Some stuff! Bottles of Canadian liquor you buy for a dollar apiece and sell for five!

TIMMY: And many more dollars the closer I get to the big city. In New York, I'm Broadway's favorite. When New Year's Eve, 1930 rolls around I'm going to be a rich man.

SARAH: Good! Only four months away. Then you can plant your backside on Broadway and not bother us any more!

TIMMY: Sarah! You hurt m'feelin's! Hey! Maybe I'll buy this town and put in sidewalks.

SARAH: Don't do us any favors! Just make your money and send us a postcard once in a while.

TIMMY: Maybe I'll include a C-note with it.

SARAH: That I believe...you sending money by postcard!

TIMMY: Be good to me, now, Sarah! I had a bad experience today!

SARAH: Your whole life's a bad experience... and it carries over to us, m'daughter Colleen and me.

TIMMY: Ah! Now there's a lovely colleen, Colleen is! A fair flower!

SARAH: Never mind your blarney... .she's my daughter.

TIMMY: And your late husband's...ya know-Black Jack Crimmins

SARAH: May the devil take him with his soul as black as his wavy hair!

TIMMY: C'mon now Sarah! You don't hate him! Sure, dead as he is, you'd hop into his bed as quick as a wink if he walked through the door.

SARAH: Mind your tongue! My life is changed. There are loftier things to think about.

TIMMY: What's this loftier talk?

SARAH: Since the blackguard went off the cliff in his car two years ago with his girlfriend beside him, Colleen and I have been comforted by our neighbors.

TIMMY: Your neighbors are close to ya, are they?

SARAH: Yes, they are. And, so's Rev. Walters. He has helped me think more of spiritual things now.

TIMMY: Spiritual things, is it? Now, who's this Rev. Walters? What happened to Father Girardeux?

SARAH: Harry Walters is a minister in town, a widower of four years and a very nice man.

TIMMY: Yeah! But, what about Father Girardeux?

SARAH: That crazy Frenchman blamed me for Jack's taking off with that round-heeled waitress from Fort Edward. He even said Mass at their funeral.

TIMMY: Well, you know these Frenchmen. She was a looker! Yes, she was!

SARAH: What would you know about a looker!

TIMMY: Believe me! I know!

(Door bursts open and Flossie appears...short skirt, tight blouse, lots of makeup and red hair)

FLOSSIE: Here I am, lover! You too, Sarah girl! *(Kisses Timmy)* The car's all safe in the barn. The cops'll never find it!

SARAH: Did you park that big Packard in the barn again! I told you last time...no more!

TIMMY: I promise, this is the last time. There are customers coming up from Saratoga, Albany, Poughkeepsie and even New York to buy the load from me.

SARAH: You'll have every cop in the county raiding my barn. No way! Find another place.

TIMMY: I can't do that, Sarah, m'gal! I've got to put some new springs in the car's rear end. That's why I don't get frisked by the cops. The springs are strong...

FLOSSIE: And comfortable too.... in the back seat!

TIMMY: That's why the cops don't give me too much trouble. I got good springs in the car so the whiskey in the trunk won't make the rear end sag. And I travel with a good lookin' doll! Those Italians always have two guys in each car with dark suits and fedoras. It's like they're wearing a sign..."Arrest Me!" With my flashy clothes and Flossie here, I breeze right through.

SARAH: I'm impressed! *(Sarcastically)* You're a wonder!

TIMMY: So I need to use the barn tonight. The guys are all comin' here later to buy m'wares!

SARAH: Well, you can take them down to the canal, for all I care. Do what the Frenchmen do, run down Lake Champlain and then move the stuff by canal down to Albany.

TIMMY: Sure! They take it by boat from lock to lock and then have to pack it in a car to get past each lock. It takes almost a week that way.

SARAH: That's their aging process! And, you have a better way?

TIMMY: You betcha! Have the guys meet me here and they take the goods south. I get my money and can head back to Canada for more.

SARAH: Well! I still want you out of here!

FLOSSIE: That's not fair, Sarah! Timmy had a bad experience today.

SARAH: A bad experience is it! His whole life is a bad experience.

FLOSSIE: No! The cops stopped us around Ticonderoga on our way from Canada.

SARAH: I thought you just said you breeze right through!

TIMMY: That's right, Sarah! I do! But I must have been a little early today. The cops mustn't have had their quota of Italians.

SARAH: What quota?

TIMMY: You know! A quota! When the cops make enough arrests for a good payday and grab enough liquor for a party, they're off the road.

SARAH: But, they didn't grab you!

FLOSSIE: No! Quick as a wink, when the cop stops us, Timmy starts looking through travel folders like we was tourists or newlyweds.

SARAH: Oh! M'god! Newlyweds. That's a joke!

TIMMY: Never mind! It was a close call.

FLOSSIE: Yeah! The cops started to give the travel folders a long look.

TIMMY: That's when Flossie used her head.

SARAH: Now, that's a trick!

TIMMY: You can be sure of that. The cops are giving the folders a close look and, quick as a wink, Flossie flashes a thigh! *(Flossie demonstrates by putting her foot on a chair and raises skirt)* The cops' sunglasses fogged up and they were sputtering all over themselves.

FLOSSIE: It was a tribute to my acting lessons!

TIMMY: They let us drive off free and clear!

SARAH: The troopers did that!

TIMMY: Sure! They're a bunch of farm kids who never saw a Broadway gal's leg before. It was like shooting fish in a barrel.

FLOSSIE: There's nothing fishy about these gams! *(Shows legs again)*

TIMMY: You know it, doll!

SARAH: Now, I'm getting sick.

TIMMY: Yeah! It must be tough to see true love on the hoof!

SARAH: Well, I don't care! You can't use my barn to sell your booze! I don't want to wind up in jail in this town. You've been storing boxes in there for two weeks now. I'd be ruined! What'll my neighbors say! And John Walters?

FLOSSIE: Oh! You got a boyfriend, Sarah?

SARAH: No! I don't have a boyfriend! The Reverend Walters is my counselor!

TIMMY: He's a lawyer too?

SARAH: No! He's a fine, upstanding clergyman who gives spiritual guidance...a counselor.

TIMMY: Hey! The only counselors I knew in New York hit you up for 20 bucks an hour and you still get 30 days in jail with good behavior.

SARAH: The reverend is talking about eternity.

FLOSSIE: Eternity? That's a long time! Isn't it?

TIMMY: Yeah! Too long for me to think about!

SARAH: Never mind! Just take your business elsewhere!

TIMMY: Look! I've got two weeks' work stashed in the barn, that's five trips to Canada and back. This could be my biggest haul. After this, I'm going to fix a milk tanker truck with a hidden door so I can store the boxes of liquor inside. The cops'll never get wise. I need the money from this load to buy a tanker. Then, I can take the stuff directly to the big city and Broadway!

SARAH: And, I suppose, your girlfriend here is going to be your helper all dressed up in overalls! That'll do things for the cops.

TIMMY: That's how much you know! She'll make believe she's a hitchhiker I picked up ten miles before the cops stopped me. Right, Flossie!

FLOSSIE: Yeah! My story will be that my boyfriend pushed me out of his car when I wouldn't let him have his way with me!

SARAH: Oh! The cops'll certainly believe that, for sure!

TIMMY: Don't worry! Flossie is a great actress with legs to match.

FLOSSIE: Thank you, Timmy doll!

(Door opens and Colleen appears. She is a beautiful fresh-faced, dewy-lipped country girl as sophisticated as a cornstalk)

COLLEEN: Hello, mother! Uncle Tim! Aunt Flossie!

SARAH: This woman's not your aunt Flossie or any aunt at all!

COLLEEN: *(To Flossie)* Oh! I'm sorry. I didn't mean...

TIMMY: It's alright girl! She can be your aunt, if you like. And, might I add that you're lookin' as lovely as ever.

COLLEEN: Uncle Tim! You're making me blush!

FLOSSIE: And, I'm getting a little warm myself!

SARAH: Enough of it, both of you!

TIMMY: Now, ladies! Don't fight. *(Laughs)* I'm only one man!

SARAH: Thank God! Another like you and this damn town'd sink into the canal.

FLOSSIE: Timmy, darling! I'm all tuckered out from the busy day. I'm going to lie down for awhile. You comin' along!

TIMMY: You go lie down and I'll get things ready for my business tonight.

SARAH: I told you that you're not doing any business around here tonight, especially with Rev. Walters visiting.

TIMMY: The reverend's here tonight? He'll cramp my style. My customers might be a little uncomfortable with a reverend hanging around.

SARAH: Well, they're not going to see him because your gangster pals are not coming here tonight! And I've got to protect Colleen from them.

TIMMY: She'll be as safe as if she was in her mother's arms.

SARAH: And that's where she'll be, not being around those ruffians you hang with.

TIMMY: Thirsty citizens, Sarah, thirsty citizens!

SARAH: No matter! Let them take their thirst to the canal! They'll not be here tonight!

TIMMY: Just this once, Sarah! Then, I'll be out of your life for good when I get my truck. I'll breeze right past this town, right past the local cops and the troopers. I won't have to be the middleman any more. I'll get top dollar!

SARAH: Don't you spoil anything for me. I look forward to the reverend's company.

TIMMY: He won't hear a thing. I'll be quiet as a mouse in the barn.

SARAH: Sure! With the cars and wagons driving up here! No way! Not tonight! Get that stuff out of the barn and sort it out with your friends somewhere else!

FLOSSIE: Ohhhh! I don't like arguments! You people work it out. I'm going to lie down and get my beauty rest.

COLLEEN: *(Innocently)* You're so beautiful! You must spend a lot of time in bed.

SARAH: You don't know the half of it, Colleen, m'girl.

FLOSSIE: *(Kisses Timmy)* Ta-ta! See you in my dreams, lover!

SARAH: That's enough of that. There's a young girl standing here!

217

FLOSSIE: Give her a couple of years and she'll start dreamin' too!

TIMMY: I'll see you later, Flossie girl! *(She blows him a kiss and ankles off)*

SARAH: *(To Timmy)* Now you! Get that stuff out of the barn and keep your friends away from here!

TIMMY: Does our cousin Mike still have that old truck?

SARAH: Yes! He has one!

TIMMY: Good! I'll borrow it and move the stuff from the barn... for your sake!

SARAH: Don't be doing me any favors but get the stuff outta here! *(To Colleen)* And you, just don't stand there! Go out in the garden and get me some carrots and potatoes.

TIMMY: *(To Colleen)* I'd help you girl but I have to be on my way to quench the thirst of thousands of my fellow citizens, those poor souls who have been denied the liquid balm that uplifts the spirit and gladdens the heart! *(He's at the door)*

SARAH: *(Shakes her head and then to Colleen)* Watch where you walk, girl, or you'll be up to your ankles in it! *(Colleen looks around, puzzled)*

TIMMY: Oh! Sarah, girl! You have a way with words! *(Laughs and exits)*

Scene Two

(Colleen is at the kitchen table, peeling potatoes and carrots, humming to herself. In a few seconds, Flossie enters from hallway)

FLOSSIE: Where's everyone, honey?

COLLEEN: Mother's gone to the store and Uncle Tim just left with a truck he borrowed from our cousin Mike.

FLOSSIE: Cousin Mike! He never told me about his cousin Mike. But, then we don't get much chance to talk about family. We're so busy with his business and being romantic.

COLLEEN: I never thought of Uncle Tim as romantic.

FLOSSIE: Then, you've got a lot to know about romance, girlie!

COLLEEN: Oh! I know about romance!

FLOSSIE: Where from, kiddo, the movies?

COLLEEN: Not always!

FLOSSIE: Learn from real men and not those pantywaists on the screen!

COLLEEN: I've had boy friends!

FLOSSIE: Why wouldn't you? You're a good-looking kid!

COLLEEN: I'm not really a kid.

FLOSSIE: That's good! So, how about those boys? Where are they now?

COLLEEN: There's one over near Rutland. We went to school together here in Whitehall.

FLOSSIE: How come he left town?

COLLEEN: He wants to be a veterinarian and he's helping one in Rutland so he can learn all about treating animals. Maybe become a doctor.

FLOSSIE: What does he know about treating girls!

COLLEEN: Oh! It's not that kind of doctor!

FLOSSIE: You don't have to be a doctor to play doctor!

COLLEEN: Oh! You mean.... play doctor!

FLOSSIE: That's it, honey! You study anatomy by the Braille system!

COLLEEN: *(Looks at her hands, gets the reference)* Oh! Oh! No! We've never played doctor!

FLOSSIE: But, you have kissed a boy?

COLLEEN: Yes!

FLOSSIE: Was it really hot and heavy? Like you had to fight him off!

COLLEEN: Oh! No! We just kissed. Randall's a gentleman.

FLOSSIE: Thank goodness your uncle Timmy's no gentleman where kissing is concerned.

COLLEEN: And you like that?

FLOSSIE: Sure, honey! I don't mind fighting for my honor...and losing once in a while.

COLLEEN: It must be something about New York City that does that to you!

FLOSSIE: New York nothing! I learned romance behind a barn in my little hometown in Pennsylvania.

COLLEEN: Is that where you're from, Pennsylvania?

FLOSSIE: Just 22 miles east of Scranton!

COLLEEN: And you learned romance behind a barn?

FLOSSIE: Sure! Sometimes, we'd play farmer and the sheep.

COLLEEN: Farmer... sheep?

FLOSSIE: Sure! When a farmer goes to buy a ewe sheep, he strokes her back and then pinches her backside to check the fat.

COLLEEN: I don't understand!

FLOSSIE: The boy would play the farmer and I'd be the sheep. Get it?

COLLEEN: Ohhh! *(Changes subject)* How did you get to New York

FLOSSIE: They had a dance contest at the local Elks club and this guy from New York was looking for dancers for his nightclub. He liked my dancing and a week later I was in a chorus line just off Broadway flashing my ankles and all points north.

COLLEEN: And, your mother didn't mind?

FLOSSIE: Listen, honey! When a woman has 14 kids and a miner for a husband who's on strike every other month, one less mouth to feed is welcome. I was 16, free to quit school, so she kissed me on the cheek, put me on the bus and that was that.

COLLEEN: Gee! All alone in a big city, I'd be scared.

FLOSSIE: Who says I wasn't scared? But, you get over it. I was a good dancer and the customers in the club, you know the guys like your uncle, all treated me good. I never missed a meal and once in a while, a guy would take me on a trip to Atlantic City and swell places like that.

COLLEEN: Did you have a chaperone?

FLOSSIE: A what?

COLLEEN: You know, a woman along to watch out for you.

FLOSSIE: Honey! I was the only woman along and I could watch out for myself. If they were sweet, I was all theirs. If they were rough, they'd be walking funny down the boardwalk and singing soprano the rest of the trip.

COLLEEN: I don't know what you mean.

FLOSSIE: Just think of your knee as your best friend, that's all!

COLLEEN: I don't understand!

FLOSSIE: Just let's say that men are not all knights in shining armor, at least below their belt.

COLLEEN: And is Uncle Tim a knight in shining armor?

FLOSSIE: Honey! He is the whole cavalry! He treats me good, loves to dance and makes me feel like I'm queen of the world. So there!

COLLEEN: I never thought of Uncle Tim that way!

FLOSSIE: Maybe some day you'll meet a guy like him.

COLLEEN: Where did you meet him!

FLOSSIE: I was dancing in a club run by Texas Guinan and Tirnmy came with some of his pals. He was working for Jack Diamond then...you know..Legs Diamond.

COLLEEN: I never heard of him.

FLOSSIE: He's pretty famous! He can be a mean son of a gun but women throw themselves at him. One of my friends, Kiki Roberts, is his girl friend when his wife's not looking. Timmy broke away from Jack's crew and is now working on his own up here. Legs is on the lam in the Catskills keeping his distance from the Dutch Shultz gang.

COLLEEN: That sounds scary ... but exciting.

FLOSSIE: That's about the way it is...scary and exciting. Legs carried a few bullet holes in him on his trip to his Catskills' hideout where he's staying with his wife and my friend Kiki.

COLLEEN: Is that proper?

FLOSSIE: I don't know if it's proper, but it works for Jack. If Timmy ever tried it, he'd get more than a knee.

COLLEEN: How come you and Uncle Tim aren't married?

FLOSSIE: Because we're too busy, your uncle says. We're sorta engaged, though. He says we'll get married the next time a filly wins the Travers.

COLLEEN: I don't understand!

FLOSSIE: Don't try, honey! That's how we get along, Timmy and me! I don't try to understand him. *(Sarah comes through the door, carrying a bag, spots Flossie)*

SARAH: And, how was your beauty sleep!

FLOSSIE: *(Frames her face with her hands)* You have to ask?

COLLEEN: Flossie was telling me how she got to New York.

SARAH: You don't have to tell me. I have a good imagination. *(To Colleen)* Where's your uncle?

COLLEEN: He drove a truck up to the barn and after awhile he drove it away.

SARAH: That's good! He's doing what I asked him to do.

FLOSSIE: And what was that?

SARAH: I told him to take all those boxes somewhere else before he did his business with them.

FLOSSIE: All by himself? He'll hurt himself! He could strain his back...or worse, rupture himself.

SARAH: Watch your language around my daughter!

COLLEEN: That's alright, mother, we had a nice talk.

SARAH: Don't you go filling this girl's head about anything you're involved in.

COLLEEN: Did you know Flossie's a dancer in New York.

SARAH: Then, what's she doing prancing around the canal in Whitehall.

FLOSSIE: I'm with the man I love, I'll have you know!

COLLEEN: Tell her about the farmer and the sheep game, Flossie!

SARAH: Never mind! I don't want to hear anything about farmers and sheep!

FLOSSIE: *(To Colleen)* Another time, honey! I have to find Timmy and give him a hand. *(Puts on her hat, and goes to door)* Or, maybe he'll give me one! *(Laughs and exits)*

Scene Three

(Sarah and Colleen are setting the table)

SARAH: Now you be respectful to Rev. Walters, you hear!

COLLEEN: Mother! I'm always respectful. I know he's a man of the cloth. Why wouldn't I be respectful. He's been good to us since father died.

SARAH: Yes, he has! And, don't you forget it.

COLLEEN: Mother!

SARAH: Yes!

COLLEEN: With the mills closed here and all that, I haven't been able to get a job to help you.

SARAH: Well, you're a help around the house and keeping the garden and helping me with the laundry I take in.

COLLEEN: I hear tell that there are jobs over in Rutland, mother!

SARAH: And, how does that concern you!

COLLEEN: Well, if I could get one, I could send you some money and maybe find something that I could do the rest of my life.

SARAH: Like what?

COLLEEN: Well, I could become a secretary in an office. I took shorthand in school, you know.

SARAH: I appreciate your consideration but Rutland's in another state.

COLLEEN: It's only about 25 miles away.

SARAH: It's out of the question. Besides, where would you live?

COLLEEN: I'm sure there are boarding houses for women.

SARAH: You'd have little enough money to send home after you pay your room and board to some widow renting out her rooms.

COLLEEN: But, I would send you something.

SARAH: You're a good girl, Colleen, not like your two brothers, running off as soon as they were old enough. One in Albany, loading ships and the other building ski lifts in Lake Placid for the Olympics! We never hear from them, one month to the next. And, they certainly don't break their necks sending a cent home. It's like they fell off the end of the earth. No! You stay here, girl, where I can look after you and you can keep me company.

COLLEEN: But, you have company with Rev. Walters!

SARAH: Now that's not the same thing. He's a man of the cloth.

COLLEEN: But, you do like him, don't you!

SARAH: I like him as a friend and spiritual counselor.

COLLEEN: And, that's all?

SARAH: That's all!

COLLEEN: But, I've heard the two of you sitting here at the kitchen table talking low and laughing softly.

SARAH: We talk low so we won't wake you! And, as for laughing, he can tell some funny tales about his life as a minister.

COLLEEN: Don't you like him, a little!

SARAH: I like him as a friend.

COLLEEN: Well, that's a start!

SARAH: What do you mean a start?

COLLEEN: Wouldn't you like him to be more than just a friend.

SARAH: If you're saying what I think you're saying, I'll....

COLLEEN: That's alright, mother! I'd be happy if he were more than a friend to you!

SARAH: We'll no more of this talk or talk about Rutland, either.

COLLEEN: But, I'd really like to find a job in Rutland, mother.

SARAH: Wait a minute! Didn't that boy who took you to the school prom go over to Rutland to take care of horses?

COLLEEN: He's studying with a veterinarian, mother.

SARAH: So, that's why you want to go to Rutland, is it?

COLLEEN: No, mother! I want to get a job and help you.

SARAH: And, help yourself to a little hanky-panky while you're at it.

COLLEEN: No! I have no intention of playing farmer and sheep!

SARAH: Farmer and sheep?

COLLEEN: Oh! Never mind, mother! I'll stay here. Forget I said anything. *(She rushes into hallway to her room as Timmy enters)*

TIMMY: Well, I'm all set, Sarah! I've moved all m'wares out of your barn!

SARAH: And where did you bring them? No, wait! I don't want to know.

TIMMY: Don't you worry, m'wares are in a nice safe place where I'll be able to do business without any interruptions.

SARAH: And, where's her highness?

TIMMY: Ah! You mean Flossie! She's m'lookout, out at the edge of town, ready to give my customers my new location. She knows them all...and, they all know her. It's a perfect set up.

SARAH: I'll bet it is. It's a wonder to have such a smart brother but, if you don't watch out, our chief of police will have you in jail before the night's out. Believe me, I won't cry a tear!

TIMMY: Chief Rooney, my old school pal, is now engaging in curing his cold, imbibing in some of the fine Canadian cough medicine I bestowed on him in his time of need.

SARAH: You're telling me that that broken down excuse for a cop is working with you.

TIMMY: Not working with me.. .just looking away from me! That's all!

SARAH: Oh! You learned some fancy tricks you did from your New York pals.

TIMMY: I'll have you know they've learned tricks from me, even Jack Diamond. He needs fast legs to keep up with me.

SARAH: You're a braggart, you are, but you're due for a fall.

TIMMY: I'm indebted for your well wishes, I am! Now, I have to get back to my place of business. Have a nice dinner with the clergy. Say a little prayer for me.

SARAH: I'm sure he doesn't know that many prayers!

TIMMY: *(Laughs)* Thank you anyway. *(Opens door and leaves as Colleen enters from hallway)*

COLLEEN: I'm sorry about arguing with you, mother!

SARAH: And, I with you! You know I'm only thinking of your own good, don't you?

COLLEEN: I know you think you do, mother!

SARAH: It's more than think I do, I know! So, no more of it!

COLLEEN: Let's leave it at that! How is Uncle Tim doing?

SARAH: Up to no good, as usual! He'll be the death of me yet!

COLLEEN: I think he's a good man, mother. He doesn't forget you. He's sent us money and I think he loves us.

SARAH: Oh! He loves us in his own way. You just have to figure out his way.

COLLEEN: Flossie surely loves him! She's told me.

SARAH: You be watching what she tells you!

COLLEEN: Oh! I know she has her ways that certainly aren't ours. But, she is her own woman who can love a man on her own terms.

SARAH: What do you know about loving a man?

COLLEEN: Nothing really! But, some day I'd like to have a man to love.

SARAH: Well, you certainly don't want one like your father, devil take him!

COLLEEN: Mother, don't say that! I have some good memories of him.

SARAH: Some memories! Running off with another woman and getting himself killed.

COLLEEN: I'm sorry about that for your sake and mine. He was a distracted man; couldn't find a job here in town when the mills closed. The wood he cut in winter and the odd canal jobs he could find in the summer, they all were difficult for a man who knew what it was to be a foreman of a mill.

SARAH: Well, he found his solace in the moonshine they made in the hills and that changed him. I guess that chickie in the diner saw more in him that I did. Good riddance!

(There is a knock on the door. Sarah opens it and Rev. John Walters stands there, hat in hand. He is medium height with strong features and a warm smile)

WALTERS: *(Enters)* Good evening, Mrs. Crimmins. And, you Miss Crimmins! It is so nice of you to invite me to dinner. *(Gives her a box of cookies)* It's just a little something to have with our coffee.

SARAH: It is our humble pleasure, Reverend. Please give me your coat and hat.

COLLEEN: It's so nice to see you again, Reverend.

WALTERS: You're growing into a beautiful woman, Colleen.

COLLEEN: *(Shyly)* Thank you, Reverend.

SARAH: We'll be ready for dinner in a few minutes. May I offer you a glass of wine, Reverend? I made it myself. You won't tell the authorities, will you? *(Laughs)*

WALTERS: My lips are sealed. I'd be pleased to have a glass.

SARAH: Colleen! Will you pour Reverend Walters a glass of wine.

COLLEEN: Yes, mother! Do you want one also?

SARAH: Well, I wouldn't want Reverend Walters to drink alone, now would I?

COLLEEN: No! You wouldn't!

WALTERS: And, I understand your uncle Timothy is in town, Colleen.

COLLEEN: Yes, he is, Reverend!

WALTERS: And, what does he do?

SARAH: He's a… He's a…a…traveling salesman!

WALTERS: And, what does he sell?

SARAH: *(Quickly)* Paint remover!

WALTERS: That's unusual. I wouldn't think there'd be that much call for paint remover to support a man traveling from town to town.

SARAH: Oh! There's plenty of call for it. Believe me, what he sells will peel the paint off any wall.

WALTERS: Well, I'm glad a man can do so well with this economy. So many people out of work, you wouldn't think that paint remover would be such a popular commodity.

SARAH: Believe me! His paint remover is in great demand. He has to turn away customers.

COLLEEN: *(Innocently going along with discussion)* Yes! He's very successful. He has a great helper, too, with his partner.

SARAH: Colleen!!!!!

WALTER: His business can support a partner, too!

COLLEEN: Oh, yes! She's a big help from what I hear!

WALTER: His partner is a "she"?

COLLEEN: Yes! Flossie met him when she was a dancer in a nightclub in New York. She's been traveling with him ever since while he sells his.... paint remover.

WALTER: That's most unusual, Mrs. Crimmins!

SARAH: My brother is an unusual man. He marches to his own cymbal!

WALTERS: That's "march to his own drum," isn't it?

SARAH: Not Tim! He's still working his way up to a drum.

COLLEEN: He's a very smart man, Reverend!

WALTERS: That's good of you think so!

(There's a commotion outside as Timmy bursts through door)

TIMMY: The troopers just raided me! They're going to bust up all my wares.

WALTERS: What are troopers doing damaging your paint remover?

TIMMY: Paint remover?

SARAH: Don't ask!

COLLEEN: How can they do such a thing?

TIMMY: I didn't stick around to ask them!

COLLEEN: Where's Flossie?

TIMMY: Oh, m'god! Flossie! She's still out at the edge of town. I've got to get her.

SARAH: Where did they find your wares?

TIMMY: Right down town! I had the stuff in the basement of an old building. They're really doing a job on the place, breaking down doors, smashing windows. It's something!

WALTERS: Where is it!

TIMMY: It looks like an old church!

SARAH: An old church?

TIMMY: Right behind the Mountain View National Bank on Main Street!

WALTERS: Good God! That's my church!

(Walters grabs his coat, runs out the door, Sarah picks up a pot to hit Timmy as Colleen just shakes her head)

TIMMY: How did I know?

(He covers his head and dashes out the door with Sarah behind him)

End of Act One

ACT TWO

Scene One

(Lights come up on Sarah's kitchen. It is early the next morning. The stage is empty. After a few moments, there is the noise of a car door slamming and the front door opens. Flossie enters, slightly disheveled.)

FLOSSIE: *(To herself)* What a night, what a night! *(She exits into bedroom, comes out with suitcase)* Gotta be ready as soon as Timmy gets out of jail so we can blow this town for good! *(She buttons her blouse, straightens her skirt and smooths wrinkles)* I never saw such commotion. The troopers busting down the doors and breaking the windows like they're lumberjacks! Then, there's this crazy guy hollering and screaming about them destroying his church. *(Fixes her garter belt and straightens her stockings)* And, there's Sarah trying to calm down the crazy guy while throwing rocks at Timmy who's explaining to the police that he's an innocent bystander. *(Goes to mirror and touches up her lipstick)* Then this hick police chief drags Timmy away with him protesting his innocence all the time! But, I got his signal to get back here and get ready to leave town. How he's going to leave town I don't know but I don't ask questions.

(There is noise offstage. Suddenly, the door burst opens and it is Rev. Walter, disheveled and almost foaming at the mouth. Flossie steps back in terror)

FLOSSIE: Oh, m'God! It's the crazy guy!

WALTERS: Crazy, am I? I'll tell you who's crazy! It's that devil of a brother Sarah has! It's him who caused the troopers to batter down my church. He's the devil's own man, that man is!

FLOSSIE: *(Innocently)* My Timmy?

WALTERS: Whosever Timmy he is! The man's a menace to society, bringing liquor into this town and then storing it in my church so's to bring the police in to accuse me of being a criminal, a bootlegger.

FLOSSIE: Oh! That's ridiculous!

WALTERS: That's what I said but they still dragged me down to the jail and it was only when police chief Rooney, I think it is, when the police chief saw me that I was freed. He told the troopers the whole story about my being the pastor of the church they just destroyed.

FLOSSIE: Well, you had somebody in your corner then!

WALTERS: A lot of good that did me! The captain of the troopers told the chief that it would be logical for me to stash—I think he said that word...stash—to stash the liquor in the basement. Chief Rooney vouched for me, and the trooper finally believed me, I think.

FLOSSIE: Well, there you are! Did they believe my Timmy?

WALTERS: No! And, why should they? But, they can't convict him because the liquor wasn't there when they broke into the church. Can you imagine? That Timmy of yours, why the man's a magician! A witness said they saw him put boxes into the church's basement last night and when the troopers broke in during the middle of the night, there wasn't a single box around.

FLOSSIE: Well, then! I'd call that a miracle! It's somebody *(looking up)* telling you that Timmy's innocent?

WALTERS: *(Still excited)* If Sarah won't believe her brother's innocent, why should I?

FLOSSIE: *(Goes to him)* There, there now! What's the saying...turn the other cheek! And what about "innocent until proved guilty"!

WALTERS: *(Still agitated)* Those things don't apply to that man! He's a charlatan!

FLOSSIE: I don't know about that! He is an Elk, if that's any help. *(Walters is still agitated. Flossie tries to comfort him)* How about a glass of water?

WALTERS: Water'll do me no good right now! I know Sarah had a bottle of her wine last night. Maybe a glass of that will do!

FLOSSIE: If you're sure the troopers won't break in and arrest us! *(Laughs. He gives her a grim look. She finds wine in the closet and pours two glasses)* You don't mind if I have a glass, do you?

WALTERS: No! Have two. I don't care! *(Takes glass)* Oh! My church's all destroyed. My good name besmirched. *(Flossie sits him down at kitchen table and sits close to him)*

FLOSSIE: *(Lifts his glass so he can take a drink)* Here! Have a little sip. It'll do you good.

WALTERS: *(Almost crying)* It's a terrible thing to lose one's good name. *(She helps him take another sip)*

FLOSSIE: Oh, I know! It's been so difficult keeping my own good name with all that swirls around me. *(Gives him another sip of wine)*

WALTERS: *(Looks at her in different light)* You were a good woman once, I bet!

FLOSSIE: Once, and still am, I'll have you know

WALTERS: But, hanging around with this Timmy McCoy man and people like him?

FLOSSIE: But, my heart is pure and that's what counts. *(She offers him another sip)*

WALTERS: But, is your heart pure? Are you free from sin? *(He raises her hand with the wine glass and takes another sip)*

FLOSSIE: Well, I've had my days...and nights! But, I think I'm good!

WALTERS: Then, you must leave this life of degradation and return to the pure world of your childhood. *(Takes another sip of wine)*

FLOSSIE: Yes! The rolling fields and the green trees and the back of the barn!

WALTERS: Back of the barn?

FLOSSIE: It was there that I learned about life, a life that brought me to this moment.

WALTERS: If you are ready to repent, then I can save you! *(Stands, takes her hands and raises her from her chair)* Are you ready to be saved?

FLOSSIE: Oh, yes! *(Moves toward him)*

WALTERS: Put yourself into my hands and I will save you! *(Draws her closer)*

FLOSSIE: Oh, yes! Oh, Yes! *(Embraces him)*

WALTERS: *(Exalted)* I will lift you up!

FLOSSIE: I'm ready!

WALTERS: *(Frenzied)* Yes! Yes! *(Moves his hand down her back and grabs her buttocks)*

FLOSSIE: *(Leans back)* Oh! You know "farmer and the sheep" too!

WALTERS: *(Dazed)* What?

(Door flies open as Sarah and Timmy enter arguing, followed by Colleen. Flossie and Walters freeze in place)

TIMMY: Now, Sarah! Will you quiet down, please!

SARAH: Quiet down....! *(She spots Flossie and Walters in a frozen embrace)* Oh. My God! I don't believe it. The world has gone to hell in a hand basket.

TIMMY: Flossie! What's all this about?

COLLEEN: Aunt Flossie! Reverend! *(Walters removes his hand as if from a hot stove)*

SARAH: Colleen! Stand back...they're evil!

WALTERS: Sarah..Colleen...I can explain!

SARAH: You can never explain this!!!!

FLOSSIE: Yes, he can! *(Thinks quickly)* I was feeling bad about Timmy and Rev. Walters here was feeling bad about his church..

235

SARAH: Oh! He was feeling bad alright!

FLOSSIE: No, really! He was trying to comfort me and I was trying to comfort him...and ..

TIMMY: Comfort, is it! Why, I ought to *(starts toward Walters)*...

SARAH *(To Timmy)* Stay out of this, you!

TIMMY: But, she's my girl!!!!

SARAH: Looks like she's everybody's girl!!!! John Walters....how could you?

WALTERS: *(Trying to gain control)* Sarah! The woman is a sinner and I was trying to save her!

SARAH: With your hand on her a....?

WALTERS: *(Quickly)* I thought she was going to faint. I was keeping her from falling.

FLOSSIE: *(Jumps in.)* That's it! I felt faint and he was trying to keep me from falling.

TIMMY: Flossie! Are you trying to con me?

FLOSSIE: No! It's true! 1 felt faint and the reverend was trying to help me.

TIMMY: That didn't look like artificial respiration he was giving you!

FLOSSIE: You know I love only you!

TIMMY: And, all I've done for you! *(Flossie moves to him, embraces him)*

SARAH: *(To Walters)* And, I thought you were a friend... trying to comfort Colleen and me! This is the image this poor girl has to carry with her all her life?

COLLEEN: Mother! Reverend Walters said he was trying to keep Flossie from fainting. That sounds like it could be true. I'm sure he'd do the same for you if you fainted. *(Sarah looks to protect her backside)*

SARAH: Not if I could help it!

COLLEEN: But, they sound so sincere!

SARAH: Honey! If you believe that story, I guarantee you're never going to leave this town, much less go to Rutland.

COLLEEN: Mother! That's not fair!

TIMMY: If the guys back in New York ever get wind of this, they'll laugh me off Broadway. My girl and a reverend playing grab ass.

FLOSSIE: *(Tries to take control)* Now, everybody! This is not doing any of us any good. It was perfectly innocent. The reverend and I were upset about what happened tonight and we were worried about you people with the police and everything.

SARAH: Sure, you were worried! A regular Salvation Army lassie! *(Spots wine bottle)* And you were saving each other with my wine!

TIMMY: What are you worried about your wine for? I just lost about 100 cases of some of the best booze those Frenchmen in Canada can make!

SARAH: Good riddance! I still don't know how you did that but at least we won't be put in jail if they can't find the booze.

TIMMY: Believe me, I'm no magician! I don't know where the stuff is any more than *(To Sarah)* you do or *(to Colleen)* you or *(Looks at Rev. Walters)*...wait a minute! How do we know you *(Points to Walters)* didn't find that liquor and sell it to someone.

WALTERS: Sir! That's a bald-faced lie and one that can bring damnation on your soul, if you have one.

SARAH: *(To Timmy)* Brother! I'm not happy with what went on here tonight with this woman of yours and a man I thought was my friend, but I will not believe that he had anything to do with the disappearance of your precious liquor.

TIMMY: You are blinded by your feelings for this man, that's all! But, look how he betrayed me with his manhandling of Flossie! I was shocked!

SARAH: Look who's shocked! The sensitive man you are!

COLLEEN: *(The peacemaker)* Why don't we all try to forget tonight and start all over!

SARAH: Oh, sure! The little peacemaker!

WALTERS: The young woman's right!

TIMMY: Colleen's right!

SARAH: *(To Timmy)* Sure! Side with her when it's to your advantage!

FLOSSIE: I agree with you, Colleen!

TIMMY: I'd feel better if I knew what happened to my liquor!

SARAH: You put your liquor above our feelings, do you?

TIMMY: Hey, sister! That liquor represents my future career!

FLOSSIE: Sarah! Why don't we all forgive and forget!

SARAH: What have you to forgive and forget?

FLOSSIE: You accused me of trying to seduce the reverend! That's what!

WALTERS: Sarah! I do feel you have misunderstood what you saw earlier. I was simply performing a mission of mercy.

TIMMY: I have another name for it!

COLLEEN: Uncle Tim! Let's forgive and forget, like Flossie said!

TIMMY: For your sake, Colleen! I'm willing to shake on it! *(Extends hand to Walters)*

WALTERS: *(Extends hand)* I'll do it as a man of peace and with the hope that Sarah believes I meant no harm.

SARAH: I'll think about it. I just want to have some peace around here.

FLOSSIE: Now, isn't that wonderful. Everybody is happy again!

SARAH: Don't push it, woman. Don't take too much for granted. *(Phone rings, Sarah answers it)* Oh! It's you. What do you want? Yes! He's here. *(Turns to Timmy)* It's the chief...Rooney!

TIMMY: *(Takes phone)* What is it, chief? What's that? Don't tell me! I'll be right there! *(Hangs up phone)* C'mon, Flossie!

FLOSSIE: Where're we going?

TIMMY *(Opens door, ushers her out)* There's been another miracle!

(BLACKOUT)

Scene Two

(Moments later, Walters is seated at the table, Sarah is at the stove, Colleen has gone to bed.)

WALTERS: Sarah! I'm sorry about what happened tonight!

SARAH: Keep your voice down, Colleen's trying to sleep! Besides, I don't want to talk about it.

WALTERS: I don't know what got into me! I really thought I was trying to help her but I became overwhelmed by her closeness, I guess!

SARAH: Maybe conversions should be made at a distance.

WALTERS: I have to admit, it must have been the wine, your wine!

SARAH: Oh! My wine is to blame now, is it?

WALTERS: No, No! I'm not saying that It's just that I'm not used to drinking wine. I'm not of the sect that drinks wine at their services.... especially homemade wine.

SARAH: You're still trying to blame it on my wine!

WALTERS: No, no, Sarah! I'm not blaming it on your wine or anything other than my own weakness....and arrogance.

SARAH: Arrogance!

WALTERS: Yes, arrogance! To believe a man like me, weak and lonely, could bring that woman back to redemption.

SARAH: She's a tough nut to crack, I'd say!

WALTERS: No! She's worthy of redemption and she seemed to be willing to change her ways.

SARAH: Look! She's my brother's girlfriend, just as tough as he is, willing to live the life at the brink of disaster, always looking for the good times.

WALTERS: But all men, and women...no matter how wicked they seem, are worthy of our efforts to reclaim them for the good life.

SARAH: Listen! They think they have the good life. We're the lost ones, according to them.

WALTERS: I cannot believe that or else my life as a clergyman has meant nothing!

SARAH: *(She sits at the table)* Look, John! I'll admit you're a good man who may take himself too seriously...

WALTERS: But, this is serious business!

SARAH: What I'm saying is that you may be in over your head! You've never met sinners like these two and the people they hang out with!

WALTERS: We are tested in strange and mysterious ways!

SARAH: Believe me! These two are strange and mysterious!

WALTERS: Since my wife died four years ago, I have only my calling to help me. I cannot admit to myself that I am not a worthy clergyman incapable of helping sinners.

SARAH: John! There are sinners and there are sinners. Timmy and his Flossie are major league sinners. These two would test the patience of Job!

WALTERS: So, you're saying my life has been a sham...a lost cause!

SARAH: No! I'm not saying that. You've done very well I would say. Certainly, your ministry here in town has been well received. Surely, in the last two years, you've been a real comfort to me...and to Colleen. I'm really grateful!

WALTERS: I've looked forward to our meetings and the conversations we've had, Sarah! They have meant so much to me. If I've brought you some comfort, then I feel rewarded by that knowledge.

SARAH: I've grown to think of you as a real good friend, not just a clergyman.

WALTERS: Have you, Sarah? I'm glad because I see you as more than a parishioner.

SARAH: You have! Even Colleen has noticed that!

WALTERS: She has? I'm glad!

SARAH: That's why I was so hurt when I saw you in the arms of that woman!

WALTERS: Oh, Sarah! I will never forgive myself. My religious ardor at the time became clouded with the wine and her exotic scent and the nearness of her body....

SARAH: You don't need to describe it again!

WALTERS: She was the first woman I've been close to since I lost my wife.

SARAH: We haven't been close?

WALTERS: No! I mean yes! I mean physically close. With Flossie, I was reduced to the basest instincts of a man!

SARAH: Well, as a woman, I'm sort of pleased to know that you have such instincts...but not to be wasted on a woman who makes a habit of arousing such instincts.

WALTERS: *(With emphasis)* Oh, Sarah! Say you'll forgive me, please!

SARAH: You have to forgive yourself first.

WALTERS: No! Only if you'll forgive me... because you mean so much to me!

SARAH: I forgive you, John! Now, let's not talk of it any more!

WALTERS: No! Let's talk of us!

SARAH: *(Coyly)* Us?

WALTERS: Yes, Sarah! I can't bear it any longer. I want you as a part of my life, a woman to share my every moment, a woman to keep my eye on my mission, and a woman I can care for and treasure as my partner in life.

SARAH: Are you saying what I think you're saying?

WALTERS: Yes, Sarah! I want you to be my wife and helpmate!

SARAH: Wife? Helpmate?

WALTERS: Yes! Wife! Helpmate!

SARAH: This is so sudden. I'm overwhelmed!

WALTERS: Please say "Yes!"

SARAH: *(Moves towards him, he embraces her)* Yes!...Yes!

(They kiss as his hand moves down her back but before it reaches her buttocks, she gently reaches for his hand and moves it back up to her shoulder blades, all without breaking the embrace or kiss while the lights go slowly black)

Scene Three

(Sarah is sitting at the table a short while later as Colleen enters room)

COLLEEN: Oh! It's wonderful!

SARAH: What is, dear?

COLLEEN: I heard enough of your conversation to know that you're going to get married.

SARAH: Married?

COLLEEN: Yes, married!

SARAH: You heard?

COLLEEN: I couldn't help it!

SARAH: Well, Reverend Walters still has to make plans and so do I.

COLLEEN: Mama! Call him John....that's his name. I heard you call him that earlier.

SARAH: Well, I didn't expect to have some busybody daughter listening in!

COLLEEN: I can't help it. Oh! Mama! I'm so happy for you!

SARAH: Well, don't go counting your chickens. We have a lot to work out before we think of getting married.

COLLEEN: Like what? You're not children. What do you have to work out?

SARAH: Where will we live, for one thing?

COLLEEN: Well, I would think we'll live in the parish house. I don't think the troopers broke into the parish house, do you?

SARAH: I don't know! But we can't be presumptuous. After all, he hasn't had any children and if we marry, he'll have a stepdaughter. He might not be ready for that.

COLLEEN: Why not? He'll be my stepfather who's a minister...isn't that wonderful?

SARAH: You'll have to act different than you do now if you have a minister for a stepfather.

COLLEEN: Why? I'm a good daughter, am I not? I haven't caused you any trouble, have I?

SARAH: *(Puts her arm around Colleen)* No! You haven't but I worry about you...about your future.

COLLEEN: We'll work that out once you're married.

SARAH: We'll have to. I don't want John to have that responsibility too.

COLLEEN: Well, he's always been helpful to both of us when we had a problem.

SARAH: Yes, he has! And, I guess that's why I think so highly of him.

COLLEEN: Highly? Admit it, mother! That's why you love him!

SARAH: Never mind your young romantic ideas! Who's talking about love?

COLLEEN: You are...even though not in so many words.

SARAH: So don't go putting words in my mouth. I'm too old for that!

COLLEEN: You're never too old for love!

SARAH: Those are some of your ideas from the motion pictures, I suppose.

COLLEEN: No! I read too. People of all ages fall in love! So, there!

(Knock on door. Sarah goes to it and opens the door. Walters enters in a happy frame of mind.)

WALTERS: Sarah! I called Rev. Maranville in Rutland...Rev. Robert Maranville. We went to the seminary together. He said he'd be pleased to marry us. Isn't that wonderful?

COLLEEN: Oh! It's wonderful...Isn't it, mother?

SARAH: Now, John! Aren't you rushing this too fast!

WALTERS: No! I took you at your word. Soon... .is ... soon!

COLLEEN: That's right, mother!

SARAH: Colleen, please! This is a matter for John and me.

COLLEEN: Alright! *(She starts to leave the room)* Don't forget I need addresses to write your invitations! *(Laughs, exits)*

WALTERS: Sarah! Robert said he'd take some services here while we went on a honeymoon! Isn't that wonderful?

SARAH: Honeymoon! I'm overwhelmed. I never even thought of a honeymoon.

WALTERS: Well, think of it please! I'd love to take a trip with you, anywhere you wanted to go.

SARAH: I can't even think of where I'd want to go. It's been so long since I've been out of Whitehall, much less on a vacation...or a honeymoon!

WALTERS: Please think of it!

SARAH: But, how could we ever repay Robert... Rev. Maranville... for helping us!

WALTER: We'll find some way. Maybe he and his wife might want to take a trip sometime and we'll cover for him.

SARAH: Yes, we could, couldn't we?

WALTERS: And, maybe I could help him find a woman to handle the secretarial work around his parish. The woman who's been with him for 15 years became ill and had to move to her sister's in Boston.

SARAH: He has a secretary? Is he that busy!

WALTERS: He has a very big parish, Sarah, very big! It's Rutland, after all!

SARAH: Yes, it is...Rutland! *(Colleen comes running out of her room)*

COLLEEN: Oh! Rev. Walters! Tell Rev. Maranville that I can take shorthand and I can do secretarial work and I...

SARAH: Colleen! What are you doing butting in like this?

COLLEEN: Oh, mother! It would be perfect. I could have a job that I would like and I'm sure I could find a nice place to live...

WALTERS: Robert's previous secretary had her own room in the big parish house. She would help his wife Martha at times too!

COLLEEN: It sounds perfect, mother!

SARAH: You're being presumptuous, Colleen!

WALTERS: Now, Sarah! It might be a very good thing. I know Colleen is an industrious young woman and would be a big help to Robert and his wife. If it's something she'd want to do and you approved, Sarah, I'd be perfectly willing to speak to Robert.

SARAH: Well, we'll see, we'll see!

COLLEEN: *(Embraces her mother, turns and starts to embrace Walters who quickly takes her hands and holds her at a distance)*

Oh, mother...Rev. Walters...I'm so happy for you and ... for me!

(Door opens quickly. Timmy and Flossie enter)

SARAH: Here goes our happiness!

TIMMY: It's a miracle I tell ya!

FLOSSIE: You're a wonder, Timmy, m'love!

WALTERS: What's a miracle?

TIMMY: I'm back in business!

SARAH: You are? I thought you lost your liquor!

FLOSSIE: He found it again!

TIMMY: Yeah! Only now I have a partner!

SARAH: A partner!

TIMMY: Yeah! Rooney...

SARAH: That run-down police chief?

FLOSSIE: That's him!

TIMMY: You see...he found out that the troopers were going to stage a raid because someone saw me put the boxes in the church basement. So Rooney took them out and hid them in the jail. When the troopers broke into the church they didn't find a thing. That's your miracle worker, reverend...Rooney!

SARAH: So, now you're partners?

TIMMY: That's right! He's taking half the profits and he worked out a deal with our cousin Michael to get an old milk truck that we can convert so we can carry boxes in the tank.

WALTERS: *(To Sarah)* Your cousin, Michael?

SARAH: Yes! We have a cousin Michael...who rebuilds cars and trucks. *(To Timmy)* So, he's in your scheme too!

TIMMY: No, not really! We will pay him so much each trip for the truck with a little interest on the side. He'll never see the liquor or touch it.

WALTERS: But, what about the chief?

TIMMY: He'll be my partner in distribution. Each trip Flossie and I make from Canada with the truck, we give him half the boxes at the price I pay and he sells them here. He gets the profits. I take the rest to good old New York City and make m'fortune.

SARAH: Oh! It's a fine scheme you have!

FLOSSIE: Isn't it wonderful? Timmy'll be a rich man and I'll be his wife.

COLLEEN: *(Blurts out)* Uncle Tim! Mother and Rev. Walters are getting married!

FLOSSIE: Married, are you?

TIMMY: Married, are you? Well, now, isn't that wonderful!

FLOSSIE: Oh, yes! Married...Sarah, you're so lucky!

SARAH: Well, I think I'm quite fortunate...yes, I do!

FLOSSIE: Timmy! Isn't that wonderful? They're getting married!

TIMMY: Yes, it's wonderful!

FLOSSIE: I always wanted to be married! Then, I met you, Timmy!

SARAH: That's the end of that dream, m'girl!

COLLEEN: Why should it, mother!

FLOSSIE: Yes! Timmy, I'll say yes, if you ask me!

TIMMY: Flossie, this is so sudden!

SARAH: Sudden! You've been with the woman for years!

TIMMY: Well, it takes time to know one another!

SARAH: I'm afraid there's very little else to know about one another.

FLOSSIE: *(Light goes on, snaps her fingers)* Timmy, who won the Travers race last week at Saratoga?

TIMMY: I think it was Wanderlust...yeah...Wanderlust...

(Without thinking) a filly!

FLOSSIE: There, it's fate! You said you'd marry me when a filly won the Travers!

TIMMY: But.. .that was just a.....!

WALTERS: To make use of your New York vernacular...are you going to welsh on your bet, Tim?

TIMMY: You got me, reverend! I'm a man of m'word. *(Turns to Flossie)* Will you marry me, Flossie?

FLOSSIE: Will I? Does the moon come over the mountain? Of course, I will, in spades!

COLLEEN: Isn't it wonderful! Rev. Walters and Uncle Tim will be brothers-in-law! And Flossie will be your sister-in-law, mother!

SARAH: Don't remind me!

FLOSSIE: I think it's wonderful! Hey! I know!! Let's have a double wedding.!

SARAH: Now, wait a minute !

WALTERS: *(Caught up with the enthusiasm)* Sarah! As long as Rev. Maranville will be here for us, he can make it a ...*(To Timmy)* how do you say...a daily double!

TIMMY: That's it, reverend! It sounds good! *(He's now caught up with enthusiasm)* I'll tell you what I'll do. *(To Walters)* As a wedding present, I'll take my profits from this trip and give it to you to repair the church.

WALTERS: That's very generous of you!

SARAH: Generous, m'eye! It's the least he can do.

WALTERS: Now, Sarah! Let's not have any more rancor. Let's be one happy family!

SARAH: *(Derisively)* I can't wait for the Christmas dinners!

FLOSSIE: Oh, Timmy! I've go to pick out my wedding dress and clothes for our honeymoon.

TIMMY: Well, let's get started downstate with the stuff so I can distribute it or we'll have no wedding.

FLOSSIE: *(Takes turns hugging Colleen and Sarah enthusiastically and Walters with some reserve)* Oh! I can't wait.

TIMMY: *(Starts towards the door)* Goodbye, folks! See you at church!

FLOSSIE: *(Follows him, turns to others)* Wait until I tell all the girls at the club. You're going to love them when they come up for the ceremony...*(as she exits)* I wonder if Kiki will be my maid of honor! *(Sarah sits at table shaking her head, Walters tries to console her and Colleen beams as lights come to blackout)*

THE END

"Christmas on the Canal"

By Martin P. Kelly

Copyright, 2004

Time: Christmas, 1933

Place: Rectory of Rev. John Walters

CHARACTERS

SARAH WALTERS … a native of Whitehall, widowed at the time when she met and married minister ….

JOHN WALTERS … a local clergyman who since married is arbiter between Sarah and her brother …

TIMMY McCOY … also a native of Whitehall who made "good" in New York City as a bootlegger but is now an almost famous Hollywood producer who lives in Hollywood as husband of Flossie who is now….

FELICIA TOVRAK … practically famous femme fatale of "B" movies, queen of the second features and beauty adviser to…

COLLEEN MEADOWS … the daughter of Sarah Walters and niece of Timmy McCoy. who is Rev. Walters' secretary and married for two years to…

RANDALL MEADOWS … a local young Whitehall veterinarian who studied in Rutland, Vermont.

Note from the Author

I had the good fortune that when my play, "Cases On The Canal," a comedy about the Prohibition era in the town of Whitehall, NY, was produced at the Bridge Theater, audiences took to the characters and the tongue-in-cheek tone of the script. I was urged to do a sequel to the play, using the same characters but at a later point in their lives.

For this play, "Christmas On The Canal," I chose five years later at a holiday time when the leading character, a bootlegger in the first play with a chorus girl as his companion, now returns as a movie producer who has filmed an early talkie movie about Whitehall as a canal port.

He has decided to premiere the film in Whitehall so his friends and relatives can see his handiwork and also view the talents of his companion, Flossie, a former night club dancer but now a movie femme fatale.

This play has not been produced to date but will be as soon as it can be scheduled at a suitable Whitehall venue.

The earlier plays in this book deal with history, either directly with the Whitehall region or nationally during the American Revolutionary period. As I view it, "Cases On The Canal" and this play, "Christmas On The Canal," provide a comic view of local Whitehall history that, quite frankly, could have been mirrored in many communities through the United States during the times in these plays.

MARTIN P. KELLY
June 19, 2010

ACT ONE

Scene One

TIME: *Two Days before Christmas, 1933*

PLACE: *Dining room of Rev. Walter's rectory. Rev. Walters is reading a newspaper, when suddenly the front door is heard opening off stage and slamming shut. Sarah enters room, carrying a letter and fuming.*

SARAH: Did you read this?

JOHN: It's the first time I've seen it!

SARAH: Right! Well, I just got it at the post office and it's the worst news ever!

JOHN: Worst news?

SARAH: Yes! My no-good brother and his floozy wife are coming to Christmas dinner.

JOHN: That's wonderful! You invited them, after all!

SARAH: I certainly did not! They're coming here without an invitation! I know that you asked them for several years but they were always too busy, thank God!

JOHN: Well, I still think it's good to have the family together.

SARAH: Family..family?

JOHN: Yes! Family! After all, he's your only brother and it is Christmas...a time for bonding and forgiveness.

SARAH: Bonding? The only thing he's bonded in his life was the bootleg liquor he sold during Prohibition.

JOHN: That's not what I mean, Sarah!

SARAH: Don't your remember the mess he created at this church six years ago when he hid cases of bootleg liquor in the basement.

JOHN: But, all turned out well, didn't it?

SARAH: But not before the troopers were ready to accuse you of hiding the liquor! We were lucky we had a fool for a police chief who got it out of the church before the troopers actually found it.

JOHN: Yes! Rooney was quite a miracle worker, wasn't he?

SARAH: He was a run-down excuse of a police chief who made money when he became my brother's partner.

JOHN: Yes! And as a result, he was able to move to Florida as head of security for a Miami Beach hotel.

SARAH: Room thieves must have a field day at that hotel!

JOHN: I wish you wouldn't get so upset.

SARAH: Upset? Who's upset?

JOHN: You are, that's who!

SARAH: Now, you're taking Timmy's side!

JOHN: I am not. Look Sarah, Timmy's your brother and I'm sure he means you well.

SARAH: He certainly knows how to show it. Aren't you forgetting that lovely double wedding we had six years ago?

JOHN: Of course I remember it. We began our life together.

SARAH: Sure! You and me and Timmy and that Flossie were a picture standing before your friend, Rev. Maranville.

JOHN: I thought we made a marvelous quartet.

SARAH: Yes, but what about the gangster Legs Diamond as my brother's best man and Legs' girl friend, Kiki Roberts, as Flossie's maid of honor.

JOHN: I remember!

SARAH: And, there was Legs Diamond's wife sitting in one of the front pews. I couldn't wait for the fireworks.

JOHN: Well, you didn't have to wait long. That was some action at the parish hall reception, I'll grant you.

SARAH: Some? Some? Sure, there was action with everyone two sheets to the wind from the bootleg gin my brother brought to the reception. Then, Legs dances up a storm with his girlfriend and Alice Diamond pulls a gun and chases Kiki into the church. Remember?

JOHN: How can I ever forget? It was good she didn't have her glasses on or we would have been burying Legs' girlfriend the next morning.

SARAH: Sure! The bullet went through the cross above the altar.

JOHN: Something heavenly was looking over us that day.

SARAH: And now there's a bullet hole.

JOHN: Be charitable Sarah! After all, Mr. Legs was killed two years later by some of his enemies.

SARAH: Good riddance!

JOHN: Sarah! Charity …charity.

SARAH: Then, his two women got it several years later. Dutch Schultz caught up with them after all.

JOHN: We should pray for their souls.

SARAH: I'm sure the angels have their hands full with them, I'd say. Legs probably has a heavenly speakeasy going full blast!

JOHN: Now, please calm down, Sarah. What did the letter say?

SARAH: It says that the two of them just arrived in New York by train from the West Coast and they'll drive up here. They're on the road now, I'd guess.

JOHN: They're driving here, you say?

SARAH: According to the postmark, they could be here anytime.

JOHN: Well, we have enough room to put them up for the holidays.

SARAH: No way, John! Let them stay at the hotel next to the railroad station.

JOHN: That's not very charitable, Sarah!

SARAH: Forget charity! I'm just trying to keep sanity in this house.

JOHN: We'll do well, Sarah, we'll do well!

SARAH: I'm trying to make sure we will!

(Door is heard opening in front hall. Colleen and Randall are laughing as they enter the dining room brushing snow off their coats.)

COLLEEN: Mother! The dogs love playing in the snow.

SARAH: I'm glad the dogs are happy!

RANDALL: Yes, Mrs. Walters! It helps in their recovery to play out in the big yard we have at the animal hospital.

JOHN: You're a good doctor, Randall.

COLLEEN: And, a wonderful husband!

SARAH: That's all very good, Colleen, but we have a problem.

COLLEEN: What problem mother?

JOHN: Now, Timmy and Flossie shouldn't be considered a problem.

SARAH: *(To Colleen)* Your Uncle Timmy and that Flossie are visiting us for Christmas!

COLLEEN: Are they, mother? Good! They got my invitation!

SARAH: You! You! You sent them an invitation? How could you! They'll spoil Christmas for us just like everything else.

JOHN: We must be charitable, Sarah!

SARAH: Must you always be a forgiving clergyman? Can't you get upset sometimes?

JOHN: It's not Christian to be angry, especially with family members!

SARAH: Family! I've got to believe he was adopted.

JOHN: Well, he wasn't, so please get a grip on yourself.

SARAH: I wish I took a grip on him when he was a kid, right around his neck!

COLLEEN: Mother! I think Uncle Timmy is a good man!

SARAH: Oh, you do! Don't you remember our wedding when you were my maid of honor standing along with those two showgirl hussies.

COLLEEN: I like Flossie! And Kiki Roberts seemed nice too as much as I knew about her.

RANDALL: They looked good in the wedding pictures!

SARAH: Sure, the wedding pictures! They could have been hung up on the post office wall. Believe me, they were trouble. You wouldn't know, you weren't in the family yet.

RANDALL: Well, if Colleen liked them, I'm sure I would.

SARAH: You're sure going to get a chance to meet this Flossie soon, no thanks to your bride here!

COLLEEN: Her name's Felicia now?

SARAH: That's all very good Colleen, but we have a problem.

JOHN: Her name's Felicia now?

SARAH: Sure! Now, she's the "big" movie star…queen of the "B" movies, the empress of the second features.

COLLEEN: She's sure popular!

SARAH: So's Rin Tin Tin!

JOHN: Now, Sarah, please let's not have any more quarreling over Timmy and Flossie..'er...Felicia!

SARAH: I'm sorry John. I still can't forget the way my brother and his friends ruined my wedding.

JOHN: We're married, aren't we? Now, isn't that all you need to remember?

SARAH: But, I'm sure our neighbors can't forget when Legs and his gang ran out of the reception when word came that Dutch Schultz's gang just passed through Fort Anne on their way to kill him.

JOHN: Chief Rooney was smart not to interfere. He called the troopers! I still don't know how Legs Diamond got away from the Schultz gang.

COLLEEN: Don't you remember! Uncle Timmy showed him a back way out of town towards Rutland. Then he went south and was in Troy before Mr. Schultz knew he had escaped.

RANDALL: Your uncle's quite a guy!

SARAH: Just wait! You still haven't met him.

RANDALL: No! But I'm sure I'll like him.

COLLEEN: Oh, you will, you will!

SARAH: *(Phone rings, Sarah answers it)*: Oh! It's you. You're what? Your car's stuck in the snow outside of town. *(Hand over mouthpiece.)* It's him! *(Into the mouthpiece)* What do you want me to do about it? Pick you up! Now, wait a minute...!

RANDALL: Colleen and I will go, Mrs. Walters!

SARAH: No, you won't. Let him get himself out of the snow.

COLLEEN: Please! It's Christmas time.

SARAH: Okay! Then, let Santa Claus pick him up..

RANDALL: We can do it!

SARAH: *(Into phone)* My son-in-law is foolish enough to come and get you. Be good! He doesn't know you! *(Hangs up. Randall and Colleen put on their coats and start to leave)*

SARAH: Randall! On second thought, why don't you send one of your St. Bernard dogs after him....one with a bad sense of direction..

(BLACKOUT)

Scene Two

(Several hours later. Randall and Colleen are sitting at the dining room table and drinking warm cocoa, trying to thaw out from their rescue trip)

RANDALL: That uncle of yours is quite a guy, Colleen!

COLLEEN: I admit he seems a little crazy but I do like him.

RANDALL: And, that Felicia is really something, too! She's beautiful and mysterious looking. Nothing like the showgirl your mother keeps talking about.

COLLEEN: Well, I don't know all the details but from what I hear, a big Hollywood producer who owns this small studio, owed Uncle Timmy a lot of money for some reason. And, it seems they worked out a deal where Flossie became the studio's star.

RANDALL: Really!!

COLLEEN: But, because other studios had Ginger Rogers and Ruby Keeler as dancers, this producer decided to change Aunt Flossie into playing an international spy. She took lessons from Gloria Swanson's acting teacher and Marlene Dietrich's vocal coach.

RANDALL: So, you have a whole different aunt!

COLLEEN: I guess so!

RANDALL: She sure looks European, doesn't she?

COLLEEN: You'd never recognize her from her dancing days!

RANDALL; I think she's really beautiful!

COLLEEN: You've said that already!

RANDALL: Well, I mean…

COLLEEN: I know what you mean! I remember seeing her with Rev. Walters. She almost seduced him!

RANDLE: She did?

COLLEEN: It was all very innocent they said, but mother was furious when she caught them in an embrace after drinking wine together…. mother's wine.

RANDALL: Wow! I guess I married into quite a family!

COLLEEN: But, I'm hoping that you bring some sanity into it. Still, we seem to put fun in dysfunctional.

RANDALL: When you came to Rutland to work as Rev. Maranville's secretary, I couldn't believe it. I missed you! You know that?

COLLEEN: And, I missed you! When you left Whitehall to study with a veterinarian, I thought maybe you'd never come back.

RANDALL: When you took that job in Rutland, I knew I wanted to come back to Whitehall with you when I finished my studies.

COLLEEN: I wanted to be with you and to help you and to let you know I missed you and I loved you.

RANDALL: You did all those things.

COLLEEN: And, when you graduated and asked me to marry you, it was the happiest day of my life.

RANDALL: Mine, too!

COLLEEN: And, I wanted to be such a part of your life.

RANDALL: Well, I know that I wouldn't have been able to establish a practice here without your help. You and your family found me an office with a large backyard that I could convert into a kennel.

COLLEEN: *(Kisses him on cheek)* You know that I really wanted to help the man I love.

RANDALL: And you're the woman I love. *(Quick kiss on her lips as Sarah enters)*

SARAH: Is that all you got to do, sit around and act like a couple of love-sick pups!

COLLEEN: We were just talking about how lucky we were being able to start the veterinary business.

SARAH: Thanks to all our animal-loving friends in Whitehall and John's parishioners.

RANDALL: We're so grateful for your assistance and Rev. Walters' help.

SARAH: Well, he certainly wanted the best for you and Colleen.

COLLEEN: And, he sure did help us.

SARAH: That's why he deserves better than he's received from my brother Timmy.

RANDALL: How so, Mrs. Walters?

SARAH: It was bad enough that my brother invited gangsters and showgirls to our wedding but he insisted on going on our honey-moon with us. It was his treat!

RANDALL: Really! That was nice of him.

SARAH: Oh, sure it was! My brother had a friend with two cottages on Cape Cod so we could spend time with him and his Flossie. John thought it was very generous but then he always sees the sunny side of everything.

COLLEEN: Well, it was a wonderful gesture.

SARAH: But, don't forget, it was still Prohibition.

RANDALL: What did that matter?

SARAH: Everything!

COLLEEN: Oh, mother!!

SARAH: Let me tell you! We got a flat tire in Bennington and a motorcycle cop tried to help us. When he took the spare tire out of the trunk, he broke a bottle of booze Timmy was carrying with about another dozen bottles in the trunk. I guess he figured he'd pay for the Cape Cod honeymoon with the sale of the liquor.

RANDALL: Did the cop do anything?

SARAH: He was ready to haul us all off to jail. Can you imagine, spending the first night of your honeymoon in jail? And, John a clergyman!

COLLEEN: But you didn't!

SARAH: No! Timmy called a former bootlegger's lawyer in Albany who contacted the Bennington judge who let us go. Before we left, the judge said something to Timmy, like "you have my address, right?" I'm sure the judge had a secret liquor delivery in a few days.

RANDALL: That certainly was a close call.

SARAH: My brother's whole life is a close call!

COLLEEN: Still, he always seems to squeeze out of trouble with a smile on his face.

SARAH: Yes, a crooked one! Listen, I certainly didn't have a smile on my face at your wedding two years ago.

COLLEEN: I was sorry he and Flossie couldn't come.

SARAH: Thankfully, they were tied up making a movie on the West Coast.

RANDALL: But, he was with us in spirit.

SARAH: I'll say! Prohibition was over but not his hi-jinks.

COLLEEN: But, he meant well!

SARAH: Why couldn't he have just sent you some money for your wedding? No! No! He has to be a big man. It certainly was a surprise.

RANDALL: I'll say!

SARAH: Sure! Hiring Guy Lombardo and his Royal Canadians to play at your wedding! He really outdid himself.

COLLEEN: But, they're the best orchestra in the country!

SARAH: And, from what I heard, he got them at half price because they were able to stop overnight to do the wedding on their way home to Canada.

COLLEEN: They really were good, playing up there on the stage at the American Legion hall.

SARAH: And, we had everybody in town trying to crash the reception to hear the band.

RANDALL: And, then Rev. Walters suggested we let them come in to listen and dance.

SARAH: *(Starts towards kitchen)* Oh! That husband of mine! They cheered him when he invited them all in. *(Stops)* And then they danced away with all the food!

(BLACKOUT)

Scene Three

(The stage is vacant when lights come up but there are sounds of noise and cheering from a crowd outside of the house. Sarah comes bustling in from stage left hallway and looks out the window. She dashes to the hallway and calls

upstairs for her husband, Colleen and Randall to come down. It is Christmas Eve afternoon)

SARAH: *(At window)* John! John! *(Moves quickly to the hallway, calls out)* John! John! Colleen..Randall! Come down quickly! *(She moves back to the window at upstage right of center, as Colleen and Randall enter room)*

COLLEEN: What is it, mother?

RANDALL: Are you alright, Mrs Walters?

SARAH: Of course, I'm alright but we won't be for long.

COLLEEN: *(Looks out window)* Why, mother, why?

SARAH: Do you see what's happening out there?

RANDALL: *(Looking out window)* Isn't it wonderful, Mrs. Walters?

SARAH: No! It's not wonderful! Up until I heard that noise outside, I had hoped my brother and his movie star wife would get another invitation to dinner… maybe in Canada.

COLLEEN: Now, mother! Look at the way all the people in town are greeting them. *(Looking out window)* They're trying to get Aunt Felicia's autograph.

SARAH: I didn't know she could write! And, she's not your aunt!!!

RANDALL: *(To Colleen)* It looks like your Uncle Timmy is throwing something to the kids.

SARAH: He's what? *(Rushes to the window)* My god, he's doing just that. The kids are scrambling all over the ground, picking up coins. *(John Walters enters)*

JOHN: What seems to be the problem, Sarah?

SARAH: That crazy brother of mine has a crowd outside and they're tying up traffic on the street. Even the horses are frightened.

JOHN: *(John goes to the window)* Oh! I see. Oh, wait!! They're coming towards the front door.

SARAH: *(Alarmed)* Who is?

JOHN: Why, Timmy and his wife.

SARAH: *(Looks out window)* And, they're bringing the crowd with them!.

(John goes to front door, and greets Timmy and Felicia)

JOHN: *(Offstage)* Oh! How good it is to see you again. *(To crowd)* Now people, thank you for your enthusiasm but my brother-in-law and his wife need their rest. They've had a very busy and exhausting trip.

(John closes door as Timmy and Felicia enter dining room. Timmy has a cashmere topcoat draped around his shoulders and a fedora with the brim turned up on one side. Felicia is wearing a long fur coat and a fur hat to match. When John and Randall take their coats out to the hall. Timmy is wearing a dark, fitted striped suit with vest and "old school" tie. Felicia is revealed in below knee length black beaded gown with a jeweled choker around her neck. She is wearing long gloves that she removes seductively.)

TIMMY: Season's greetings to everyone!

FELICIA: *(Broad German accent)* Oh! My dears! It is so good to see you again!

JOHN: Welcome to our humble home! *(Felicia brushes his cheek with her hand while Timmy gives him a hearty hand shake.)*

TIMMY: *(With feeling)* It's great to be back in the village of my birth!

SARAH: Oh, God! Are we in trouble!

JOHN: Now, Sarah!

FELICIA: *(Embraces Sarah)* Oh, Sarah! It makes my heart full to see you again.

SARAH: It's full alright..full of cr…

JOHN: Now, Sarah, please!

TIMMY: Yes, dear sister of mine! It's the holidays and we've left our busy schedule to spend them with you.

FELICIA: And, where's my divine niece!

(Colleen and Randall enter room)

COLLEEN: Here I am aunt Fl...oh, it's Aunt Felicia now!

FELICIA: *(Kisses Colleen's cheek)* Yes! My dear!

SARAH: I told you, Colleen, she's not your aunt!!!!

COLLEEN: *(Ignores her mother)* Uncle Timmy, Felicia! I'd like you to meet my husband, Randall Meadows.

TIMMY: *(Shakes Randall's hand)* Great to meet you! You've got a wonderful girl there!

RANDALL: I know that, Mr. McCoy!

TIMMY: Let's forget the formality, Randall. It's just Uncle Tim from now on!

FELICIA: *(Seductively to Randall)* My! Aren't you handsome! *(Embraces him)* You ought to be in the movies! *(Randall is embarrassed, mutters "Gee, thanks!)*

SARAH: Colleen, keep your eye on this one!

FELICIA: I want to make a film about Christmas!

COLLEEN: Well, there's "A Christmas Carol!"

FELICIA: Ah! A wonderful story! Timmy is trying to get the author to make Scrooge a woman's role.

SARAH: Charles Dickens has been dead for 50 years.

TIMMY: No matter! Felicia is a bigger star than Dickens! Did you see her in "Murder in Shanghai?"

COLLEEN: Yes! It was wonderful and scary! You were so good playing the Chinese woman forced to choose between your family and that handsome English spy.

FELICIA: Yes! Osgood was wonderful to work with except he talked funny...you know an accent and all that!

TIMMY: Listen, folks! Felicia has her choice of leading men.

SARAH: Working for that flea-bitten studio in Hollywood! Why, I swear I saw a cowboy on a horse in the background of that London scene.

RANDALL: Yes! I saw that. It was funny!

FELICIA: It was not supposed to be funny, my dear!

TIMMY: We were working next to the set of a Hoot Gibson picture, that's all. We didn't have time to re-shoot it.

FELICIA: Yes! And that Hungarian film editor forgot to cut it out! I was totally embarrassed at the world premiere in Milwaukee.

COLLEEN: Milwaukee? Why there, Uncle Tim!

TIMMY: I was able to get a tie-in promotion with Stutts beer. Old man Stutts put up a good portion of the money to make the film.

SARAH: You never go far from beer, do you?

TIMMY: Experience counts for everything, dear sister!

SARAH: And, you got plenty of that!.

FELICIA: My Timmy has made me a star. *(Dramatically)* I am on top of the world.

SARAH: Sure! You're the queen of the "B" movies, every man's dream in the second feature.

TIMMY: It was my plan, Sarah, m'girl! We carved out a piece of the Hollywood action. Let Warner Brothers, Columbia, MGM and 20th Century Fox fight it out for screening the first features. We, at World-Wide Films, will make our mark with the films for the masses, those people who want full value for their ticket money...the second feature.

JOHN: It seems like a good business decision, Tim!

TIMMY: You can bet on it, Reverend.

COLLEEN: We are proud of both of you, Uncle Timmy! You left town six years ago...

SARAH: ...One step ahead of the cops....

COLLEEN: *(Ignoring her mother)*...on your way to New York to make your fortune in illegal liquor and now you return a big business man with Flossie as a...

FELICIA:... Felicia, my dear! Felicia!

COLLEEN: Why did you change you name from Flossie Travell to Felicia Tvorak?

FELICIA: Well, my dear, Felicia Tvorak is far more continental. Besides, Timmy bought me a beautiful set of monogrammed matched luggage for our honeymoon and I didn't want to change the initials!

COLLEEN: Uncle Timmy, you helped change a night club dancer into an international star.

SARAH: But they'll never get out of that broken down studio on the shady side of Hollywood. International star, my eye!

TIMMY: Our films tell stories of adventures all around the world with Felicia as an international beauty matching wits with enemy spies as they attempt to take over the good old U.S. of A.

RANDALL: How did you go from "paint remover" salesman to a Hollywood producer.

TIMMY: Paint remover?

SARAH: Do you think I was going to tell the boy Colleen's uncle sold illegal bootleg liquor. Now, that they're married that's another thing!

TIMMY: No matter! Well, as we were coming back from our honeymoon after that near miss getting arrested in Bennington, I looked at my beautiful Floosie sitting there beside me in the car and decided she deserved better than flashing her legs at cops to get bootleg gin past them.

JOHN: That is very inspiring!

SARAH: Inspiring? Have you lost your mind, John? He just saw the handwriting on the wall. Prohibition was a dying duck once President Roosevelt took office.

JOHN: Reformation for any reason is still praiseworthy!

SARAH: John! You always seem to be talking in sermons.

COLLEEN: *(To Timmy)* Well, I'm glad you changed your profession. I can boast to all my friends about you and Aunt Felicia!

SARAH: She's not your aunt!!!

FELICIA: Yes, my dear! I'm too young to be your aunt.

COLLEEN: But you were my Aunt Flossie!

FELICIA: Yes! But Felicia Tvorak belongs to everybody! She is a woman for the world.

SARAH: Nothing's much changed! Flossie belonged to everybody, too!

TIMMY: Never mind, Colleen! When I found that I could strike a deal with old man Stutts, I took my chances with the movies.

COLLEEN: How did you meet Mr. Stutts?

TIMMY: Well, I saved him from getting killed by Al Capone's gang in Chicago.

RANDALL: Really! How?

TIMMY: Well some of Legs Diamond's old gang told me that Harry Stutts was due to be rubbed out in a garage in Chicago on Valentine's Day.

COLLEEN: How awful!

TIMMY: And, he owed me a lot of money because of the booze I got him from Canada for his speakeasy!

JOHN: And that was the reason you're making movies?

TIMMY: When I tipped him off about Capone, he made sure he was in Milwaukee for Valentine's Day. I saved his life and he still owed me money.

JOHN: It was that simple?

TIMMY: Simple! He moved to California to get away from the Capone gang and got out of bootlegging by investing in a small business. A guy who owned it was making films wherever they could and with whom ever they could get in front of a camera.

JOHN: I'm still puzzled!

TIMMY: Look! In trade for the money he owed me and in gratitude for saving his life, he gave me a quarter share of the film studio he bought. Stutts' Cinema Company. He even had a slogan for his films: "If it's a Stutts, it's the nuts!"

SARAH: Now, I've heard everything. Where's Al Capone when you need him?

TIMMY: I wanted the slogan to be: "Stutts' films are the real McCoy!"

SARAH: You're kidding!

TIMMY: I only had a quarter share of the company so I was voted down. But, I was able to get Stutts to agree to make Flossie the studio's star.

FELICIA: Yes! They changed my name and got me the Russian director from the Moscow Art Theater.

TIMMY: He was a refugee from the Revolution…

FELICIA: *(Dramatic)*…who taught me to emote from my heart, my very being, to expose my inner emotions to the world…

SARAH: Oh! My god! So that's what you're exposing now?

FELICIA: He taught Gloria Swanson every movement she did, every glance of her smoky eyes, and every sly smile.

TIMMY: You can see the Swanson influence in Felicia's work.

SARAH: *(Sarcastically)* Oh, I know!

COLLEEN: That's who it was. Remember, Randall! I said to you Felicia reminded me of someone.

TIMMY: Then I got Marlene Dietrich's vocal coach…

SARAH: No wonder I couldn't understand what you were saying in that Shanghai film!

FELICIA: And once Timmy got me that dramatic help, the rest is history.

TIMMY: You said it, baby! The rest is history.

COLLEEN: I'm so proud of you, Aunt Felicia!

FELICIA: *(Turns to Colleen)* Thank you, my dear! And, I am proud of you. You have married a very handsome young man! No?

COLLEEN: Oh! Yes, Aunt Felicia.

SARAH: Watch your step! Listen, Flossie or Felicia or whoever you are, keep your hands off!

JOHN: Oh! It's time we went to evening services!

SARAH: Good! Church will be a welcome relief.

(Randall and Colleen get all the coats and everyone gets ready to leave as they start for the door. Felicia stops them with an announcement.).

FELICIA: Tonight! I'm going to present everyone with a great gift. *(She rubs her stomach)*

SARAH: On! My God. Don't tell me she's preg….

FELICIA: *(Moves hands to throat)* My vocal coach says I'm ready to make my debut. Tonight, I will sing the Christmas hymns solo!

(Colleen and Randall are bemused. Timmy appears proud while Rev. Walters seems puzzled, Sarah is aghast!)

SARAH: Oh, my god! Now, we'll really have to leave town!

(BLACKOUT)

ACT TWO

Scene One

(It is shortly after midnight service. There are a few moments when the stage is dark with only the Christmas tree lighted. There's a burst of people coming in, led by Sarah who turns the switch for the dining room lights. John Walters, Colleen and Randall follow)

SARAH: I can't believe that Felicia or Flossie or whatever she calls herself!

JOHN: Now, Sarah! Don't get yourself excited.

SARAH: Excited, excited! Why wouldn't I? These are people who are my neighbors and your congregation! And, that wife of my crazy brother embarrassed all of us.

JOHN: She was moved by the moment, that's all!

SARAH: It wasn't bad enough that she had to make her grand entrance with her fur coat and outlandish gown! She also started to give out autographs to the people in the pews.

JOHN: They were pleased to see a celebrity. She is very popular, you know.

SARAH: But, tonight wasn't a movie opening; it was a church service!

COLLEEN: She participated in the service very well, I thought.

RANDALL: She sings loud for sure.

SARAH: And off-key! I was never so embarrassed! Even the organist was thrown off-key. The poor woman'll probably give up music for the rest of her life.

JOHN: But, look at the new parishioners we had tonight. They all wanted to see Felicia.

SARAH: They were supposed to be attending a church service.

JOHN: The Lord operates in strange ways.

SARAH: She's certainly strange alright!

JOHN: No! I mean we had the biggest collection that this church has ever had at Christmas.

RANDALL: I heard a minister's wife from another congregation say her husband was really upset that his parishioners were attending your service, Rev. Walters.

SARAH: Where did you see her?

RANDALL: At our service! She wanted to get Felicia's autograph. But, she said her husband was going to demand that Rev. Walters' Rotary Club membership be revoked.

SARAH: See, there! Now, you're going to be barred from the Rotary Club. What'll be next, the Elks?

JOHN: But, don't you see. If some of these new people come back to my church, I can save more souls.

SARAH: Including the other minister's wife?

JOHN: I'm sure he'll understand!

SARAH: Of course! The biggest collection of the year and his parishioners are all at your church...including his wife. That'll make him real happy!

COLLEEN: And, Uncle Tim was very popular after church service. He was passing out candy and cupcakes and all sorts of sweets.

RANDALL: He even cut up a rum cake to give them some.

SARAH: My lunatic brother was giving the kids rum cake???

RANDALL: He said it wouldn't hurt them!

COLLEEN: And, he was telling them all about Santa Claus.

SARAH: I'll bet he was!

COLLEEN: I heard him tell the children that Santa Claus brought gifts to the Infant that first Christmas.

JOHN: That doesn't make sense!

SARAH: Now, you're catching on, John! *(Hall door opens, with carols being sung outside. Timmy and Felicia enter.)*

TIMMY: Merry Christmas! Merry Christmas!

FELICIA: Joyeux Noel, you all!

SARAH: What did you do, bring the Mormon Tabernacle Choir with you?

TIMMY: Nah! They're kids from church. I gave them money to go around town singing. Felicia taught them how to sing the carols!

SARAH: Those kids are ruined! *(Singing is heard outside window. The kids are singing a Christmas carol off-key)*

FELICIA: Don't they sound angelic?

SARAH: Angelic?

JOHN: Now, Sarah! I think Timmy's idea had the right intention... to bring joy to the town.

SARAH: *(To John)* Doesn't anything ever upset you?

TIMMY: Yeah! We gave candy and cakes to the kids after services and they had a wonderful time.

FELICIA: Yes! They were so good in sharing. Most of them gave some of the cake to the animals in the live manger. It was so sweet!

SARAH: *(To Colleen)* Didn't you say your uncle was passing out rum cake to the kids.

COLLEEN: It looked like it!

TIMMY: Hey, the cakes are only five proof.

JOHN: Five proof?

SARAH: Yes! That's alcohol…five percent!!

FELICIA: It's good for them…they won't catch cold!

JOHN: But what will their parents say?

TIMMY: Oh! The kids were sharing some of the rum cakes with their parents!

FELICIA: *(Dramatically)* It was really so wonderful! Christmas…. it is better to give than to receive!!

TIMMY: We gave the candy and cakes to the kids who shared them with their parents and the animals.

SARAH: The animals?

FELICIA: It's what I always dreamed Christmas should be!

(Phone rings. Colleen answers it.)

COLLEEN: Randall! It's for you. *(Randall crosses to phone)*

RANDALL: This is Randall Meadows! Yes, the veterinarian! What happened? You're kidding! All right! I'll be right there! *(Hangs up phone and dashes for his coat)*

COLLEEN: Randall! What is it?

RANDALL: I've got to get down to the church right away!

COLLEEN: Why?

RANDALL: The animals in the crèche are sick! The sheep just threw up on the Wise Men. *(Dashes out.)*

(BLACKOUT)

Scene Two

(It is just past noon as dinner is being prepared. Colleen is setting the table along with Sarah. Felicia is lounging on a chair, talking about her life in the movies.)

FELICIA: Yes, Colleen, it is so dreadful having to get up so early in the morning for the filming. Why, it takes an hour for makeup!

SARAH: That's all? I would have...

COLLEEN: ...Mother!

FELICIA: When we are doing outdoor scenes we take a rest in the early afternoon...a siesta...it is too hot in Hollywood. But, when we are filming in the studio, they have fans blowing air over large cakes of ice to keep us cool.

SARAH: What a waste of ice!

FELICIA: It's all done for the art. My muse is the depth of emotion I experience from those wonderful scripts.

SARAH: Your muse is it?

COLLEEN: Mother! All great artists have a muse; don't they Aunt Felicia?

(During this dialogue, Felicia is in another world, oblivious to Sarah)

FELICIA: You are right, dear one! It is our guiding beacon that draws us up to the moment when we are connected with our audiences...our fans....our dreams!

SARAH: I think I liked you better as a two-bit dancer!

COLLEEN: Mother!!!!! *(To Felicia)* Which is your favorite film you've made?

FELICIA: They are all my children, my dear! How can you choose one above the other? Ah!!! You will know when you have children, my dear one.

SARAH: Never you mind...!

FELICIA: Yet! Each mother does have one that's closer than all the others...and I, too, have my favorite.

COLLEEN: I knew you would!

FELICIA: It is my newest film..."The Streets of Venice!"

SARAH: What???

FELICIA: Imagine, if you will...dark romantic shadows beneath the many bridges in that fascinating, mysterious city. Venice, where everyone speaks Italian, that melodious language that rolls from the tongue like a vibrant stream. The canals speak volumes about the romance that is in the city's very fiber.

SARAH: I feel like I'm under water already!

COLLEEN: Mother!!! *(To Felicia)* You speak Italian, too?

FELICIA: No, my dear! They hire an Italian extra to dub in my voice. She takes inspiration from my physical emoting so familiar to my many fans.

SARAH: I'll bet she does!

COLLEEN: When will we be able to see the film?

FELICIA: When my director can come to this country!

SARAH: Where is he now?

FELICIA: He's in Paris...France, that is... making the final editing of the film and then he will come here.

COLLEEN: Will he come soon?

FELICIA: Timmy will know more about that!

(Just then, Timmy enters the room to announce that dinner is ready. Rev. Walters and Randall follow him)

TIMMY: We wish to announce that the finest Christmas dinner will be served this noon, better than any man or woman ever ate.

SARAH: What are you now, Tiny Tim?

RANDALL: That's good, Mrs. Walters! Tiny Tim, right out of "A Christmas Carol."

TIMMY: Don't encourage her, Randall, m'boy. She is just jealous that we men have taken over the kitchen and have prepared a sumptuous meal.

FELICIA: I'm sure it will be a fine repast, my love, and one suitable for our gustatory pleasures!!

SARAH: Gus ta what?

TIMMY: Pay her no mind, my sweet Felicia! You are correct, dear Felicia, we will find new pleasures in dining.

COLLEEN: Isn't that wonderful mother...the men cooked the meal.

SARAH: I'm astounded! But, we better wait for the serving of it first.

TIMMY: The spices are from the Orient! And, the vegetables are from the gardens of delight!

SARAH: Listen to the former bootlegger! Have you been hitting the cooking sherry?

JOHN: He has inspired us to new heights, dear Sarah! Yes, he has!

SARAH: Were you into the sherry, too?

JOHN: Sarah! Please!!

RANDALL: I know I didn't have any sherry and I think the dinner will be wonderful. I peeled the potatoes, cut up the turnips and removed the turkey's innards!

SARAH: Well, at least you have experience working with animals!

TIMMY: No matter! I want you all to take your seats while we serve you as you wonderful women deserve!

SARAH: Will he ever stop?

TIMMY: Come, gentlemen…we are now mere servants. *(They exit following Timmy)*

SARAH: I've lost control of my own home!

COLLEEN: Now, mother! I think it's wonderful that they are being so gallant to us. *(The women sit)*

FELICIA: Yes! We shall be the Queens of the day!

(Randall, followed by John, enters carrying trays filled with vegetables, bread and assorted condiments)

TIMMY: *(Calls from the kitchen.)* Prepare you for the feast of a lifetime…the prize turkey. *(There is a loud crash in the hallway. The rest turn to one another in shock as the turkey tumbles into the room)* I'll be a son of a bit…

SARAH: *(Covers Timmy's outburst)* You're damn right you are!

(BLACKOUT)

Scene Three

(The six people are sitting around the table following dinner. It is obvious that all has not gone well following Timmy's dropping the turkey in the previous scene.)

TIMMY: Well, I thought we saved the day…at least John here did!

JOHN: I was only too happy to help!

SARAH: Well, we wouldn't have had to wash off a cooked turkey if twinkle toes here *(Points to Timmy)* hadn't been so clumsy.

TIMMY: It was the turkey's fault. He was a slippery fellow, that tom was!

SARAH: You should have let Randall carry it in. He's more used to working with animals.

FELICIA: But, Timmy was anxious to have us enjoy our Christmas dinner…and we did, Timmy dear!

SARAH: Speak for yourself, your highness!

COLLEEN: Now, mother! We've just had a wonderful time together. Isn't that something?

JOHN: It's a proud thing it is to cook dinner for our women!

TIMMY: Oh! That it is, Reverend.

RANDALL: It was the first real meal I ever helped cook.

COLLEEN: And, I'm going to remember that in the future!

TIMMY: There you go, Randall, m'boy! You're going to be chained to the kitchen for the rest of your life.

RANDALL: No! I will enjoy helping out, just as Colleen helps me at the animal hospital.

SARAH: Now, isn't that a fine arrangement.

JOHN: Oh! I think it is, Sarah!

SARAH: And, I suppose you'll want to be helping in the kitchen from now on.

JOHN: It would be my pleasure, Sarah dear!

COLLEEN: Oh! How wonderful! Everybody has the Christmas spirit!

FELICIA: It's so much like movies when we all must work together to create great art!

SARAH: Oh! Here we go again!

TIMMY: No! Sarah, m'dear! Felicia is right. It takes teamwork to make a fine movie. And, my Felicia makes it all work because she is our star!!!

JOHN: Here, here!

COLLEEN & RANDALL: Here, here!

SARAH: How come you're not working at the big studios with Clark Gable. Federic March, Claudette Colbert and all the famous stars?

TIMMY: Oh! But Felicia is able to select her roles and she is more famous because of her special talent for thrilling people in the spy movies she makes.

COLLEEN: Oh! You're so right, Uncle Timmy!

RANDALL: I've only seen one of your movies, Felicia, and I was on the edge of my seat.

SARAH: Probably to make a quick getaway!

COLLEEN: Mother!!!

FELICIA: Which one did you see!

RANDALL: It was "Dawn in the Desert!"

FELICIA: Oh, yes! We made that in Death Valley with all the sand and the heat! But, it was worth all the discomfort to make that wonderful film.

TIMMY: And, we were able to get that great Egyptian star, Momar Tarniff.

SARAH: I heard he was a waiter in a Hollywood restaurant!

TIMMY: Only until he learned English! He's an international star.

SARAH: Well, I understand he didn't learn all that much English!

TIMMY: Enough to convey his deep devotion to Felicia as his Arabian princess!

FELICIA: He was a natural as a romantic lover! I felt so secure in his arms!

TIMMY: I had a little trouble with that!

COLLEEN: Well, Uncle Timmy, they were only acting.

SARAH: I'll bet!

JOHN: Sarah! Timmy has every confidence in Felicia. She's an actress who also has a deep devotion to her marriage vows!

SARAH: John! You're talking about Hollywood. Don't you read the papers with all the scandal out there?

COLLEEN: Oh! Mother! Aunt Felicia loves only Uncle Timmy!

FELICIA: You are quite correct, my dear! He is the man who made what I am today….an international star!

TIMMY: Oh! It is the least I could do for a woman I've treasured as my companion all these years!

SARAH: Will you listen to this baloney? It's enough to make you sick

RANDALL: I think it's great! He has taken Felicia to the heights of fame and fortune!

TIMMY: Well, we're still working on the fortune!

SARAH: I'll bet you are!

JOHN: Don't worry, Timmy! With you behind her, Felicia will be the biggest star in Hollywood.

SARAH: At least the tallest!

TIMMY: We call it statuesque, m'girl!

SARAH: Call it what you will, she's still a broken down chorus girl in my eyes!

JOHN: Now, that's not nice, Sarah!

SARAH: Oh! I'm sick of this pretense and all their high-faluting ways.

JOHN: Sarah! Jealousy is a sin!

SARAH: Jealous! Jealous! Huh!

COLLEEN: Mother! We should be proud we have such a famous person in the family. Everybody in town has been impressed.

SARAH: Sure! She creates a commotion in church, teaches children to sing off-key and gets the animals in the crèche sick by feeding them rum cake.

TIMMY: It's all an exuberance of spirit! Felicia enjoys the adulation of her fans and wants to reciprocate.

RANDALL: And, they certainly did!

TIMMY: *(Stands)* And, now for our Christmas gift to the family!

COLLEEN: Oh! How wonderful!

RANDALL: You didn't have to!

SARAH: Don't bother! Dropping the turkey was enough!

JOHN: Please, Sarah, let Timmy continue.

TIMMY: Felicia, my dear, do you want to tell them!

FELICIA: *(Stands beside Timmy)* Our great Russian director, Mischa Bognadorf, is on his way from England with "Streets of Venice!" and we could not think of a better place to do the world premiere than here in Whitehall…the American Venice.

SARAH: The what?

TIMMY: Sure! Venice is famous for its canals and so is Whitehall. It's our Christmas gift to the town!

COLLEEN: How wonderful! When will it be shown?

RANDALL: Where will you show it?

TIMMY: Why, right down town in the Capitol Theater.

JOHN: Now, won't that be an event! That's a wonderful present for the whole community.

FELICIA: Yes! All our friends will come from Hollywood for the premiere.

TIMMY: I'm going to book a special train that will come from Hollywood right to Whitehall.

RANDALL: Wow! That's quite a long ride, isn't it!

TIMMY: That's publicity, m'boy! It's how you build up interest in the movie! Felicia and I will go back to Hollywood to board the train there and ride all the way to New York and then up to Whitehall here in our special car. We'll greet fans at every stop across the country and tell them about the greatest little town in the nation... Whitehall!

SARAH: Must you?

JOHN: What a wonderful idea! We can have a great celebration here in town when you arrive with your Hollywood people! The Chamber of Commerce will love it!

COLLEEN: How many people will be coming from Hollywood?

TIMMY: Why, I'd say at least 200!

FELICIA: Maybe more!

SARAH: Glory be to God! Whitehall will never be the same!

RANDALL: It's a great boost for our town.

TIMMY: And, Randall, I'd like you and Colleen to be our representatives here.

COLLEEN: Really!

TIMMY: Yes! You can make arrangement for rooms for the premiere's out-of-town guests!

SARAH: You damn fool! There isn't that much hotel space in the town!

FELICIA: We thought you'd like to encourage the people in town---my fans---to open their homes to our Hollywood friends.

SARAH: Oh, God! Now you've done it!

JOHN: We'll manage and besides, I think the townspeople will enjoy helping out!

SARAH: You do, do you? *(Phone rings, Colleen answers)*

COLLEEN: Hello! Who? I'm afraid I don't understand you! Tim! Oh! You want to talk to my uncle Timmy! *(Turns phone to Timmy, to others)* He has a thick accent!

FELICIA: Oh! It must be Mischa Bognadorf! How wonderful!

TIMMY: *(On phone)* Mischa, my friend! *(Listens)* Great! We'll start right away. We'll see you in New York tomorrow night!

FELICIA: Let me talk to him! *(She takes phone from Timmy)*

TIMMY: *(Explains to others)* That's our director, Mischa! He just arrived in New York with the film. Now we can meet him there and start our trip to Hollywood to prepare for the cross-country trip back to Whitehall.

SARAH: Oh! That must make sense somehow but it beats me!

FELICIA: *(On phone)* Oh! I'm so glad you are back, my dear Mischa! I am ready to put myself in your hands once more! *(Blows him a kiss through the phone audibly and hangs up)* Oh! I love that man and what he does for me!

SARAH: Obviously!

TIMMY: Now! We must be off so we can meet Mischa tomorrow night. He just got off the boat from England. He's been trying to get us on the phone for an hour. Our operator in town here kept hanging up on him. I guess it's his accent!

FELICIA: Yes! We must rush to his side. *(Crosses around the room, hugging everybody and saying "Goodbye and Merry Christmas")*

TIMMY: Merry Christmas, to all! We had a great time!!

(They exit as Colleen and Randall follow to the door, calling out.."Drive Carefully")

SARAH: *(Sits at the table, head in hands)* Why the hell couldn't I have been an only child?

(BLACKOUT)

THE END